Both Here and There

Both Here and There

Studies in Concentric Parallelism
in the Gospel of Luke

Dennis W. Chadwick

WIPF & STOCK · Eugene, Oregon

BOTH HERE AND THERE
Studies in Concentric Parallelism in the Gospel of Luke

Copyright © 2018 Dennis W. Chadwick. All rights reserved. Except for brief quotations in critical publications or reviews, no part of this book may be reproduced in any manner without prior written permission from the publisher. Write: Permissions, Wipf and Stock Publishers, 199 W. 8th Ave., Suite 3, Eugene, OR 97401.

Wipf & Stock
An Imprint of Wipf and Stock Publishers
199 W. 8th Ave., Suite 3
Eugene, OR 97401

www.wipfandstock.com

PAPERBACK ISBN: 978-1-5326-1802-4
HARDCOVER ISBN: 978-1-4982-4321-6
EBOOK ISBN: 978-1-4982-4320-9

Manufactured in the U.S.A. New Testament quotes in English are used by permission from *The Holy Bible, English Standard Version* (Wheaton, IL: Crossway/Good News, 2011), unless otherwise noted. Transliterated Greek words are transliterated from *Novum Testamentum Graece 28* (Stuttgart: Deutsche Bibelgesellschaft, 2008). Unless otherwise noted, Old Testament quotes in English are from *A New English Translation of the Septuagint*, NETS, (New York: Oxford University Press, 2007). Old Testament text in transliterated Greek is transliterated from Alfred Rahlfs, *Septuaginta*, 8th ed. (Wurttemburg: Wurttembergische Bibelanstalt, 1965).

*For Judy,
Joyia, and Merry*

Contents

Preface | xiii

Introduction | 1
  Identifying Literary Forms in Gospel Narratives
  Identifying Concentric Forms in Gospel Narratives
  Discern the Author's Intent to Use Concentric Parallelism:
    Seven Methods
  Who Intentionally Wrote History This Way?
  Luke's Larger Intentions

Part 1 The Galilee Narrative | 15

1. Disciples and Apostles: Luke 4:40–6:19 | 17
  Luke's Unique Perspective
  Documenting the Form
    Jesus Heals Them All (Section A, 4:40—5:1a, and A′, 6:17–19)
    Jesus People (Section B, 5:1b–11, and B′, 6:12–16)
    Jesus' Healing Hand (Section C, 5:12–16);
      Jesus Heals a Hand (Section C′, 6:6–12a)
    The Authority of the Son of Man
      (Section D, 5:17–26, and D′, 6:1–5)
    Jesus Calls Sinners to Repentance (Section E, 5:27–39)
  Interpreting the Form
    The Unpaired Center Section
    Terminal Sections
    Interior Sections
  Summary
  The Story Continues

2. Take Care How You Receive the Word: Luke 7:1—8:56 | 35
    Documenting the Form
        The Lifegiving Word (Section A, 7:1–17, and A′, 8:40–56)
        The Reported Word (Section B, 7:18–35, and B′, 8:26–39)
        The Godlike Word (Section C, 7:36–50, and C′, 8:22–25)
        The Operative Word (Section D, 8:1–3, and D′, 8:19–21)
        Hearing the Word (Section E, 8:4–18)
    Interpreting the Form
        Receiving the Word (Section E, 8:4–18)
        Jesus' Word in Narrative Context
        Jesus' Powerful Word (Section A, 7:1–17, and A′, 8:40–56)
        Trampled on the Path (Section B, 7:18–35, and B′, 8:26–39)
        Roots Among Rocks (Section C, 7:36–50, and C′, 8:22–25)
        Maturing Among Thorns (Section D, 8:1–3, and D′, 8:19–21)
    Summary

3. Apostolic Non-Leadership: Luke 9:1–50 | 63
    Twelve Unready Men
    Documenting the Form
        Sharing Jesus' Ministry (Section A, 9:1–3, and A′, 9:49–50)
        Status Borrowed from Jesus (Section B, 9:4–5, and B′, 9:46–48)
        Scandalized by Jesus (Section C, 9:6–11, and C′, 9:43–45)
        Ministry With and Without Jesus
            (Section D, 9:12–17, and D′, 9:37–42)
        Identifying Jesus (Section E, 9:18–22, and E′, 9:28–36)
        Dying and Rising (Section F, 9:22, and F′, 9:23–27)
    Interpreting the Form
        Sharing Jesus' Ministry
        Status Borrowed from Jesus
        Scandalized by Jesus
        Ministry With and Without Jesus
        Identifying Jesus
    Luke 9:1–50 as Introduction to the Journey Narrative in
        9:51—19:46

Part 2 The Journey Narrative | 83

4. Go Follow | 87
    Leaving and Arriving
        (Section A, Luke 9:51–56, and A′, Luke 18:28–46)
    Kingdom Regimen
        (Section B, Luke 9:57–62, and B′, Luke 19:11–27)
    He Comes (Sections C and C′)
        Hospitality (Luke 10:1–7 and 19:1–10)
        Blockade (Luke 10:8–16 and 18:35–43)
        Grasp (Luke 10:17–24 and 18:31–34)
    Overview of Sections A–C and A′–C′

5. Simply Saved | 97
    Signs of Life (Section D, Luke 10:25–37, and D′, 18:18–30)
    Nearing the Life-Giver (Sections E and E′)
        The Women and the Men (Luke 10:38–42 and 18:9–14)
        The Sisters and the Censure (Luke 10:38–42 and 18:15–17)
    Overview of Sections D–E and D′–E′

6. Petition the Giver (Sections F and F′) | 103

7. Kingdom Come | 105
    Signs of the Kingdom (Sections G and G′)
        Gifted Voices (Luke 11:14 and 17:11–19)
        Reign (Luke 11:15–23 and 17:20–21)
        Return (Luke 11:24–26 and 17:22–24)
        Life and Passion (Luke 11:27–28 and 17:25)
        Judgment (Luke 11:29–32 and 17:26–33)
        Readiness (Luke 11:33–36 and 17:34–37)
    Review of Parallels between Sections G and G′
    Censure (Sections H and H′)
        Affront and Exposure (Luke 11:37–41 and 16:14–15)
        Authority (Luke 11:42 and 16:16–18)
        Finger Work (Luke 11:43–48 and 16:19–26)
        Warned but Intransigent (Luke 11:49–51 and 16:27–31)
        Obstructors (Luke 11:52 and 17:1–6)
        Carefully Chosen Words (Luke 11:53–54 and 17:7–10)
    Review of Parallels between Sections H and H′

8. Stuff and Money | 118
    Shelter (Sections J and J′)
        Exposure (Luke 12:1–3 and 16:1–2)
        Eternal Welfare (Luke 12:4–7 and 16:3–9)
        Undivided Hearts (Luke 12:8–12 and 16:10–13)
    Review of Parallels between Sections J and J′
    Wealth (Sections K and K′)
        Shares (Luke 12:13–15 and 15:11–12)
        Fare Well (Luke 12:16–21 and 15:13–14)
        Want (Luke 12:22–31 and 15:15–17)
        Father's Pleasure (Luke 12:32–34 and 15:18–24)
        Giving Accounts (Luke 12:35–40 and 15:25–28)
        Settling Accounts (Luke 12:41–48 and 15:28–32)
    Review of Parallels between Sections K and K′

9. Alignment | 128
    Line in the Sand (Sections L and L′)
        Division and Decision (Luke 12:49–53 and 14:25–27)
        Discernment (Luke 12:54—13:5 and 14:28–33)
        Discarded (Luke 13:6–9 and 14:34–35)
    Review of Parallels between Sections L and L′
    Guest List (Sections M and M′)
        Release (Luke 13:10–17 and 14:1–6)
        Rise (Luke 13:18–21 and 14:7–11)
        In or Out (Luke 13:22–30 and 14:12–24)
    Review of Parallels between Sections M and M′

10. Luke the Stylist | 136
    Luke and Rhetorical Practice
    Luke the Communicator

11. Context of the Journey Narrative | 140
    Aspects of the Kingdom of God in Luke
    Aspects of the Kingdom of God in the Journey Narrative
    Kingdom of God in the Chiastic Center of the Journey Narrative

12. Inside Out | 144
    Killers (Sections N and N′)
    Setting Out (Luke 13:31–33 and 9:51–56)
    Lamenting (Luke 13:34–35 and 19:41–44)

13. Jesus' Journey and David's Progress | 151
    Preparation
    Luke 13:31–33, 9:51–56, and 1Reigns 19:11–18
    Luke 13:34–35, 19:28–46 and 2 Reigns 6:1—7:17
    Luke 13:31–33 and 1 Reigns 31:1—2 Reigns 1:16
    Luke 13:34–35 and 2 Reigns 1:17–27
    Overview of the Textual Relations of Sections N and N′

Conclusion | 169

Appendix 1: Glossary | *173*
Appendix 2: Jesus' Journey and Elijah's Journey | *176*
Bibliography | *179*

Preface

My listening friend, a long-time student of the Bible, a seasoned teacher, and an experienced study group leader, paused a few moments to consider what I had just pointed out to her in the earlier chapters of Luke's Gospel. Her serious eyes began to sparkle as her lips parted in a smile. "Isn't God humorous!" she exalted. "He sneaks in the fun along with the serious!"

The scriptures we had compared were chapters 7 and 8 of Luke, chapters showing a sweeping mirror-like repetition of themes, plot, and details. My friend acknowledged these doublets and leapt to an explanation for why Luke or God might bother to include them in holy writ. Fun, she concluded; it must be an expression of dry humor, as no other likely explanation came to mind.

There are indeed historical, theological, and literary reasons why Luke would compile the teachings and doings of Jesus in that way, and he may well have had fun doing it. It was also fun to discover the result of Luke's careful work. The discoveries documented in this book came over many years with the help not only of biblical scholars who wrote up their observations, but also with the help of friends, volunteer readers, print professionals, and family members.

In 1984 a friend, Lewis Toland, urged me to read a book on Luke. Some observations and ideas in that book fastened my interest and imagination on the way the Lukan narrative of Jesus' journey to Jerusalem was composed and what Luke's unique journey account means. My burst of curiosity grew into a thirty-four year study project.

Many volunteers have provided additional eyes as well as wise guidance for the project. Helpers contributed in the following approximate order over the years: Those who first interacted with my rudimentary observations were an adult Sunday school class at First Christian Church, Lawrence, Kansas. Pastor George Stulac (Memorial Presbyterian Church, St. Louis, Missouri) encouraged the Lukan journey project and traded insights on it during the years 2000–2001. A community study group on Luke gathered weekly in the early 2000s over the course of several months, helping discover several important observations in the Lukan travel narrative. The group included Liz Topp, Judy Chadwick, John Espy, Jim Musser, Joe Potts, Scott Rask, James Schaefer, and Marlin Schaich.

Joy Moore, then newly hired as an associate dean at Duke Divinity School, gave key encouragement in 2008 to pursue publication of the project. From that year I began to seek out professional advice and opinions from academic authors, including exploratory conversations with John Breck, Darrell Bock, Robert Tannehill, Bernard A. Taylor, and Steve Walton. Kevin Lee, then a graduate student at the University of Kansas, persevered through several years of Lukan analysis with me as a weekly study partner.

In more recent years, fellow congregants at Grace Evangelical Presbyterian Church of Lawrence, Kansas, hosted an adult Sunday school class and a men's Bible study group in which I was asked to present a portion of the following material. And as I began to write up the project for eventual publication, various individuals kindly agreed to review the manuscript or provide other guidance: Garwood Anderson, Jenny Read-Heimerdinger, Terry Morrison, Timothy Nicholls, Brent Yorgey, David Brack, and, once again, George Stulac. They have contributed immensely to the essence and clarity of the essays.

What I offer in this book is less formal and more idiosyncratic than the conventions of theological academic writing. As I finally set out to write in my sixth and seventh decades, I face some limitations of advancing age: poor memory for resources I have read and lack of time and energy for what I haven't read. As the result, this book has almost no subject survey or literary theory, and lacks most of the saber-crossing with potential critics that is standard in academic writing. The proposals in the body and the rabbit-trails in the footnotes arise mostly from my own concerns and from the few resources with which I interact. I believe, however, that I have something to offer to the academy as well as to pastors, but my ideal audience for these studies is a Greek-reading pastor or student.

I thank Matt Wimer, my project manager at Wipf & Stock, and all the other WS staff who so professionally brought this book to print. Betty Talbert gave patient, perceptive, and creative editorial guidance in shaping the manuscript. And Judy Chadwick, my dear wife of fifty years, read drafts and advocated for the concerns of lay readers and non-academic pastors who may turn to this book for instruction. Her sacrificial love is crucial to this project, hand in hand with that of the gracious King who prompted it and who reigns over it.

Introduction

These studies assist Bible teachers to prepare authoritative lessons from portions of the Gospel of Luke. The Evangelist structured certain portions of his narrative using a large-scale literary form that today's reader does not readily recognize. This book aids Bible interpreters to see these structures and discern the author's intention for creating them, allowing interpreters to craft authoritative messages and appropriate applications.

Christian traditions that emphasize short devotional and liturgical scripture readings as the basis for one's spiritual walk seem to suggest that one should drink the wine of the word in small glassfuls. Reading short epistle paragraphs or narrative episodes for liturgy, devotion, or as sermon texts, feeds our souls, connects us with a community of similar readers and with a tradition, perhaps an ancient tradition, but it may divert us from what biblical authors intend to teach through extended discourses.

For a brief example, some mistakenly take Psalm 46:10a, "Be still, and know that I am God," to mean that God's people should nurture the interior life or meditation. In the context of Psalm 46, however, the exhortation means that God's people should stop being despairing alarmists: their prayer life should exhibit peaceful confidence in God's cosmic power and purposes.

> God is our refuge and strength, a very present help in trouble. Therefore we will not fear though the earth gives way, though the mountains be moved into the heart of the sea, though its waters roar and foam, though the mountains tremble at its swelling. *Selah* (Ps 46:1–3)

Effective students read biblical narrative extensively as well as intensively. By reading the broad context of liturgical or devotional selections, rather than only smaller isolated portions, students learn to question artificial breaks in a narrative such as topical headings arranged by editors and breaks necessitated by page-turns. Chapter and verse numbering for Old and New Testaments provides valuable assistance; however, in some cases chapter and verse breaks, headings or subheadings, can cloak the structure and flow of the text. But practically speaking, only a little can be done in print to help us overcome such obstacles. The best help resides in the reader herself: a reader who reads past artificial boundaries, who expects her peripheral vision to grasp connections in the text, who practices poetic and theological memory in the act of reading.[1] These are skills for studying biblical narrative that unveil the author's meaning.

Ancient readers (and listeners) of Luke and of the other New Testament writings lived in a world saturated with many literary conventions and standard literary styles. The Hebrew Old Testament contained similar literary styles, especially in its poetry and poetic prose. Literary method and style manuals, along with rigorous exercises to emulate the conventions, were part of the ancient Greek and Roman educational system. New Testament authors reveal their literary training by following many of these conventions while also developing their unique literary styles. The first four verses of Luke's Gospel, for example, are one of the finest examples of ancient rhetorical style in the New Testament:

> Inasmuch as many have undertaken to compile a narrative of the things that have been accomplished among us, just as those who from the beginning were eyewitnesses and ministers of the word have delivered them to us, it seemed good to me also, having followed all things closely for some time past, to write an orderly account for you, most excellent Theophilus, that you may have certainty concerning the things you have been taught. (Luke 1:1–4)

Ancient readers might know well or sense that Luke was writing a new story in literary forms familiar to them. But modern readers might not recognize such forms, especially in English translations. These studies will guide pastors, teachers, and other Bible students (1) to identify an ancient literary form in portions of Luke's Gospel, intentionally composed by the author, and (2) to interpret these texts authoritatively.

---

1. Cell phones or tablets are portable and instantly accessible, but create a great disadvantage for careful students when they use the devices to read scripture. When we read a printed Bible, our semi-conscious or conscious mind processes connections between words lying in the center of our gaze and words lying further above, below, and across the page. A tablet or cell phone view-screen prohibits peripheral integration that the brain naturally does.

INTRODUCTION

Identifying Literary Forms in Gospel Narratives

Identifying biblical literary structures may seem unhelpful to those who read for devotional or sermon preparation purposes. Yet, when we think about it, we structure our own sermons in literary forms we call "outlines," hoping to help our listeners understand the scriptures, because form reveals meaning. Thus, digging out textual details by identifying ancient rhetorical forms will only bring us greater understanding of the the author's intention. Gospel authors used form to reveal meaning.

The Evangelists tell connected linear stories of Jesus, selecting from among the many episodes of the oral tradition available to them (John 20:30, 21:25). Concurrently they also engage in evangelistic/theological discourses about Jesus. Indeed, this is a reason why the synoptists and John wrote their Gospels: they intend to "catch men" instead of fish (Luke 5:10), not simply to write out a history of Jesus. Thus Mark's Gospel begins, "The beginning of the gospel of Jesus Christ, the Son of God" (1:1); Luke writes his narrative so that Theophilus and other readers "may have certainty concerning the things you have been taught" (1:4); and John writes "so that you may believe that Jesus is the Christ, the Son of God, and that by believing you may have life in his name" (20:31). As the author discourses on Jesus, he selects and orders episodes to tell the story and to do his own "fishing," stitching episodes together in his own unique way using literary forms.[2] For the Gospel writers as well, form reveals meaning.

For example, Luke's parallel structures (clearly literary forms) tell the story and teach its meaning. Respective birth announcements (1:5–25; 26–56) and birth stories (1:57–80; 2:1–52) of John the Baptist and Jesus extensively run parallel to show that Jesus is greater than John the Baptist. On a much smaller literary scale, beatitudes in Luke's Sermon on the Plain follow parallel structure: "Blessed are you . . ." (6:20–23) and "Woe to you . . ." (6:24–26), the four beatitudes being topically matched in the same order by the four woes. Luke and the other Gospel authors utilized literary forms in their accounts of Jesus, even concentric forms.

---

2. God the Holy Spirit mysteriously worked upon Luke's intellectual resources in a way that uniquely inspired a trustworthy and authoritative account of Jesus. In this book I refer simply to what Luke has written, keeping the above in mind.

Identifying Concentric Forms in Gospel Narratives

The Evangelists could organize the story using concentric parallelism in addition to other literary stuructures. Teachers of the Gospels need eyes trained to see concentric parallelisms.

One can see concentric parallelism most readily in poetic biblical language as in the example below. In the example, the phrases of 1 John 3:9 are set apart and indented to show their poetic relationship. The right-hand column gives an analysis of the poetic structure and attaches letter identifiers to matching structural members.

1 John 3:9	Structural scheme
No one born of God	A: *born of God*
makes a practice of sinning,	B: *practice of sinning*
for God's seed abides in him,	C: *God's seed abides*
and he cannot keep on sinning	B: *keep on sinning*
because he has been born of God.	A: *born of God*

This example contains a concentric parallelism on a small poetic scale, the scale perhaps the most common in ancient literature.[3] Further, writers could and did apply the principle of *mimesis*, or imitation and adaptation of form, and produce large-scale prose compositions having extensive prose sections that correspond in an ABCBA fashion, or indeed, in a form extended even longer, such as ABCDEDCBA.[4]

Ancient rhetoricians did not establish a nomenclature for concentric parallelism even though it can be readily observed in ancient literature, so modern rhetoricians and exegetes use a variety of older terms and newer terms to describe it.[5] Concentric parallelism as I use the term is an ancient, wide-spread rhetorical form (still used today) by which a poet or author expresses him-/herself in a connected series of words, phrases, statements, topics, personae, or episodes. The author then reframes and develops similar episodes, personae, topics, statements, phrases, and words *in the reverse order* to complete the idea. By doing so, sometimes an author creates an

---

3. Some concentric parallelisms have a doubled middle section, which, for example, might be analyzed as ABCCBA.

4. Or longer yet. Often those who analyze these forms will distinguish the sections of the last half of the scheme by adding the prime symbol (') after those identifiers, such as ABCB'A'. See the glossary at the end of this book.

5. Greek and Roman orators and writers developed rhetoric into a craft having handbooks, into a profession, even into a public office. Ancient Hebrew writers also practiced artistic structuring of language in their poetry and prose, but they learned it by imitation and apprenticeship. By Luke's time, however, Greco-Roman literary culture had mostly engulfed Hebrew literary culture.

unpaired center section. Such a center section (or a pair of center sections) typically carries the main meaning or focus of the entire literary device. In the example above, "God's seed abides in him" is both the source of spiritual birth and the power restraining sin. The form serves a variety of rhetorical purposes, including filling out the thesis with illustrations, exceptions, contrasts, alternatives, special emphases, or development; adding nuance; establishing continuity for a subdivision of text (or the continuity of a whole text); and holding the listener's or reader's attention.

Concentric parallelism may describe the form of a short poem, teaching, or slogan. "Do not give dogs what is holy, and do not throw your pearls before pigs, lest they trample them underfoot and turn to attack you" (Mt 7:6, ABBA) offers a fairly brief example. Still shorter and more elegant is "Whoever sheds the blood of man, by man shall his blood be shed" (Gen 9:6, ABCCBA). John Kennedy urged Americans to "Ask not what your country can do for you, but what you can do for your country" (ABCCBA).

On the other end of the scale, concentric parallelisms can extend to huge proportions. These texts are not poems or even remotely poetic, but prose. A whole book, i.e., chapter, of Virgil's *Aeneid* might have this form, as might a whole battle in a description by Thucydides in his *History of the Peloponnesian War*. Chapter 17 of Genesis provides an example of a large concentric parallelism.

Genesis 17	Structural Scheme
1a When Abram was ninety-nine years old	A
1b The Lord appeared to Abram	B
1c–2 I make my covenant between me and you	C
3 Abram fell on his face	D
4–8 Abram's new name; his offspring	E
9–14 Keeping covenant	F
15–16 Sarai's new name; her offspring	E
17–19a Abraham fell on his face	D
19b–21 I will establish my covenant with Isaac	C
22–23 God went up from Abraham	B
24–27 Abraham was ninety-nine years old	A

Ancient readers expected to encounter such things, even in histories. Contemporary readers can find more theological richness in the Gospels and in other biblical narrative when they become aware of occasions of concentric parallelism. But many readers instead have come to expect the Gospels to report the life of Jesus in the way that they experience their own lives: moving from hour to hour, event to event, and place to place with little sense of cohesion or perceivable meaning. Contemporary literary culture (meaning not just theorists but everyday readers such as you and I) may reject literary symmetries as being too contrived and not life-like. Authors in classical and biblical antiquity, however, often wrote their narrative after considering the greater meaning of the narrative, and then shaping the story literarily to reveal its meaning in the telling.

Careful modern readers of the Gospels, on the other hand, avoid granting concentric parallelism a dominant place in their expectations. Unfortunately, an infatuation with this form and a delight in its beauty can misguide students of the Bible in a way that allows concentric parallelism to take on a life of its own so that it becomes a form-in-waiting that looks for any text to inhabit. It is all too easy to wish this form onto a text . . . and then suddenly "discover" evidence of its presence in a few of the words, phrases, or concepts in the text. The discoverer then expresses these findings with tidy interpretive headings that name discovered parallels. Indeed, this interpretive foible is why some critics place rigorous demands on any who claim to glimpse concentric parallelism in biblical text. They ask, can you show a high probability that the author intends the reader to see this form in the selected portion? And they set out a series of tests to assess this probability.[6]

We contemporary readers who glimpse such a structure in our study and meditation on biblical narrative should resist our enthusiasm to show it and explain it right away to those under our teaching.[7] There is work to be done in validating our observations because biblical authority matters, because authorial intention matters, and because seeing the text like the original recipients would have seen it matters. The rush to preach or teach what we've glimpsed, or to push ahead in publishing that article, likely undercuts our responsibility to God who authorizes the scriptures. This rush also undercuts our responsibility to those who follow our personal model as

---

6. One set of tests for claims that narrative textual units correspond to one another was developed by Douglas McComiskey for his book *Lukan Theology in the Light of the Gospel's Literary Structure*. He develops his own tests and takes into account tests proposed by other authors. I heavily depend on his presentation in the following chapters. McComiskey, however, remains hesitant to accredit any large concentric structures in Luke. His own structural proposal is not a concentric one. McComiskey himself separates his eleven tests into four levels of importance. I have selected from among his tests, with my selection guided by how likely a pastor or a lay Bible student would be to have the skills and resources to apply these individual tests. I have also adapted and clarified some of the tests. By applying these tests to the texts under consideration in this book, we show how results from particular tests point to the possibility that Luke, with theological intent, assembled elaborate concentric parallelisms from the words and acts of Jesus. See McComiskey, *Lukan Theology*, 12–13.

7. I am writing particularly for pastors, teachers, and Bible students who hold the authority of the biblical text and of the biblical author's vision above the authority of the reader.

teachers, and further, it undercuts our responsibility to those who anticipate hearing the authoritative voice of the Lord in our preaching and teaching.[8]

This book explains how Luke deployed such rhetorical literary devices as structural schemes to tell the story of Jesus, especially how he arranged large-scale concentric parallelisms. In the midst of telling that linear story, he arranged pieces of his discourse as clusters of episodes with concentrically parallel shapes, like the rings around the place where a pebble is dropped in calm water. At the story level, the narrative moves forward by means of the usual linear connectives such as "then," "after that," or "when they arrived," yet through the very same episodes the author organizes a symmetrical balance that catches the reader's attention and theological interest upon close reading. Some readers glimpse among the episodes parallel phrases, words, actions, topics, metaphors, motifs, etc. These parallels invite the reader to compare episodes, bringing the story to a temporary standstill at essential points while a reader scans backward to find the extent of a parallel and its meaning. This book claims that Luke employed the literary strategy of large-scale concentric parallelism in his Gospel, but how can we be confident that he did so?

Discern the Author's Intent to Use Concentric Parallelism: Seven Methods

Since discerning the author's intention more clearly is key to proper interpretation, what methods should we use that help us isolate and then validate potential correspondences between passages in biblical narrative before we begin to interpret it?

First, note attention-getting literary correspondences. Was a word, an action, a topic, a metaphor, or a motif obvious in both passages? For example, in Luke's journey narrative there are two times when someone asks Jesus, "What must I/shall I do to inherit eternal life" (10:25; 18:18). Similar attention-getting features add to the probability that the author intended correspondence. But note: such devices are primarily surface details catching the eye of the general reader, rather than theological subtleties to which we are attuned.

Further, features restricted to two apparently corresponding passages add to the probability that the author intended correspondence. "Restricted" means that a discrete word or feature occurs in the whole text, i.e., the entire Gospel of Luke, only in two places. If the feature is widely distributed

---

8. Phyllis Trible (*Rhetorical Criticism*, 106) admonishes authors (and by implication, classroom Bible teachers and preachers) not to focus on the literary structures discovered in a text, but on the message arising from the structures: "present . . . the finished product, leaving the reader to puzzle how it came forth."

in the narrative and not just in the passages at hand, it is less valuable to verify an intentional parallel.

Second, identify other significant words, phrases, actions, and concepts occurring in both of the passages that seem to correspond. Resist the urge to immediately apply a title to your analysis of the corresponding passages. If we do so, we begin to consider our creative title as a significant correspondence, *which it isn't*! A title is the *very last step* of any biblical analysis, or *maybe isn't needed at all*. Summary titles written too early undercut validation of the literary device, and blind exegetes to careful consideration of the text. I wrote all interpretive titles in this book only at the very end of the project.

Third, use a concordance to check each primary word identified in the two texts that seem to correspond. Do this in Greek if you can. If you don't work in Greek, try to use a resource like *The Englishman's Greek Concordance* that helps you know the Greek word behind the English translation. Find the distribution of each of the above primary words within the whole biblical book that you are studying. If a word or other feature occurs only in the two texts we are comparing, or only occur rarely elsewhere, it adds to the probability that the author intended the structure. If the word is widely distributed in the narrative and not just in the passages at hand, this word will be less valuable on its own in verifying an intentional parallel. I found, for example, that the word "manure" occurred only in the very two passages I was comparing (13:8; 14:35). While both episodes have a word for "ground" or "soil," that word occurs in Luke so frequently that it's presence in any episode does not signal any special literary arrangement.

Fourth, scan the two passages for obvious parallel subdivisions based on shared significant corresponding words, phrases, actions, or concepts. The more one passage corresponds directly to (or parallels) another passage in its detailed development (without skipping over anything, placing anything in parentheses as an aside, reintroducing "lost" wording, or moving anything), the more likely it is that the author intended the alignment. If we can do this work in Greek, we may find even more significant correspondences and our work will move even closer to discovering authorial intention.

Fifth, consider what deliberate editing a Gospel writer does to his sources in order to produce his Gospel. A telling factor in favor of author intentionality is when the Evangelist edits his source text to provide the same word or phrase in corresponding sections or when he rearranges what was in his source text (perhaps a portion of the Gospel of Mark) to create sequential corresponding subdivisions in his own narrative. Checking the editorial process of biblical authors can in some cases lead to strong validating evidence for concentric parallelisms.

Sixth, carefully examine the center section(s). Ask, what is this all about? Interpretation of a concentric parallelism in biblical narrative begins with interpretation of its center section or sections as viewed in connection with the literary/theological context of the entire structure, particularly in light of material in the outer sections (often tagged as Sections A/A'). Close analyses are needed because authorial purposes are unique to any concentric form various authors create, and there is no patterned way to find the meaning of the center. Close readings should also bear in mind narrative emphases of the text that fall before the beginning of the discovered literary form. When interpreted well, the center section or sections should clearly connect to the illustrations, nuances, or instances provided in all of the concentric sections arrayed around it. Repeated close readings of this material are essential and often productive.

Seventh, read two or more commentaries that identify main theological themes. As we consider the meaning of the correspondences (before we try to make up section titles, if we do) read commentaries that identify the main themes of theology in the biblical book we are studying. The biblical author labored to express certain themes. Scholars have discerned these over time and written them up for our benefit. Commentaries can provide likely conceptual directions and needed boundaries for confirming and interpreting what we have glimpsed. Commentaries also give invaluable help, of course, in the earlier steps listed above.[9]

Commentary authors and other biblical specialists disagree in a variety of ways with the propriety of identifying large concentric literary structures in biblical narrative. Joel Green believes that short-term memory of a reader/listener could not sustain an integration of such a lengthy literary complex.[10] Joseph Fitzmyer claims (regarding the Lukan journey narrative) that "it is impossible to detect a structure in this account or any genetic or logical development."[11] It is not my purpose to counter such objections with any answer other than the cumulative validity of the chapters in this book.

Who Intentionally Wrote History This Way?

Trained authors anywhere in the Greco-Roman and Hellenized world might employ concentric parallelism as one of their many rhetorical devices. For

---

9. Commentators who do literary or narratological analysis include Joseph Fitzmyer, David Tiede, Luke Timothy Johnson, Charles H. Talbert, and Robert Tannehill. I find Joel Green's volume, *The Gospel of Luke*, especially helpful.

10. Green, *Luke*, 399, n. 20.

11. Fitzmyer, *Luke I–IX*, 825.

example, Josephus, a Hellenized Jewish historian of the first century, organized portions of his *Wars of the Jews* concentrically.[12] Luke clearly shows that he belongs to the cohort of trained authors.

The author of the Third Gospel did not attach his name to the narrative: the work is anonymous. Only in the late second century Luke's name became associated with the narrative that tradition now calls "the Gospel according to Luke" (affirmed by Justin Martyr, about 160 CE; and by Irenaeus, about 180 CE). I follow the tradition. He no doubt had thorough training (and excellent ability) in Greek literary culture and yet was intimately aware of Israelite scripture, culture, and traditions. Luke was male, although he was (atypically for his time) quite concerned and articulate about responses of women to the kingdom of God. The Evangelist also wrote the anonymous Acts of the Apostles as volume two of his opus. Luke appears to have been a companion of Paul, given that Luke narrates portions of Acts using the pronoun "we" (16:10–18; 20:4—21:19; 27:1—28:30).

Luke was not an apostle of Jesus (as distinguished from being a follower of Jesus). Nor does he attribute his work to any apostle of Jesus to establish the work's authority. Luke's primary claim to authorial and editorial credibility lay in his literary introduction: the narrative is written to Theophilus as one more among many accounts that the man might have access to, but this one being a careful and orderly narrative to show the truth of what others taught (1:1–4). The narrative was written in the early sixties of the first century from an unknown location. In the early chapters of his work Luke writes and edits in the style of the Septuagint (LXX), possibly in order to seek further credibility by stylistic association with that widely known Greek Old Testament. Luke borrowed from Mark and from additional sources, certainly written ones (Luke 1:1) and possibly oral ones.[13]

Although unstated in the narrative, Luke implies that he is speaking with the authority of God. Compiling these episodes about Jesus in the selected order, Luke claims to tell a story on God's behalf about God's Son. As compiler from sources and literary stylist, the Evangelist avows to proclaim the nature and ways of God's kingdom as revealed in Jesus of Nazareth. Narrating episodes in the life and ministry of Jesus, Luke asserts an insider's perspective having divine authority. Never, apart from the introductory verses (1:1–4), however, does Luke address the particulars of his authority. But even there, Luke explicitly claims only an authority of a careful observer and of a disciplined writer (1:3).

---

12. Feldman, *Flavius Josephus*, xx–xxii.
13. We can identify this approach theoretically as the "Mark-plus theory."

INTRODUCTION   11

The author of the Third Gospel shows no evidence of seeking personal notice. Neither does he silently flaunt his literary ability: Luke's literary art must be sought out. He remains an unidentified literary craftsman and historian-theologian with a compelling larger vision.

Luke's Larger Intentions

Traditional outlines reveal the third Gospel's big picture, outlines that contain a mixture of thematic and geographical divisions: birth narratives of John and Jesus, Galilean ministry, journey southward, Jerusalem ministry, crucifixion, and resurrection. These outlines rightly feature Luke's role as a historian giving an account of the life and ministry of Jesus.

Luke was also a theologian and evangelist presenting truth to Theophilus, truth about the significance of Jesus. The following outline features Luke's narrative theology of Jesus.[14]

1:1–4	Introduction
1:5—3:22	Jesus and John
3:21–22	(transition)
3:21—4:15	Jesus and God
4:14–15	(transition)
4:14–44	Jesus and Authority
4:42—5:3	(transition)
4:42—6:19	Jesus the Master
6:17–19	(transition)
6:17–49	Jesus the Teacher
6:46–49	(transition)
6:46—9:2	Jesus the Lord
9:1–2	(transition)
9:1–50	Jesus and the Coming Crisis
9:51—19:46	Jesus the King
19:45–46	(transition)
19:44—22:6	Jesus the Priest
22:1–6	(transition)

14. Luke systematically connects these theological themes using the literary strategy of rhetorical transitions. For a thorough explanation of Greek rhetorical transitions, see Longenecker, *Rhetoric at the Boundaries*. Such short transitions artfully blend preceding and following themes.

22:1—24:12	Jesus and the Cross
24:1–12	(transition)
24:1–53	Jesus and the Resurrection
(Acts 1:3–5)	(transition)

The outline above schematizes certain important observations about how Luke folds Christology into his narrative, but the outline is arbitrary and incomplete. The theme of Jesus' relation to God, for example, often appears outside of Luke 3:21—4:15. The Gospel elsewhere contains a variety of statements and questions about Jesus' identity, questions about whether he is the Son of God and whether he is the Christ of God, and statements that indeed he is.

I have summarized the theme of Jesus' identity vis à vis God in a table below. The list of statements and questions starts with an angelic introduction followed by two cycles of identity discovery regarding Jesus. Cycle one begins with "You are my beloved Son" (3:22) and ends with "This is my Son, my Chosen One" (9:35), filled with affirmations and inquiries on the same theme in between. Peter's confession that Jesus is "the Christ of God" (9:20) begins the second cycle of discovery. The cycle ends with the series of unanswered questions in Luke 23 asking whether Jesus is the Christ of God, the king of the Jews.[15]

1:32	He will be great and will be called the Son of the Most High.
2:11	Unto you is born . . . a Savior, who is Christ the Lord.
3:22	You are my beloved Son
4:3, 9	If you are the Son of God
4:22	Is not this Joseph's son?
4:34	I know who you are— the Holy One of God
4:41	You are the Son of God; knew that he was the Christ
5:21	Who is this who speaks blasphemies? Who can forgive sins but God alone?
7:16	A great prophet has arisen among us!
7:19	Are you the one who is to come, or shall we look for another?
7:39	If this man were a prophet, he would have known . . . .
7:49	Who is this who even forgives sins?

---

15. Luke 9:1–50 serves literarily as a transition between themes, first bringing up the topic of kingship and then completing the cycle of identifying Jesus as God's Son (except see Luke 4:41 and 22:70).

INTRODUCTION   13

8:25   Who then is this, that he commands even winds and water, and they obey him?
8:28   What have you to do with me, Jesus, Son of the Most High God?

9:9   John I beheaded, but who is this about whom I hear such things?
9:18   Who do the crowds say that I am?
9:20   But who do you say that I am?
9:20   The Christ of God.
9:35   This is my Son, my Chosen One, listen to him.

22:67 If you are the Christ, tell us.
22:70 Are you the Son of God then?
23:3   Are you the king of the Jews?
23:35 He saved others; let him save himself, if he is the Christ of God, his Chosen One.
23:37 If you are the King of the Jews, save yourself.
23:39 Are you not the Christ?

This theological outline and these identity cycles help provide a big picture of Luke's narrative project.

We have described large-scale concentric parallelism, with methods that serve simultaneously to identify its presence in Lukan narrative and to confirm its intentionality. We touched only briefly on interpretation of concentric parallelisms under the sixth method listed above. The remainder of this book provides examples both of interpreting and documenting structures in the Gospel of Luke. Chapters 1–3 (Part 1) identify and interpret three large concentric structures within the Galilean ministry portion of the narrative. Chapters 4–14 (Part 2) document one far larger concentric form that structures the entire Lukan journey of Jesus from Galilee to Jerusalem, taking up the middle third of the Gospel.

Part 1

The Galilee Narrative

Luke's Galilee narrative describes the period in Jesus' ministry from his return to Galilee (4:14) after John's baptism and the devil's temptation to the moment when Jesus departs from Galilee toward Jerusalem (9:51). Rumors swirl around about Jesus (4:22, 23c, 37; 5:15; 7:18) and people come from near and far to see what he is doing and hear for themselves what he says.

Luke provides for Theophilus an account of Jesus' early ministry, an account aimed at convincing Theophilus of Jesus' uniqueness and of a requisite response to Jesus. Luke's presentation of Jesus' ministry in Galilee for Theophilus includes episodes arrayed in three large concentric parallelisms. These structures gather the story of Jesus up into theological units for a discerning reader.

Part 1 of this book identifies and interprets three concentric parallelisms in the first third of Luke's Gospel, with our chapters 1, 2 and 3 offering detailed validations and systematic interpretations. Readers should study these three concentric structures well before moving on to the fourth structure in Part 2.

1

Disciples and Apostles
Luke 4:40–6:19

Luke writes his narrative to a person he calls "most excellent Theophilus" in order to clarify for him a variety of teachings about Jesus that were circulating. He intends to provide Theophilus with "certainty" about the person and activity of Jesus (Luke 1:1–4). For Theophilus and for any other readers, certainty about what God is up to in the "word" about Jesus (2) warrants theological and practical consequences. Perhaps more on the practical side is the question, how does one become a follower of Jesus?

In order to answer this question, Luke organized a concentric prose discourse in Luke 4:40–6:19, that erects the following structure.[1]

4:40–5:1 Jesus heals them all.	A
5:2–11 Jesus takes his first disciples.	B
5:12–16 Jesus' healing hand	C
5:17–26 Authority of the Son of Man	D
5:27–39 Jesus calls sinners to repentance.	E
6:1–5 Authority of the Son of Man	D′
6:6–12a Jesus heals a hand.	C′
6:12–16 Jesus names his apostles.	B′
6:17–19 Jesus heals them all	A′

The justifications for dividing the text of Luke in this way make up a significant portion of this chapter, followed by an exposition on what Luke consequently teaches (through Jesus' words and actions) about following

---

1. The chapter introduction, sectional titles, and chapter subtitles were added only at the end of the study process, as aids for the reader.

Jesus as his disciples. In the course of our analysis we address Luke's unique perspective on disciples. Next we document the form. Finally we interpret the form.

Luke's Unique Perspective

Luke alone among the Gospels presents Jesus as calling disciples after a distinct time of individual ministry. Matthew, Mark, and John all describe Jesus as calling a band of disciples after his baptism and temptation. Matthew and Mark place the call of Simon Peter, Andrew, James, and John just after Jesus' withdrawal from the Judean wilderness to Galilee (Matt 4:12–22, Mark 1:14–20). John states that Simon Peter and others "came and saw" Jesus while all were still in the vicinity of John the Baptist (John 1:39). Subsequently Jesus calls them, renames Simon, and welcomes them to stay with him (1:29–51). Luke, however, uniquely places the gathering of disciples by Jesus as happening only after a period of unaccompanied ministry.

In Luke, Jesus returns to Galilee from the time of temptation in the Jordan wilderness, news about him spreads, he teaches in synagogues and then in the Nazareth synagogue. Later, in the Capernaum synagogue, he drives out a demon from a man, but leaves there in favor of ministry in Simon's home, where he heals diseases and casts out more demons until there is reason for Jesus to seek out temporary solitude (Luke 4:14–44).

Luke describes all of this as happening after Jesus' baptism and temptation in the wilderness, but before Jesus calls any disciples. At first Luke shows Jesus as a people's prophet, but not as the kind who gathers a band of followers. He seems to be like Elijah and Elisha (4:24–27), although not yet having any followers analogous to the "sons of the prophets."[2] But unlike those prophets he attracts crowds of the curious and the needy. "All" were transfixed by his teaching (4:20), "all spoke well of him and marveled" at his words (22), "all" were "amazed" at his authoritative power (36), people brought "all" the sick and diseased to him for healing and Jesus healed "every one" (40). "The people" want access to Jesus and to his amazing power; they would keep him for themselves (42).

Then Luke tells of Jesus beginning to call out (from 5:2) a band of disciples, some of whom Jesus will eventually, after a period of training, send out to broaden his ministry (9:1–6, 10:1–24). The story of whom he gathered and Luke's concurrent discourse on how persons become disciples extends through a long portion of text from 4:40 through 6:19, a portion which begins with Jesus having no disciples and ends with having twelve

---

2. See 2 Kg 2:3–18; 4:38–44; 6:1–7.

designated apostles (6:12–16) and "a great crowd of . . . disciples" (17), a portion centered on the statement "I have not come to call the righteous but sinners to repentance" (5:32).

Luke's unique presentation of this period in Jesus' ministry is made up of concentrically parallel rings of narration. These rings of encounters radiate out from a central teaching section in which Jesus teaches about calling disciples and becoming disciples. Luke organized and edited his sources to underline that Jesus had a period of ministry without disciples, and to further stress that the change from lacking disciples to having them contains important theological and practical concepts for the listener/reader. From Luke's unique perspective we turn to documentation of his concentric form.

Documenting the Form

In various ways Luke marks the transition from a linear description of Jesus' solo ministry to a concentric discourse on Jesus' gathering of disciples. First, the final episode of Jesus' ministry alone (4:40–41) contains indicators of a concluding statement. For one, Luke here densely clusters the words "all," "every," and "many." Luke frequently concentrates some or all of the words "all," "every," "many," and similar in a brief length of text as a formula to mark narrative boundaries. Further, "the sun was setting" provides a standard literary ending gesture. What is more, in 4:41 the Lukan narrator provides a summary explanation of repeated demonic outbursts about the identity of Jesus: "they knew he was the Christ."

Second, the next episode (4:42–44) signals a beginning. It is now morning. Jesus moves on, first to an isolated place for prayer (see 5:16) and then to other towns under a newly clarified sense of purpose.[3] Here Luke begins a new discourse.

At the other end of his discourse (6:17-19) Luke again deploys a rhetorical transition, also containing his typical section-ending formula ("all," "all," "all"). As a rhetorical transition, these verses have some of the feel of an introduction to the "Sermon on the Plain" (6:20–49), with its "stood on a level place" and its "all . . . who came to hear him." On the other hand, this transition echoes the beginning of our concentric structure in 4:40—5:1. Both texts summarize Jesus' healing of "diseases" (4:40; 6:18) and exorcisms, both speak of a *topos* ("place," 4:42; 6:17) where people throng to Jesus.

---

3. Luke may have seen, followed, and adapted a concentric structure already existing in Mark. If this is so, an additional degree of validation comes to structure we glimpse in Luke. See Rhoads, *Mark as Story*, 52–54, for a concentric approach to Mark 2:1—3:6 that is similar to our approach to Luke 4:40—6:19.

Furthermore, in 6:20 Luke departs from his practice of drawing on details and outline from Mark's Gospel, beginning his so-called "lesser interpolation" (6:20-8:3), with the possible implication that Luke intends 6:19 as a narrative boundary.

Luke 4:40–6:19 recounts a series of events in the early ministry of Jesus. As such, the story is propelled along by circumstantial connectives introducing many of these episodes: "And when it was day" (4:42), "On one occasion" (5:1), "when he had finished speaking" (4), "While he was in one of the cities" (12), "On one of those days" (17), "After this" (27), "On a Sabbath" (6:1), "On another Sabbath" (6), and "In these days" (12). Luke tells a linear episodic story about Jesus.

There is evidence, however, that he also concurrently (interlaid in the very same episodes) makes a concentrically organized discourse about how Jesus calls disciples and apostles. In this statement he organizes episodes into a shape having four pairs of corresponding sections plus an unpaired center section. Section A seems to correspond to Section A′ in certain important ways, Section B seems to correspond to Section B′ in other important ways, and so on. But what is the evidence for such correspondences?[4]

Jesus Heals Them All (Section A, 4:40–5:1a, and A′, 6:17–19)

In Section A Jesus heals "every one of them" (4:40); then, in a time of solitude that arises from the demands of the brief urban ministry, he discerns the necessity to shift location. He prepares to "preach the good news of the kingdom of God to the other towns" (43). The other section, Luke 6:17–19, places great stress on the quantity of people around Jesus, many of both disciples and other supplicants, who come to hear him and be cured by him. All experience Jesus' power.[5]

---

4. The following subheads are topical only (not theological). The subheads reflect features that justify seeing parallels in the text of Luke. I address the *meaning of the parallels* near the end of the chapter. This book is narrowly focused on the evidence for and meaning of concentric parallelisms in Luke's Gospel. For the meaning of other details that interest you, see traditional commentaries.

5. In tables having columns for comparison, I put an English word or phrase in italics when it conceptually corresponds to a word or phrase in the opposite column. Transliterations of Greek words are also in italics, transliterations being used instead of the Greek words themselves so that Bible students who do not read Greek can also see the lexical similarities between designated words.

Luke 4:40 Now when the sun was setting, *all those who had any who were sick with various* diseases *(nosois) brought them to him, and he laid his hands on every one of them and healed them.* ⁴¹ And demons also came out of many, crying, "You are the Son of God!" But he rebuked them and would not allow them to speak, because they knew that he was the Christ. ⁴² And when it was day, *he departed and went into a desolate place. And the people sought him and came to him, and would have kept him from leaving them,* ⁴³ but he said to them, "I must preach the good news of the kingdom of God to the other towns as well; for I was sent for this purpose." ⁴⁴ *And he was preaching in the synagogues of Judea.* 5:1 On one occasion, while the crowd was *pressing in on him* to hear the word of God, he was *standing by the lake* of Gennesaret,	Luke 6:17 *And he came down with them and stood on a level place, with a great crowd of his disciples and a great multitude of people from all Judea and Jerusalem and the seacoast of Tyre and Sidon,* ¹⁸ *who came to hear him and to be healed of their* diseases *(nosōn). And those who were troubled with unclean spirits were cured.* ¹⁹ And all the crowd *sought* to touch him, for power came out from him and healed them all.

Potential correspondences catch our eye. In Section A the people "seek" Jesus (4:42), while in Section A' the crowd seeks to touch him (6:19). Further, 4:42–44 shares with 6:17 movement of Jesus toward certain rural places, and both scriptures tell of other movement to and from towns, including named ones. In 4:42 Jesus comes to a specific *topos* (a "desert place"), and in 6:17 he comes to another specific *topos* (a "level place"). The region "Judea" is specified in both texts.[6] Our glance takes in similarities between 4:40 and 6:18–19: large groups of people come to Jesus to benefit from his powers of healing and exorcism, and indeed they all find the release they seek. Jesus' practice of placing his hands on those whom he is healing (4:40) gets noticed so that subsequently the crowd attempts to commandeer such power by reaching out to touch him (6:19).

Such possible correspondences draw us to look closer. What other evidence of author intentionality is here? Luke uses the word "diseases, *nosoi*" in both 4:40 and 6:18, a word he uses only two other times in his Gospel (7:21; 9:1). Adapting from the Second Gospel, Luke borrowed the Markan term *nosoi* for 4:40, but while in A' the Markan source had a different term for "diseases," Luke changed it to *nosoi* (6:18), apparently to help shape the correspondence of Sections A and A'. This appears to be intentional use of vocabulary of limited distribution in these two healing sections for the purpose of providing signposts to help the reader/listener discern a concentric discourse.[7]

---

6. Luke may in both A and A' use the place name "Judea" in a broad sense, meaning highland Palestine generally. See Luke 23:5 and Acts 10:37.

7. Luke 5:1 serves both to complete the themes of Section A and to begin the plot of Section B.

Jesus People (Section B, 5:1b–11, and B′, 6:12–16)

These sections recount key events as Jesus gathers an inner circle of disciples. First, he changes their identity from fishermen to fishers of men (B), and he formalizes their tie to him by designating them as apostles (B′). Most prominently, the call to catch men (5:10) is furthered in B′ by naming twelve as apostles or "sent ones" (6:13-16).

Two sets of restricted vocabulary in the sections raise the probability of intentional literary alignment. First, both Jesus' calling of the first disciples and his naming of the Twelve follow a night of toil. In Section B Simon objects when Jesus urges him to go back out and resume fishing, saying that "we toiled all night (through the whole night, *di' holes nuktos*) and took nothing" (5). This verse contains the only occasion in his Gospel where Luke uses the preposition *dia* with the noun for night, *nuktos*. Analogously in Section B′, using a verb that denotes intense effort, Luke narrates that Jesus "all night . . . continued in prayer" (*dianuktereuōn*, 12) before selecting his apostles. This verb occurs only here in the entire Gospel. Thus the phonemic sequence *dia . . . nukt—* is restricted in the Gospel to these two texts.

Luke 5:1 On one occasion, while the crowd was pressing in on him to hear the word of God, he was standing by the lake of Gennesaret, [2] and he saw two boats by the lake, but the fishermen had gone out of them and were washing their nets. [3] Getting into one of the boats, which was Simon's, he asked him to put out a little from the land. And he sat down and taught the people from the boat. [4] And when he had finished speaking, he said to Simon, "Put out into *the deep* and let down your nets for a catch." [5] And Simon answered, "Master, we toiled all night (*di' holes nuktos*) and took nothing! But at your word I will let down the nets." [6] And when they had done this, they enclosed a large number of fish, and their nets were breaking. [7] They signaled to their partners in the other boat to come and help them. And they came and filled both the boats, so that they began to sink. [8] But when Simon Peter (*Simōn Petros*) saw it, he fell down at Jesus' knees, saying, "Depart from me, for I am a sinful man, O Lord." [9] For he and *all who were with him* were astonished at the catch of fish that they had taken, [10] and so also were *James and John*, sons of Zebedee, who were *partners* with Simon. And Jesus said to Simon, "Do not be afraid; from now on you will be catching men." [11] And when they had brought their boats to land, they left everything and followed him.

Luke 6:12 In these days he went out to the mountain to pray, and all night (*ēn dianuktereuōn*) he continued in prayer to God. [13] And when day came, he called his disciples and chose from them twelve, whom he named apostles: [14] Simon, whom he named Peter (*Simōna hon kai ōnomasen Petron*), and *Andrew his brother*, and *James* and John, and Philip, and Bartholomew, [15] and Matthew, and Thomas, and James the son of Alphaeus, and Simon who was called the Zealot, [16] and Judas the son of James, and Judas Iscariot, who became a traitor.

Second, the narrator states in 6:14 that Jesus gave Simon the name Peter (*Simōna hon kai ōnomasen Petron*); in the Lukan narrative this may mean that Jesus did so when he selected Simon as an apostle. The narrator, however, first uses the dual name "*Simōn Petros*, Simon Peter" at 5:8, after referring to the fisherman as "Simon" three times. Such a deliberate placement of the apostle's dual name in the earlier text signals correspondence of Section B to Section B′. Further, these are the only two places in Luke's Gospel where he employs the full name "Simon . . . Peter," adding to the possibility that the sectional correspondence is intentional. So far in our study of Luke 4:40–6:19, we have documented two instances of correspondence between concentric sections based on restricted vocabulary. There are more in other sections.

Jesus' Healing Hand (Section C, 5:12–16); Jesus Heals a Hand (Section C′, 6:6–12a)

Luke in chapter 5 presents a leper who knows the power of Jesus to heal, but harbors doubts about whether Jesus would heal in his case. Jesus cleanses him and sends him off to seek an official "all clear" from the priest. Word gets out, bringing even more inquirers, from whom Jesus occasionally isolates himself for private prayer. In the other section, Luke 6:6–12a, Luke says that on a Sabbath Jesus encounters a man in the synagogue, a man having paralysis in his right hand. Jesus also encounters there a group of Sabbath rigorists gathering evidence against him, and they watch to see what Jesus will do about the man's hand. Jesus heals the hand, sending the prosecutors into a fury of plans against Jesus because he healed on the Sabbath. Luke adds that Jesus habitually sought out seclusion for prayer during that time. [8]

---

8. Luke in 6:12 artfully closes this section by its general first clause and introduces Section B′ by its specific second clause.

Luke 5:12 While he was in one of the cities, there came *a man full of leprosy.* And when he saw Jesus, he fell on his face and begged him, "Lord, *if you will*, you can make me clean." ¹³ And Jesus stretched out his hand (*ekteinas tēn cheira*) and touched him, saying, "I will; be clean." And immediately *the leprosy left him.* ¹⁴ And he charged him to *tell no one*, but "go and show yourself to the priest, and make an offering for your cleansing, as Moses commanded, for a proof to them." ¹⁵ But now even more the report about him went abroad, and great crowds *gathered to hear him and to be healed of their infirmities.* ¹⁶ But *he would withdraw* to *desolate places* and *pray.*

Luke 6:6 On another Sabbath, he entered the synagogue and was teaching, and *a man was there whose right hand was withered.* ⁷ And the scribes and the Pharisees watched him, to see *whether he would heal on the Sabbath, so that they might find a reason to accuse him.* ⁸ But he knew their thoughts, and he said to the man with the withered hand, "Come and stand here." And he rose and stood there. ⁹ And Jesus said to them, "I ask you, is it lawful on the Sabbath to do good or to do harm, to save life or to destroy it?" ¹⁰ And after looking around at them all he said to him, "Stretch out your hand (*ekteinon tēn cheira sou*)." And he did so, and *his hand was restored.* ¹¹ But they were filled with fury and *discussed with one another* what they might do to Jesus. ¹²ᵃ In these days *he went out* to *the mountain* to *pray* . . . .

The general parallel is striking. In each section Jesus heals a man who has a non-life-threatening disease and validates that healing to local Israelite authorities. We glimpse a few other surface indicators of correspondence between the sections. In particular, there seems to be a tandem sequence of five parts within the sections: a man's body bears a condition likely placing him in social and economic privation (5:12a; 6:6); someone challenges Jesus' integrity (5:12b; 6:7–9); a hand is extended, resulting in healing (5:13; 6:10); short-term and longer-term responses take shape (5:14–15; 6:11); and Jesus departs to a remote area to pray (5:16; 6:12a).

There is sub-surface evidence of correspondence between the two sections in the verb "stretch out, *ekteinein*," which Luke uses only three times in his Gospel, two of them here, the third elsewhere in a different meaning: "lay hands on" (22:53). In Section C Jesus "stretched out his hand" (*ekteinas tēn cheira*, 5:13) and, significantly, for a potentially contagious and ritually unclean disease, touched the leper making him "clean" (12). In the corresponding part of Section C′, Jesus told the man with the withered hand, "Stretch out your hand" (*ekteinon tēn cheira sou*, 6:10), and, significantly, while under scrutiny by the Pharisees lest Jesus do any work of healing on the Sabbath, did not touch the man to heal him. Clearly, Luke counterbalanced the verb "stretch out" (in this meaning) only in these two places. In Sections D/D′ to follow, Luke once again distinctively restricts one expression to two discrete sections.

The Authority of the Son of Man
(Section D, 5:17–26, and D′, 6:1–5)

An episode from Luke 5 displays a scene inside a house full of seated Pharisees and scribes evaluating Jesus; it is also full of onlookers; it is fuller still of the power of the Lord to heal; and it becomes even fuller when four men provide creative access through the roof for their paralyzed friend. They lower him right in front of Jesus. Instead of healing the man immediately, Jesus pronounces the man's sins forgiven, which stirs up thoughts of accusation against Jesus among the religious rigorists present. Jesus makes it clear to them that he, the Son of Man, has authority both to forgive sins and to heal. The paralytic gets up and leaves, healed and forgiven.

Luke 6:1–5 also takes place on a Sabbath (see 6:6), but outdoors in the fields. Pharisees challenge the propriety of the disciples, who have gleaned some heads of grain and hand-winnowed them for a snack. Jesus answers by drawing upon the life of David, pointing out that David had authority in a time of need to take priestly bread for his men to eat. Likewise Jesus, having the authority of the Son of Man, can provide for his men in an exceptional way.

Luke 5:17 On one of those days, as he was teaching, Pharisees and teachers of the law were sitting there, who had come from every village of Galilee and Judea and from Jerusalem. And the power of the Lord was with him to heal. [18] And behold, some men were bringing on a bed a man who was paralyzed, and they were seeking to bring him in and lay him before Jesus, [19] but finding no way to bring him in, because of the crowd, they went up on the roof and let him down with his bed through the tiles into the midst before Jesus. [20] And when he saw their faith, he said, "Man, your sins are forgiven you." [21] And the scribes and the Pharisees began to question, saying, "Who is this who speaks blasphemies? Who can forgive sins but God alone?" [22] When Jesus perceived their thoughts, he answered them, "Why do you question in your hearts? [23] Which is easier, to say, 'Your sins are forgiven you,' or to say, 'Rise and walk'? [24] But that you may know that the Son of Man has authority on earth to forgive sins" —he said to the man who was paralyzed—"I say to you, rise, pick up your bed and go home." [25] And immediately he rose up before them and picked up what he had been lying on and went home, glorifying God. [26] And amazement seized them all, and they glorified God and were filled with awe, saying, "We have seen extraordinary things today."

Luke 6:1 On a Sabbath, while he was going through the grainfields, his disciples plucked and ate some heads of grain, rubbing them in their hands. [2] But some of the Pharisees said, "Why are you doing what is not lawful to do on the Sabbath?" [3] And Jesus answered them, "Have you not read what David did when he was hungry, he and those who were with him: [4] how he entered the house of God and took and ate the bread of the Presence, which is not lawful for any but the priests to eat, and also gave it to those with him?" [5] And he said to them, "The Son of Man is lord of the Sabbath."

Plot movements occur in the same order in both passages. Some men, because they apparently trust Jesus, unwittingly create a controversy between Jesus and some on-looking Pharisees (5:18–20; 6:1). The Pharisees consequently challenge Jesus' authority by questioning him (5:21; 6:2). Jesus responds to their challenges by his own questioning (5:22–24; 6:3–5), claiming the authority of the Son of Man. Jesus clarifies to the Pharisees that he is the Son of Man who "has authority on earth to forgive sins" (5:24a) and the Son of Man who authoritatively interprets scripture as the "lord of the Sabbath" (6:5).

A lexical feature shared by both of these accounts increases the possibility that Luke intentionally aligned these sections. Pharisees object that only God can act with divine authority, "Who can forgive sins but God alone?" (*ei mē monos ho theos*, 5:21). Jesus forgives anyway. Similarly in the opposite section, Pharisees protest that Jesus' disciples (by his permission) breach God's Sabbath law by plucking, cleaning, and eating grain on that day. Jesus affirms their behavior. He teaches that a precedent that priestly privilege was set aside by the needs of David and his men as they took and ate bread that "is not lawful for any but the priests to eat" (*ei mē monous tous hiereis*, 6:4).

In both cases, God's anointed one acts with unexpected authority. The sequence of Greek words *ei mē mono—* ("except only . . .) occurs in Luke only at these two places. Further, with Luke still adapting his Markan source as he assembles both of these passages, in Section D he changes Mark's *heis* (Mk 2:7) to *monos* (Luke 5:21), and then in Section D' adds *monous* (6:5) where the Markan text lacked it (Mk 2:26), with the result that both sections contain this unique sequence of words. When Luke edits his sources to create such a restricted lexical correspondence, we conclude that Luke intentionally counterpoised these two controversies about Jesus' authority with religious authorities.

We have finished now with the architecture of the last of the large corresponding sections in our text, Luke 4:40–6:19, and move on to Section E, which stands alone at the center of the literary structure.

Jesus Calls Sinners to Repentance (Section E, 5:27–39)

In the middle section Jesus clarifies to both friends and critics what it means to follow him as a disciple. Jesus calls Levi the tax collector to follow him, and Levi does so immediately. Levi then throws a large feast for Jesus, with Levi's friends and professional contacts as other guests, but on-looking critics object that Jesus should not fraternize with such irreligious people. Jesus compares his relationship to Levi, that of calling the unrighteous to repent, to the relationship of a physician to his sick patient.[9] The critics then change their approach to criticize the piety of Jesus and his disciples, claiming that really religious people don't party, they fast and pray. Jesus counters that exceptional behavior (feasting) is now appropriate because of the exceptional guest they are celebrating. Honoring Jesus is like honoring a bridegroom. Further, new repentance and a new Lord require in the disciple a new form of life. The old ways are no longer appropriate to a changed life, as used wineskins cannot bear the ferment of new wine and as new unshrunk cloth cannot successfully patch an old garment. This is the essential profile of following Jesus.[10]

But before we interpret the section, it is appropriate to ask whether the section discloses its own interior concentric structure that can be validated by the criteria listed in chapter 1. Large structures such as Luke 4:42—6:19 may indeed have small structures within them.[11] This author sees a compact concentric structure here (*abcb'a'*) in which 5:27–29 corresponds to 36–39, 30–31 corresponds to 33–35, and 32 stands alone as *unit c*. Can such an observation be validated as intentional on Luke's part?

Luke 5:27 After this he went out and saw a tax collector named Levi, sitting at the tax booth. And he said to him, "Follow me." 28 And leaving everything, he rose and followed him. 29 And Levi made him a great feast in his house, and there was a large company of tax collectors and others reclining at table with them.

Luke 5:36 He also told them a parable: "No one tears a piece from a new garment and puts it on an old garment. If he does, he will tear the new, and the piece from the new will not match the old. 37 And no one puts new wine into old wineskins. If he does, the new wine will burst the skins and it will be spilled, and the skins will be destroyed. 38 But new wine must be put into fresh wineskins. 39 And no one after drinking old wine desires new, for he says, 'The old is good.'"

---

9. Jesus' metaphor implies that following Jesus (5:28) also means repenting of sin (31–32).

10. The center material, 5:27–39, of this large concentric parallelism constitutes "a single scene" centered on Jesus' words, "I came not to call the righteous but sinners to repentance" (32). See Green, *Luke*, 245.

11. We subdivide Section E using lower-case italic letters as unit designations. I refer to these small passages as "units" to distinguish them from the larger "sections" in the previous discussion.

5:30 And the Pharisees and their scribes grumbled at his disciples, saying, "Why do you eat and drink with tax collectors and sinners?" [31] And Jesus answered them, "Those who are well have no need of a physician, but those who are sick.

5:33 And they said to him, "The disciples of John fast often and offer prayers, and so do the disciples of the Pharisees, but yours eat and drink." [34] And Jesus said to them, "Can you make wedding guests fast while the bridegroom is with them? [35] The days will come when the bridegroom is taken away from them, and then they will fast in those days."

5:32 I have not come to call the righteous but sinners to repentance."

Levi's radical positive response following Jesus' call (27b–28) seems to correspond to the main thrust of Jesus' parable: the disjunction of new and old cloth or fresh and old wineskins (36–38). New must go with new. Levi expressed his new relationship to Jesus in a new action of abandoning his tax-gathering table and perhaps abandoning his lucrative franchise. Further, the great feast in which many recline at Levi's table with Levi and Jesus (29) finds an echo in the drinking of new and old wine and in attending to how *good* the wine is (36–39). Similarly, one might at first glance consider units to cohere by an accumulation of similar elements in the same order. This order includes the observation that in both units the Pharisees (with their scribes in unit *b*) indirectly challenge Jesus' righteousness through criticism of his disciples. Second, the Greek text of both challenges places the words *eat and drink* at the end of the sentence (30, 33). And finally, in terms of corresponding figures of speech, Jesus indirectly answers in each case by the use of metaphor (31, 34–35).

We tried in the paragraph above to draw out evidence that Section E exhibits its own internal concentrically parallel structure, but we cannot adequately show that Luke intended such a structure within Section E. When we apply the "due diligence" tests from chapter 1, our effort falls short due to lack of first-order evidence. When we seek validation for concentricity in the ordinary vocabulary, the concepts, and the figures of speech occurring in both halves of this Section, our proposal lacks potent correspondences. Our "seeing" is not in fact truly "seeing." Glimpses of concentric structure must be tested for validity.

Considering 5:27–39 as a whole, however, v 32 still stands out as a summary statement, naming the issue of righteousness and repentance as central to Jesus' purpose. Luke's large structure requires a center between its double line-up of other episodes: Section E, with Jesus' purpose statement in its very midst, marks the center.

We are now ready to interpret what we have validated as concentric literary architecture. We have shown that a series of four episodes aligns with another series of four episodes. Between lies a middle section highlighted by Jesus' teaching that he came to call sinners to repentance. A pastor's or teacher's patience and discipline in validating this suspected concentric parallelism brings an opportunity for that leader to teach authoritatively based on knowing Luke's compositional intention.

Interpreting the Form

Going back to an earlier explanation, at the level of story the narrative moves forward by means of the typical circumstantial connectives such as "then" or "after that" or "when they arrived." Linear biblical narrative advances its own meanings, both within episodes and in the sequencing of episodes. Bringing out these meanings is the purpose of most traditional biblical commentaries.

In some portions of the Bible, however, concurrently with a linear narrative the author might also organize a concentrically balanced narrative, its ring structure intended to arrest the reader's attention and theological interest. The theological discourse arising from such a structure is *concurrent*; that is, the meaning of such a discourse normally does not displace the meaning of the individual episodes or of the collective linear story of the narrative. As we now begin to interpret the concentric form validated above, we look for a Lukan discourse that *stands alongside* the meaning of the linear narrative (the story about Jesus), not in place of it.

The Unpaired Center Section.

In concentric parallelisms, particularly in those that have an unpaired center section, the center section provides the main theme of the overall form and the concepts needed for interpreting it.[12] In our current study, Section E (5:27–39) is that unpaired center section. The section holds its own lexical and syntactic ties to all the sections arrayed around it, but more significantly, it contains the conceptual keys that explain the meaning of the whole concentric structure from Luke 4:40 to 6:19. Every part of this section's concentric discourse connects theologically to (1) those who do or may respond to Jesus by following him, (2) the identity and authority of the Lord and prophet who calls them into his band, or (3) to ways to respond to him.

Potential followers include, for example, opportunists (tax collectors, 5:27–30), sinners in general (30, 32), and the highly religious (Pharisees along with their scribes; 30, 33). Following Jesus involves at least hearing

---

12. Some authors limit the term "chiasmus" to this form.

and then heeding his call to follow (Levi, 27–28), table fellowship with him (Levi, 29; metaphorical wedding guests, 34), repentance from sin (32), and (metaphorically) putting the new product in a new and appropriate container (new cloth and new wine, 36–38). The one who calls people to follow him appears here as "he" (27), "Jesus" (31, 34), "I" (32), and metaphorically as a physician (31) and a bridegroom (34–35). The relation of the called to this caller is that they follow (27–28), they host him (29), they recline and eat with him (29–30), they need him (31–32), they submit morally to him (32), and (metaphorically) they are hosted by him (34–35). Those here who do not follow Jesus react to his choice of friends (29–30) and to his lack of visible piety (33).

Such details of this central Section put forward a group of key concepts. First, Jesus calls and gathers disciples; becoming a disciple involves following Jesus. Then, following him means a moral and sometimes physical departure from one's past ways to be with Jesus. Further, becoming a disciple means responding to Jesus' call, receiving restoration from him, and fellowshipping at his table. And fourth, it means submitting to Jesus as the authoritative interpreter of how to please God.

Terminal Sections

The eight paired sections arrayed concentrically around this center contain illustrations and clarifications of these main concepts. Sections A and A' begin and round off Luke's discourse on (the first phase of) disciples being included in Jesus' ministry: the sections show general movement from no disciples (4:40–44) to many disciples and even to a few apostles (6:17). The crowd gains a key new insight: that as disciples they are to go with him (6:17), rather than he come to them or stay with them (4:42b). They begin to realize that to follow Jesus is to follow God's prophet (4:43; 6:18a).

Interior Sections

Sections B and B' particularize: Jesus calls certain named men from an identifiable place plying a common trade (5:1–3, 10) to follow him, and then to represent him as apostles (6:13–16). Peter's response to divine power mediated by Jesus, a response of desolate humility before the holy and then a response of unconditional commitment to Jesus' assuring call, brings the particularization to a sharp focus. Simon Peter is a normal person whose life is radically changed by encountering and then following Jesus. Luke also clarifies through his characterization of Peter how disciples should view

Jesus. He is more than a "master" (5:5) given temporary leadership, he is the "Lord" (8) whose word is to be trusted and followed, just as Jesus trusts and follows what God reveals to him in prayer (6:12).[13] These four sections (A, A', B, B'), the outer four Sections of the concentric literary form, unambiguously display the concepts of Section E, the center of the form.

The next four sections moving toward the interior of the structure also display the concepts described above, but less transparently. In the linear story, Jesus' disciples and those clearly becoming disciples mostly disappear from the spotlight and move into the background. Secondly, new themes in the linear story seem to subvert the "following Jesus" theme of the concentric discourse: Sections C and D appear to be about healing, not about calling or becoming disciples; likewise, Sections C' and D' at the surface appear to be about an ongoing debate with the scribes and Pharisees over sabbath-keeping regulations, not about disciple-making or following Jesus. Yet on the conceptual level, Luke's discourse on discipleship continues.

Sections C and D illustrate how Jesus' physician metaphor (5:31) directly links to "sinners" and "repentance" (32): Jesus chooses to "cleanse," both physically and spiritually, one who is full of scars and wounds (12–16); and paralysis happens on both the physical plane, needing his healing, and the spiritual plane, needing his forgiveness (17–26). Jesus gives his followers release from bondage. This restoration is basic to following Jesus.

Sections D' and C' clarify further who it is that Jesus calls – *he also calls these scribes and Pharisees*, a call whose reception hangs in the balance because, while we read here that they are furious with Jesus and want to impede him in some way, we never read the end of their story in Luke's Gospel. We never read that Pharisees and scribes finally reject Jesus.[14] Luke leaves the question open.[15] In the Third Gospel Jesus never closes his call to sinners of any kind. A call to scribes and Pharisees means, as a first step, that they would submit their understanding of the letter and spirit of the scriptures to Jesus. He would be their authoritative rabbi, and they would leave aside other authorities just as clearly as Peter left aside the boat. Thus these four sections surrounding the center section clarify further both *what* life-change can happen to those who follow Jesus and, indeed, *whose* lives can be changed.

---

13. Jesus too is one "set under authority," as recognized by a centurion (Luke 7:8).

14. See Green, *Luke*, 300–302, 305–308, and 537–38. See also Acts 5:34-39 and 23:9.

15. Whereas in Mark 3:6 they immediately set about planning how to destroy Jesus. We, however, are limiting our analysis to Luke's Gospel only and not attempting a harmonizing interpretation, because Luke provides to Theophilus a unified narrative adequate for him (and today's reader) to "have certainty concerning the things you have been taught," 1:4.

For the reader ready to see it, in 5:27–39 Luke gathered words of Jesus about calling disciples to himself and about the nature of following him. Around those verses Luke arrayed pairs of episodes from Jesus' early ministry which, concentric pair by concentric pair, help readers "have certainty about the things" (1:4) that we and Theophilus may have been taught about following Jesus.

Summary

Luke provided Theophilus a narrative on an already-familiar story of Jesus: his antecedents, his preparation, and his inclusion of disciples into God's mission. But the period of unaccompanied ministry in Luke's narrative would, perhaps, be unanticipated by Theophilus, based on other oral or written accounts of Jesus that Theophilus encountered. Its substantial presence in Luke's account postponed and thereby highlighted the time when Jesus began to gather disciples. Further, narrative tension in the unaccompanied ministry period between ministry to people who want to "keep him" in their locale (4:40–42) and Jesus' commitment to purposeful ministry-on-the-move to other places (43–44) leaves the sympathetic reader wondering how the tension will be resolved. Will Jesus stay or go?

The Gospel writer answers by means of a concentrically structured discourse made up of episodes from Jesus' early ministry. The structure is a large concentric parallelism of episodes arrayed around an axis. *The answer to the reader's question which Luke articulates through this device is that Jesus calls individual people, brings their lives into God's healing, wholeness, and kingdom, and keeps the people with him as he pursues God's purpose elsewhere. Going with him involves abandonment of competing loyalties, trust in Jesus' protection and provision, and submission to the kingdom of God.*

The Story Continues

The outworking of these episodes, Luke 4:40—6:19, in the rest of the Gospel, however, remains anything but clear and simple. Do healed people actually follow him? Must the healed and the repentant leave home and follow Jesus? What will the "great crowd" of disciples and "great multitude" (6:17) of curious and needy people do in response to Jesus? Does the concentric discourse about becoming disciples and apostles of Jesus serve as the base line for what follows in the Gospel?

In chapters seven through ten, multitudes come to Jesus and follow him for various reasons (7:11, 8:1–3, 9:11, 10:1), and in 9:14 the crowd increases to "five thousand men." Yet by the end of Luke 23 the corpus of followers apparently has not multiplied, but possibly diminished substantially (22: 39–46; 23:49). In the latter reference, followers are called "acquaintances, *gnōstoi*," adding to Luke's unclear distinctions between "the twelve," "disciples," and "crowds" as the narrative proceeds. In many places, Luke mentions that only Jesus goes or comes, with silence about his disciples or apostles or the crowds. They seem to disappear for lengthy portions of narrative.

Various people who experience God's kingdom through the ministry of Jesus are told to go home or go away rather than to join his band (5:14, 24-25; 7:22; 8:48; 14:4; 17:19), and one who pleaded to continue with Jesus was instructed to go home and carry out there a veritable apostolic role (8:39). In Luke's Gospel, after the end of our text in 6:19, Jesus' followers may or may not stay with Jesus and may or may not be identified as disciples or apostles.

How are we to understand these observations in the light of Luke's discourse on becoming disciples in 4:40–6:19 with its center in 5:27–39? What could a preacher or Bible teacher put forward to learners that would be consistent with both the discourse described above and with details in the rest of the narrative?[16] First, departure to follow Jesus may indeed mean geographic dislocation, but it certainly means redirection into the rule of God through Jesus. Further, such a departure may include release from a degrading bondage and some kind of restoration to wholeness, flourishing, and life in God's kingdom. Third, since Jesus sends his followers on "ahead" to places Jesus himself is about to come, being his disciple today means not only being with Jesus to hear, pray, be healed, and worship, but also venturing in Jesus' name into lives and places where his word and kingdom do not yet reign.[17] These summary statements might adequately nuance our conclusions from Luke 4:40–6:19.

As students of the Gospels, Acts, and of Old Testament narratives, pastors and other careful readers of the Bible sometimes recognize that a familiar word, theme, or scenario comes back into the story we are studying. For that phenomenon, one approach to analysis and interpretation that we can consider is the *possibility* that the authors/editors employed concentric parallelism to express a theological discourse concurrently with the story. Between glimpsing features of a potential concentric parallelism and eventually proclaiming its message, however, awaits a process of carefully

---

16. Apart, that is, from harmonizing with other Lukan texts about being Jesus' disciples: 9:57–62, 14:25–33, for example.

17. "Messengers" in 9:52 are called "disciples" in 9:54; "others" in 10:1 are called "disciples" in 10:23; "disciples" in 19:29 are called "those who were sent" in 19:31. See also 8:39.

validating the presence of such a structure and systematically interpreting it.[18]

---

18. Wisdom of others indicates that teachers should teach the results of their study, but not try to lead one's students through all the steps of analysis and discovery that the teacher has taken. When intellectual curiosity of students craves more detail for the basis of your interpretation, show them sparingly, to the extent that their curiosity is satisfied. See Trible, *Rhetorical Criticism*, 106.

2

Take Care How You Receive the Word
Luke 7:1–8:56

IN LUKE'S CHAPTERS 4–6, crowds of eager listeners jostle closer to hear Jesus' riveting teaching on the ways and purposes of God, and on how to live under Jesus' lordship. In Luke 7–8 Jesus calls for much more than casual curiosity about his words and works, he calls for embracing them as the source of life. His words and his works together constitute his *word*. Jesus calls people to conform daily to what they hear from him, following him with tenacity and hope. Jesus calls people to delight in and embrace the logic (*logos*) of what they see him do. Luke organizes a concentric theological discourse in chapters seven and eight (7:1–8:56) of his narrative to emphasize that disciples of Jesus must heed the word they hear or experience from him.

Let's consider for a moment how ancient storytellers and historians wrote. Virgil in his *Aeneid* and Thucydides in his *History of the Peloponnesian War*, for example, wrote in and for a literary culture for whom it was normal to read or hear stories arranged in complex concentric forms. The Gospel of Mark boasts a similar mix of narrative and design.[1] Luke, as a highly articulate and capable writer of Greek, entirely steeped in the Hebrew scriptures and culture as well, compiles and edits his narrative for Theophilus primarily within the practices of Greco-Roman literary culture. Such practices included the blending of story with theological discourse by the artful and purposeful structuring of material within the narrative.

Accordingly, Luke styles what we know as chapters seven and eight of his Gospel as an extensive concentric parallelism of episodes. Earlier episodes about Jesus' word thematically match episodes about it later in the

---
1. Rhoads, *Mark as Story*, 52–54.

portion. Luke arrays outer episodes around other episodes that serve as the center or axis. The whole structure is calculated by Luke to urge a living, dynamic relation to Jesus and his word, not a passive or static one. The overall topic radiates from the center section of the concentric form (8:4-18): what does it mean to bear fruit for the kingdom of God in a continuing way, having once received the word of God. The following form in 7:1–8:56 structures Luke's discourse:[2]

7:1–17 The Lifegiving Word	A
7:18–35 The Reported Word	B
7:36–50 The Godlike Word	C
8:1–3 The Operative Word	D
8:4–18 Hearing the word	E
8:19–21 The Operative Word	D′
8:22–25 The Godlike Word	C′
8:26–39 The Reported Word	B′
8:40–56 The Lifegiving Word	A′

Luke's "Sermon on the Plain" (6:20–49) forms an introduction to the discourse in 7:1–8:56. Jesus addresses his teaching on the plain primarily to his disciples (6:20, 27, 39, 46), his words in the sermon being about behaviors and behavioral motivations in Jesus' new community.[3] Jesus emphasizes that his disciples must live out all of their relationships in the counter-cultural ways of the Jesus community: daily life in the kingdom of God is predicated on it, the justice of the coming eschaton calls for it, and personal submission to Jesus the Lord demands it. Jesus' simile comparing trees and their fruit to his hearers and their behavior prepares the reader/listener of the Sermon for the core metaphor of 7:1–8:56: God's word as seed yielding (or not yielding) fruit in the lives of those who encounter Jesus.[4]

Documenting the Form

In these accounts Jesus gives life to those who trust him, both to social insiders and social outsiders, to the dying, the dead, and the good-as-dead. The stories inform us as well as confront us with hope in Jesus. Luke continues narrating the ministry of Jesus and concurrently fashions in them a

---

2. The chapter introduction, sectional titles, and chapter subtitles were added only at the end of my study process, as aids for the reader.

3. This perspective on the Sermon on the Plain depends heavily on the insights of Green, *Luke*, 265–71.

4. The teaching of Jesus was previously identified as the word of God (5:1).

discourse about the "word" of God coming to Israel in the ways and words of Jesus (see 7:7, "but say the word").[5]

The Lifegiving Word (Section A, 7:1–17, and A′, 8:40–56)

Twice in Luke 7 and 8 Jesus commands dead bodies to resume living. Luke 7:1–17 and 8:40–56 contain these commands plus an array of additional parallel features. The sustained similarities and oppositions show that Luke placed them in an intentional correspondence.[6]

Luke 7:1 After he had finished all his sayings in the hearing of the people, he entered Capernaum. ² Now a *centurion* had a servant who was sick and *at the point of death*, who was highly valued by him. ³ When the *centurion* heard about Jesus, he sent to him elders of the Jews, asking him to come and heal his servant. ⁴ And when they came to Jesus, they *pleaded with him* earnestly, saying, "He is worthy to have you do this for him, ⁵ for he loves our nation, and he is the one who built us our *synagogue*."

Luke 8:40 Now when Jesus returned, the crowd welcomed him, for they were all waiting for him. ⁴¹ And there came a man named Jairus, *who was a ruler* of the *synagogue*. And falling at Jesus' feet, he *implored him* to come to his house, ⁴² for he had *an only daughter*, about twelve years of age, and she was *dying*.

---

5. In light of Greek discourse analysis, Section A actually begins at 7:2. Verse one concludes the previous section.

6. In the quoted biblical text I put an English word or phrase in italics when it conceptually corresponds to a word or phrase in the opposite section. Transliterations of Greek words are also in italics. Additionally, words that qualify as restricted or highly limited vocabulary are in italics.

⁶ And *Jesus went* with them. When he was not far from the house, the centurion sent friends, saying to him, "Lord, *do not trouble yourself,* for I am *not worthy to have you come under my roof.* ⁷ *Therefore I did not presume to come to you.* But say *the word,* and let my servant *be healed.* ⁸ For I too am *a man set under authority,* with soldiers under me: and *I say to one,* 'Go,' and he goes; and *to another,* 'Come,' and he comes; and *to my servant,* 'Do this,' and he does it." ⁹ When Jesus heard these things, he marveled at him, and turning to the crowd that followed him, said, "I tell you, not even *in Israel* have I found *such faith."* ¹⁰ And when those who had been sent returned to the house, they found the servant *well.*

¹¹ Soon afterward he went to a town called Nain, and his disciples and a great crowd went with him. ¹² As he drew near to the gate of the town, behold, a man who *had died* was being carried out, *the only son of his mother,* and she was a widow, and a considerable *crowd* from the town was *with her.* ¹³ And when the Lord saw her, *he had compassion* on her and said to her, *"Do not weep."* ¹⁴ Then he came up and *touched the bier,* and the bearers stood still. And he said, *"Young man,* I say to you, *arise."* ¹⁵ And the dead man *sat up and began to speak,* and Jesus *gave* him to his mother. ¹⁶ *Fear seized them all,* and they *glorified* God, saying, "A great prophet has arisen among us!" and "God has visited his people!" ¹⁷ And this *report about him spread* through the whole of Judea and all the surrounding country.

As *Jesus went,* the people pressed around him. ⁴³ *And there was a woman who had had a discharge of blood for twelve years, and though she had spent all her living on physicians, she could not be healed by anyone.* ⁴⁴ She came up behind him and *touched the fringe of his garment,* and immediately *her discharge of blood ceased.* ⁴⁵ And Jesus *said,* "Who was it that touched me?" When all denied it, Peter said, "Master, the crowds surround you and are pressing in on you!" ⁴⁶ But Jesus said, "Someone touched me, for I perceive that power has gone out from me." ⁴⁷ And when *the woman saw that she was not hidden,* she came trembling, and falling down before him *declared in the presence of all the people why she had touched him,* and how she had been immediately healed. ⁴⁸ And he said to her, *"Daughter, your faith* has made you *well*; go in *peace."*

⁴⁹ While he was still speaking, someone from the ruler's house came and said, *"Your daughter is dead*; do not trouble the Teacher any more." ⁵⁰ But Jesus on hearing this answered him, "Do not fear; only believe, and she will be well." ⁵¹ And when he came to the house, he allowed *no one* to enter *with him,* except Peter and John and James, and *the father and mother of the child.* ⁵² And all were *weeping and mourning* for her, but he said, *"Do not weep,* for she is not dead but sleeping." ⁵³ And they *laughed at him,* knowing that she was dead. ⁵⁴ But *taking her by the hand* he called, saying, *"Child, arise."* ⁵⁵ And her *spirit returned,* and she *got up at once.* And he directed that something *should be given* her to eat. ⁵⁶ And her parents *were amazed,* but he charged them to *tell no one what had happened.*

The first thing that catches our eye is the "sandwich" ordering of the accounts in 8:40–56.⁷ The episode about the woman with a discharge of blood is surrounded by the one about Jairus and his daughter. Such a method of storytelling insists that the listener/reader consider the two accounts

---

7. Or intercalation.

together. In important ways they are about the same thing and to some degree supplement each other. Two stories tell one story.

Two stories together? As we read chapters seven and eight of Luke closely, one possible question to ask about this account is whether there are two *other* adjacent stories here that tell one story. There are no other "sandwiched" accounts. But is it possible that there are two other adjacent univocal accounts, and might such accounts in some way "balance off" or correspond to aspects of 8:40–56?

Two other such adjacent stories occur in 7:1–17: the healing of the centurion's servant and raising the widow's son. The verses correspond to 8:40–56 in multiple ways. In both double stories Jesus responds to pleas for help from respected leaders (7:2–5; 8:41). He draws near the leaders' homes but is nevertheless told not to trouble himself (7:6; 8:49) by any further approach to the dead or dying household members (7:2; 8:42). Parents having only one child have lost their child to death (7:12; 8:42, 49). Jesus rebukes weeping mourners, and he makes physical contact with the dead person (thus ritually polluting himself). He commands each corpse to "rise" (7:13–14; 8:52, 54). Both bodies immediately come alive in good health (7:15; 8:55). Enough surface evidence accumulates here to propose that the two adjacent stories of Luke 7:1–17 correspond to the two "sandwiched" stories of Luke 8:40–56. Deeper evidence further confirms our observation.

Tightly restricted vocabulary also validates correspondence between Sections A and A'. The verb "do not trouble yourself" (*mē skullou*) of 7:6 occurs elsewhere in Luke only in 8:49, "do not trouble the Teacher any more" (*mēketi skulle*). The adjective "only-born" (*monogenēs*) of 7:12 and 8:42 occurs elsewhere in Luke only at 9:38 (the pleading of a man whose son is demonized). Restricted and highly limited vocabulary such as these indicates that text surrounding Luke 7:6 and 12 was intended by Luke to correspond in some way to text around 8:42 and 49.

Other deep confirmation of our thesis comes from Luke's editing of his Markan source for the episode about Jairus and his daughter. His editorial work on the sources for Luke 7:1–17 is inaccessible to us because those sources are not extant, but for the Jairus story and the story of the woman with the hemorrhage, Luke clearly uses Mark.[8] Of the three times that Luke moves Markan material to a different location in his own account of the story, one of them is significant for our validation process. Luke moves the last clause of Mark's version (*and told them to give her something to eat*, Mark 5:43b) forward to a position ahead of the parents' amazement and ahead of

---

8. Many speculate that Luke took episodes about the centurion and about the widow of Nain from a theoretical source commonly called "Q."

Jesus' charge to remain silent about the resuscitation (Luke 8:55, 56). As the result, the word *be given* (*dothēnai*, 8:55c) in Section A′ stands in correlation to the word *gave* (*edōken*, 7:15b) in Section A, the narrator's statement about Jesus giving the revived son to his mother. This is a plausible reason for Luke, in appropriating Mark's account for his own, to change the ending in that way.

The evidence above shows that Luke aligned 7:1–17 to correspond with 8:40–56. In both sections Jesus' powerful word gives mortal life back to dead people (a man and a woman) and vigor back to languishing people (a man and a woman). Each of them receive vitality directly from Jesus: his word enlivens them without mediation. An indirect word from Jesus, however, informs the plots of the next sections toward the interior of the structure.

The Reported Word (Section B, 7:18–35, and B′, 8:26–39)

Sections B and B′ highlight the word of God as reportage, as indirect exposure to words and doings of Jesus. John the Baptist (Section B) and the peope of Gerasa (Section B′) hear reports of Jesus' actions, reports fraught with his expectation that the report warrants positive response.

In Section B′ we read two additional responses to Jesus as he comes ashore in Gentile territory. The demon-possessed man had been naked, wild, and out of his mind, but after Jesus heals him he is clothed, composed, and in his right mind. He wants to follow Jesus wherever the boat would take him, but accedes to Jesus' command to return to his own people to become a preparer of the way. Section B′, as in Section B, features an individual believer in Jesus and a group of those who do not believe the visible evidence about Jesus. The Gerasene crowd fear Jesus and his powers; they want him to leave. Luke in effect urges readers of these accounts to align themselves with the purpose of God shown in the life and ministry of Jesus, even when those in control promote questioning him, resisting him, bargaining with him, or fearing him.

Luke 7:18 The disciples of John reported all these things to him. And *John*, [19] calling two of his disciples to him, sent them to the Lord, saying, "Are you the one who is to come, or shall we look for another?" [20] And when the *men (andres)* had come to him, they said, "John the Baptist has sent us to you, saying, 'Are you the one who is to come, or shall we look for another?'"

[21] In that hour he healed *many (polloi)* people of *diseases and plagues and evil spirits*, and on *many (polloi)* who were blind he bestowed sight.

[22] And he answered them, "*Go and tell* John what you have seen and heard: *the blind receive their sight, the lame walk, lepers are cleansed, and the deaf hear, the dead are raised up*, the poor have good news preached to them. [23] And blessed is the one who is not offended by me."

[24] When John's *messengers had gone*,

Luke 8:26 Then they sailed to the country of the Gerasenes, which is opposite Galilee. [27] When Jesus had stepped out on land, there met him *a man (anēr)* from the city who had demons. For a long time *he had worn no clothes, and he had not lived in a house but among the tombs*. [28] When he saw Jesus, he cried out and fell down before him and said with a loud voice, "What have you to do with me, Jesus, Son of the Most High God? I beg you, do not torment me." [29] For he had commanded the unclean spirit to come out of the man.

(For *many (polloi)* a time it had seized him. He was *kept under guard and bound with chains and shackles*, but he would break the bonds and be driven by the demon into the desert.)

[30] Jesus then asked him, "What is your name?" And he said, "Legion," for many demons had entered him. [31] And they begged him *not to command them to depart* into the abyss. [32] Now a large herd of pigs was feeding there on the hillside, and they begged him to let them enter these. So he *gave them permission*. [33] Then the demons came out of the man and entered the pigs, and the herd rushed down the steep bank into the lake and drowned.

[34] When the *herdsmen* saw what had happened, they *fled and told it* in the city and in the country.

Jesus began to speak to the crowds concerning John: "What did *you go out into the wilderness to see?* A reed shaken by the wind? ²⁵ What then did *you go out to see?* A man *dressed in soft clothing?* Behold, those who are *dressed in splendid clothing* and live in luxury are in kings' courts. ²⁶ What then did *you go out to see?* A prophet? Yes, I tell you, and more than a prophet. ²⁷ This is he of whom it is written, "'Behold, *I send my messenger before your face*, who will prepare your way before you.'

²⁸ I tell you, among those born of women none is greater than John. Yet the one who is least in the kingdom of God is greater than he." ²⁹ (When *all the people* heard this, and the tax collectors too, they declared God just, having been baptized with the baptism of John, ³⁰ but the Pharisees and the lawyers *rejected the purpose of God for themselves*, not having been baptized by him.) ³¹ "To what then shall I compare *the people of this generation*, and what are they like? ³² They are like children sitting in the marketplace and calling to one another, "'We played the flute for you, and you did not dance; we sang a dirge, and you did not weep.' ³³ For John the Baptist has come eating no bread and drinking no wine, and you say, 'He has a demon.' ³⁴ The Son of Man has come eating and drinking, and you say, 'Look at him! A glutton and a drunkard, a friend of tax collectors and sinners!' ³⁵ Yet wisdom is justified by all her children."

³⁵ Then *people went out to see* what had happened, and they came to Jesus *and found* the man from whom the demons had gone, sitting at the feet of Jesus, *clothed* and in his right mind, and they were afraid. ³⁶ And *those who had seen it told them* how the demon-possessed man had been healed.

³⁷ Then *all the people of the surrounding country of the Gerasenes asked him to depart from them*, for they were seized with great fear. So he got into the boat and returned. ³⁸ The man from whom the demons had gone begged that he might be with him, but Jesus sent him away, saying, ³⁹ "Return to your home, and declare how much God has done for you." And he went away, proclaiming throughout the whole city how much Jesus had done for him.

Corresponding details connect these episodes.[9] First, compare the person of John the Baptist to the person of the demoniac. John ministers under the Spirit's prophetic call in the barrens of Judea (Luke 1:80; 3:2, 3), while the demoniac lives among the tombs (8:27) and in the desert (29). John wears camel's hair sackcloth (7:24–26, Mark 1:6), while the demoniac wears nothing (Luke 8:27). John eats locusts and wild honey (Mark 1:6), while the demoniac must eat whatever he can scavenge, perhaps including

---

9. In light of Greek discourse analysis, Section B actually begins at 7:18b. Luke 7:18a concludes the previous section. Similarly, Section B′ actually begins at 8:27. Verse 26 concludes the previous section.

locusts. The man lacks a call and message at first, but Jesus gives him both, eventually bringing him into a rough alignment with the role of John in Israel, but in Gentile territory.

Second, verbs of 'seeing' appear prominently in both 7:24–27 and 8:34–36.[10] Third, words meaning "all the people" occur as the subject at a similar point in each episode (7:29a, 8:37a). Fourth, also in a similar position in each episode, the narrator comments in the midst of a question-and-answer exchange between Jesus and others by providing commentary about the wider chronological context of Jesus (7:21) and of the demon-possessed man (8:29). Finally, the narrator gives prominence to the quantity "many" (*polloi*, 7:21a, 21b; 8:29b). Since we have found surface parallels here, meeting one of our tests for aligned episodes (chapter 1, method 2), let us investigate at a deeper level.

Luke 7:18–35 and 8:26–39 contain no corresponding restricted vocabulary. But Luke's appropriation of textual sources provides evidence that he intentionally aligned and expanded his source text in Matthew so that Luke 7:20–21 might correspond in various ways to a similarly edited source text at 8:27–29. We assume here that, on the one hand, Luke 7:18–35 is based on the same source as Matt 11:2–19, and on the other hand that Luke 8:26–39 is based on Mk 5:1–20.

Matt 11:2 Now when John heard in prison about the deeds of the Christ, he sent word by his disciples [3] and said to him, "Are you the one who is to come, or shall we look for another?"	Luke 7:18 The disciples of John reported all these things to him. And John, [19] calling two of his disciples to him, sent them to the Lord, saying, "Are you the one who is to come, or shall we look for another?" [20] *And when the men (andres) had come to him, they said, "John the Baptist has sent us to you, saying, 'Are you the one who is to come, or shall we look for another?'"* [21] *In that hour he healed many people of diseases and plagues and evil spirits, and on many who were blind he bestowed sight.*
[4] And Jesus answered them, "Go and tell John what you hear and see: [5] the blind receive their sight and the lame waLuke, lepers are cleansed and the deaf hear, and the dead are raised up, and the poor have good news preached to them. [6] And blessed is the one who is not offended by me."	[22] And he answered them, "Go and tell John what you have seen and heard: the blind receive their sight, the lame waLuke, lepers are cleansed, and the deaf hear, the dead are raised up, the poor have good news preached to them. [23] And blessed is the one who is not offended by me."

---

10. The word "behold" (*idou*) (7:25, 27) and the phrases "before your face" and "before you" (27) are part of the prominence of 'seeing' in 7:24–27.

The first few verses of Section B contain this significant editing. Luke derived 7:18–23 from (the source of) Matt 11:2–6, and he added a seemingly unnecessary repetition of John's question to Jesus (7:20) after the men arrive. He also added a summary narration in v 21 about "many" healings. Verses 20–21 in Luke separate John's question from Jesus' immediate answer as given in Matthew, and provide other additional material. In this way Luke expands his account of John the Baptist to correspond with an edited account of the demoniac, as described below.

Luke edits the Markan source to appropriate it for the demoniac account (Section B'). He transposes the narrative position of Mark 5:6–8 to move the demonized man's question, "What have you to do with me, Jesus, Son of the Most High God?" earlier in the narrative. He also changes *anthrōpos* ("a man") of Mark 5:2b into *anēr* ("a man") of Luke 8:27b.[11]

Mark 5:2b immediately there met him out of the tombs a man (*anthrōpos*) with an unclean spirit. ³ He lived among the tombs.	Luke 8:27b there met him a man (*anēr*) from the city who had demons. For a long time he had worn no clothes, and he had not lived in a house but among the tombs.
	²⁸ When he saw Jesus, he cried out and fell down before him and said with a loud voice, "What have you to do with me, Jesus, Son of the Most High God? I beg you, do not torment me." ²⁹ For he had commanded the unclean spirit to come out of the man.
And no one could bind him anymore, not even with a chain, ⁴ for he had often been bound with shackles and chains, but he wrenched the chains apart, and he broke the shackles in pieces. No one had the strength to subdue him. ⁵ Night and day among the tombs and on the mountains he was always crying out and cutting himself with stones.	(For many a time it had seized him. He was kept under guard and bound with chains and shackles, but he would break the bonds and be driven by the demon into the desert.)
⁶ *And when he saw Jesus from afar, he ran and fell down before him.* ⁷ *And crying out with a loud voice, he said, "What have you to do with me, Jesus, Son of the Most High God? I adjure you by God, do not torment me."* ⁸ *For he was saying to him, "Come out of the man, you unclean spirit!"*	

---

11. The Greek word *anēr/andres*, however, occurs frequently in Luke and is not restricted vocabulary in these sections.

Luke intentionally aligns an expanded Luke 7:20–21 to correspond in various ways to an edited 8:27–29. By his appropriation of sources for sections B and B' the Evangelist establishes the first part of a continuing parallel sub-structure of events and narration. Thus, ascetic men (*andres*) or an ascetic man (*anēr*) come to Jesus. They ask, in effect, "What can we/I expect from you?" (7:19–20; 8:27–29a). Here the Lukan narrator steps in to provide relevant background histories containing "many" similar events (7:21; 8:29b–d).

Returning to the action, Jesus sends both the messengers and the demons away with implied answers to their questions (7:22–23; 8:30–33). Messengers depart (7:24a; 8:34). The crowd "goes out to see" (7:24b–27; 8:35–36). A parallel sub-structure in six parts adds another potent validation of correspondence between Section B (7:18–35) and Section B' (8:26–39). Having seen, some embrace the importance of what they see and some reject or deny it (7:28–35; 8:37–39).

When intermediaries report what Jesus says or does, that mediated "word" bears Jesus' authority and call to belief. Both initial and subsequent listeners in these sections face unavoidable choices regarding Jesus. His word is urgent, often unanticipated and sometimes scandalous. Further, Jesus acts in ways befitting God himself.

The Godlike Word (Section C, 7:36–50, and C', 8:22–25)

Jesus' jolts the plausibility structures of his hearers when he matter-of-factly speaks and acts in Godlike ways. Only God forgives all of one's unspecified sins and controls nature by fiat, yet Jesus does both in Sections C and C'.

The sections 7:36–50 and 8:22–25 make an unlikely pair. In 7:36–50 Jesus receives expressions of passionate gratitude for his forgiveness of the sins of "a woman of the city" (37) and Jesus reproves Simon the Pharisee for Simon's loveless welcome, contrasting Simon's welcome to the woman's welcome.[12] The other section, 8:22–25, takes place on the lake and features a dangerous storm. Jesus orders the storm to stop, and the resulting calm amazes the others in the boat. One wonders whether Section C' offers any parallel at all to the dinner host or the dinner intruder in Section C. On the other hand, 7:36–50 lacks a boat and a storm, and indeed, it never mentions any of Jesus' disciples as participating in the dinner. Section C' is also much shorter, only twenty-five percent as long as section C. What evidence of

---

12. In light of the Greek discourse analysis, Section C actually begins at 7:36b. Luke 7:36a concludes the previous section.

correspondence, if any, presents itself on the surface, and what can be found below the surface?

Luke 7:36 One of the Pharisees asked him to eat with him, and *he went into the Pharisee's house* and *reclined at the table.*	Luke 8:22 One day *he got into a boat* with his disciples, and he said to them, "Let us go across to the other side of the lake." So they set out, [23] and as they sailed *he fell asleep.*
[37] And behold, a woman of the city, who was a sinner, when she learned that he was *reclining* at table in the Pharisee's house, brought an alabaster flask of *ointment,* [38] and standing behind him at his feet, *weeping,* she began to *wet his feet with her tears* and wiped them with the hair of her head and *kissed his feet and anointed them* with the *ointment.*	And *a windstorm came down on the lake, and they were filling with water*
[39] Now when the Pharisee who had invited him saw this, he said to himself, "If this man were a *prophet,* he would have known who and what sort of woman this is who is *touching him, for she is a sinner.*"	and were in danger. [24] And they went and woke him, saying, "*Master, Master,* we are *perishing!*"
[40] And Jesus answering said to him, "Simon, I have something to say to you." And he answered, "Say it, Teacher." [41] "A certain moneylender had two debtors. One owed five hundred denarii, and the other fifty. [42] When they could not pay, he cancelled the debt of both. Now which of them will love him more?" [43] Simon answered, "The one, I suppose, for whom he cancelled the larger debt." And he said to him, "You have judged rightly." [44] *Then turning toward the woman he said to Simon, "Do you see this woman? I entered your house; you gave me no water for my feet, but she has wet my feet with her tears and wiped them with her hair.* [45] *You gave me no kiss, but from the time I came in she has not ceased to kiss my feet.* [46] *You did not anoint my head with oil, but she has anointed my feet with ointment.*	And he awoke and *rebuked the wind* and the raging waves,

⁴⁷ Therefore I tell you, her sins, which are many, are forgiven—for she loved much. But he who is forgiven little, loves little." ⁴⁸ And he said to her, *"Your sins are forgiven."* Then those who were at table with him began to *say among themselves, "Who is this (tis houtos estin), who even (kai) forgives sins?"* ⁵⁰ And he said to the woman, "Your *faith (pistis sou) has saved you; go in peace."*

and they ceased, and *there was a calm.* ²⁵ He said to them, "Where is your faith? (*pistis humōn*)" And they were afraid, and they marveled, *saying to one another, "Who then is this (tis ara houtos estin), that he commands even (kai) winds and water, and they obey him?"*

Significant lexical correspondence between these sections lies in their endings, 7:47–50 and 8:25. The woman exercises saving faith but the disciples in the boat were saved despite their lack of faith. Second, in response to Jesus' assertions of God-like authority (forgiving sins, 7:47–48; quelling a windstorm, 8:24b), stunned observers of Jesus ask, "Who is this?" (*tis houtos estin*). Finally, those in both accounts contemplating what they have just heard and seen from Jesus add the word "even" to their question (*kai*), an expression that refers to his already remarkable exhibitions of authority in other contexts. The observers imply, "This tops them all!" None of these Greek words qualify as restricted or limited-use vocabulary, so *our claim for counting them as a correspondence lies in the thematic interrelated and clustered presence of all three expressions at the ends of both accounts.*[13]

The remainder of 7:36–50 and 8:22–25 contain linking evidence of another kind, a kind below the surface and invisible to the reader or listener encountering both sections. Luke edited his source in Mark's fifth chapter so that events in 8:22–25 would appear in the same order as the events in 7:36–50.[14]

These sources, Mark and the other one, offered accounts that told quite different stories, but told them in almost the same thematic order. First, Jesus enters an environment unusual for him to enter (a special guest at a Pharisee's dinner, 7:37a–b; a passenger on a boat, 8:22a–c). Having arrived there, Jesus reclines (the posture appropriate to dining at a *triclinium*, 7:36c–37c; the posture appropriate to falling asleep on a lengthy boat ride, 8:23a).[15] Third, while thus reclined, a danger for that environment appears out of nowhere (a probable prostitute ritually "contaminates" Jesus by

13. Restricted vocabulary is the exclusive use of a Greek word in only two places in the entire Gospel. Limited-use vocabulary is the rare but not exclusive use of a Greek word. Restricted and limited-use vocabulary appearing in texts suspected of being parallel adds weight to the evidence in favor of a parallelism between the texts.

14. Luke seems to have taken 7:36–50 from some other source known to him from his research.

15. The *triclinium* was a Roman style of dining that had been widely adopted in Israelite society among those of means.

touching him, 7:37d–38; a sudden windstorm and waves threaten to sink the boat, 8:23b–c).

Both episodes continue further in parallel thematic order, but our concern here is with the second and third parts of this shared order described just above. Luke edits the order of events from Mark's account to establish the above-described thematic parallel in Section C'. He edits Mark's account, Mk 4:37–38a, so that his own account of the same event, Luke 8:22d–23, appears in the same order as events in Simon's house, namely, that mention of his reclining came before the description of approaching danger. As the result of such editing, in one story Jesus reclined for dinner and then the "sinner" woman came. And in the other, Jesus reclined to sleep and then the windstorm came.[16] *Identifying such editing adds evidence to our claim that Luke intentionally aligned 8:22–25 to correspond with 7:36–50 as Sections C' and C in an extensive concentric parallelism.*[17]

Mark 4:35 On that day, when evening had come, he said to them, "Let us go across to the other side." ³⁶ And leaving the crowd, they took him with them in the boat, just as he was. And other boats were with him.	Luke 8:22 One day he got into a boat with his disciples, and he said to them, "Let us go across to the other side of the lake."
³⁷ And a great windstorm arose, and the waves were breaking into the boat, so that the boat was already filling.	So they set out, ²³ and as they sailed he fell asleep.
³⁸ But he was in the stern, asleep on the cushion.	And a windstorm came down on the lake, and they were filling with water and were in danger.
And they woke him and said to him, "Teacher, do you not care that we are perishing?"	²⁴ And they went and woke him, saying, "Master, Master, we are perishing!"

Quite similar endings of both sections plus editing to bring about parallel thematic alignment point toward an intentional concentric shaping of

---

16. Mark's account provides the same information, but in a different order, an order that Luke improved for his purposes.

17. Luke makes other edits of Mark 4:35–40 to appropriate it for his narrative, but only this edit seems to be based on the strategy of making an alignment with Luke 7:36–50.

these passages in Luke's Gospel. If we have successfully demonstrated this, our two accounts in Luke take their place as Section C and C' inside of A/A' and B/B' in the concentric structure. The Evangelist then brings together a further pair of episodes into the literary architecture he intentionally builds, episodes about Jesus' followers putting into action the word from Jesus.

The Operative Word (Section D, 8:1–3, and D', 8:19–21)

Women provided their healing by Jesus enact the mercy they received by providing for the band of disciples out of their own means. The woman who gave birth and nurture to the infant Jesus must also enact the word of her grown son.

If Sections C and C' look at first consideration to be unlikely corresponding sections, the opposite is true of Sections D and D': a comparison of Luke 8:1–3 and 8:19–21 finds clear similarities. First, both sections reintroduce individuals who are tied to Jesus in culturally recognized bonded relationships. The "twelve" (1) have become much more than temporary hangers-on and more than committed followers: Jesus called, chose, and named them as his apostles (6:12–16). They are bonded to Jesus in somewhat the same manner as a school of disciples would be attached to a rabbi or as sons of the prophets might be bonded to a prophet. In the other section the bonded relationship is that of family. Jesus' mother and brothers come for a visit, expecting that their family relationship to Jesus would provide them privileged access to him (8:20).

Our observation of similarity in bondedness does not extend to how Jesus or others express that bond in the accounts, only that such a bond is assumed. David Brack points out that "A key theme in both of these sections is also the breaking of traditional boundaries in order for the word of God to spread. Luke 8:1-3 highlights the unique inclusion of women into Jesus' ministry. Likewise, Luke 8:19-21 shows that familial boundaries are no longer determinative of our primary allegiances."[18]

Second, the gender distinction of mother and brothers 8:19–21 finds its parallel in 8:1–3. The twelve are all male and the other listed followers are all female: in addition to named women (v 2–3), the "many others" is feminine plural as well. Jesus' mother and brothers in one section are paralleled by male apostles and female followers in the other.

---

18. From personal correspondence with David Brack.

Luke 8:1 Soon afterward he went on through cities and villages, *proclaiming and bringing the good news of the kingdom of God*. And *the twelve were with him,* [2] *and also some women who had been healed of evil spirits and infirmities*: Mary, called Magdalene, from whom seven demons had gone out, [3] and Joanna, the wife of Chuza, Herod's household manager, and Susanna, and many others, who *provided for them out of their means*.

Luke 8:19 Then *his mother and his brothers* came to him, but they could not reach him because of the crowd. [20] And he was told, "Your mother and your brothers are standing outside, desiring to see you." [21] But he answered them, "*My mother and my brothers* are those who *hear the word of God and do it.*"

Further, the theme of embodiment or "putting into action" unites the sections. The arrival of Jesus' brothers and mother (vv 19–21) becomes an object lesson for the dense crowd listening to Jesus. According to Jesus in v 21, those who can claim an important bond to Jesus are those who not only hear his word but put it into practical action, who "do" the teaching they accept from him. In the opposite section (vv 2–3) women who received healing, who were freed from bondage by Jesus, now put received mercy into action by serving Jesus and the apostles. Jesus, of course, could provide daily food (see 9:10–17), instead he accepts the women's service as their appropriate response to the powerful word that healed them.[19]

All of the similarities above between 8:1–3 and 8:19–21 do not qualify under our methodological standards as proven correspondences, even granting the accumulation of features that they share in common. These passages do, however, stand in the gap between other sections (C and C' on one side and E on the other) that have strong parallel features. Such robust structures on both sides of Sections D and D' lend an additional degree of definition and credibility to possible correspondences between 8:1–3 and 8:19–21. The reader of scripture and of this chapter will decide whether the similarities between Sections D and D' pointed out above are sufficient to

---

19. Another instance of embodiment theme might be found in the second participle of 8:1b, along with its direct object: "bringing the good news of the kingdom of God." The verbs "proclaiming and bringing" of 8:1 can be understood as an example of *hendiadys*, or using two verbs to state one idea, as in "May God lead and guide us": "proclaiming" (*kērussōn*) always signifies public communication of important information and the verb for "bringing" (*euangelizomenos*) can mean the same. But (in the Greco-Roman cultural context) it can mean something substantially more. *Euangelizomenos* can combine the idea of announcing along with the act of bringing into being: the announcement of a new king's accession to the throne was also the launch of his reign. The very announcement of such "good news" brought into being a new sovereignty over the hearers of the announcement. Consistent with this, "*euangelizomenos*" in 8:1b stipulates "the kingdom of God" as its object. Luke may mean that Jesus in 8:1b is not only telling about the kingdom of God, but inaugurating it in his own presence, words, and actions. In terms of "embodiment," Jesus would be both announcing and embodying God's kingdom.

establish their sectional correspondence and, as a consequence, their place as the fourth pair of sections in a large concentrically corresponding literary structure.

Two short thematically parallel episodes from Luke 8 affirm that love for Jesus manifests in acting on the grace that he gives, whether the grace of healing or the grace of teaching. Putting into action Jesus' word (whether heard, seen, or experienced) demonstrates that one truly "hears" his word.

Hearing the word (Section E, 8:4–18)

Section E (8:4–18), the middle section, contains the interpretive principle of the large concentric form we have been identifying in Luke 7:1–8:56. For concentric literary forms longer than four lines of poetry, the center line or lines of more compact forms, and the center section or sections in long forms, typically define the main theme or main point of the composition. *The center is both the hub of meaning and the axis of organization for concentric compositions such as the episodes making up chapters seven and eight of the Third Gospel. Upon seeing paired concentric sections in a composition, the reader should turn first to the center for explicit information or implicit clues about the composition's meaning.*

Readers recognize in Luke 8:4–18 the so-called The Parable of the Soils (4–8a), followed shortly thereafter by Jesus' also-familiar allegorical interpretation of the parable (11–15). The four "soils" or landing-places represent four sorts of people who have heard the word of God and who respond to it differently. Immediately after the parable (8b–10) and again immediately after Jesus' interpretation of the parable (16–18) come brief comments by Jesus on hearing and knowing. Luke adapts these short comments from Mark's longer versions of the sayings (Mark 4:2–25) appearing there in the same context.

Luke 8:4 And when a great crowd was gathering and people from town after town came to him, he said in a parable: ⁵ "A sower went out to sow his seed. And as he sowed, some fell along the path and was trampled underfoot, and the birds of the air devoured it. ⁶ And some fell on the rock, and as it grew up, it withered away, because it had no moisture. ⁷ And some fell among thorns, and the thorns grew up with it and choked it. ⁸ And some fell into good soil and grew and yielded a hundredfold." As he said these things, he called out, "He who has ears to hear, let him hear."

Luke 8:9 And when his disciples asked him what this parable meant, ¹⁰ he said, "To *you* it has been *given* to know the *secrets* (*mystēria*) of the kingdom of God, but for others they are in parables, so that '*seeing* they may not *see*, and *hearing* they may not *understand*.'

Luke 8:11 Now the parable is this: The seed is the word of God. ¹² The ones along the path are those who have heard; then the devil comes and takes away the word from their hearts, so that they may not believe and be saved. ¹³ And the ones on the rock are those who, when they hear the word, receive it with joy. But these have no root; they believe for a while, and in time of testing fall away. ¹⁴ And as for what fell among the thorns, they are those who hear, but as they go on their way they are choked by the cares and riches and pleasures of life, and their fruit does not mature. ¹⁵ As for that in the good soil, they are those who, hearing the word, hold it fast in an honest and good heart, and bear fruit with patience.

Luke 8:16 "No one after lighting a lamp covers it with a jar or puts it under a bed, but puts it on a stand, so that those who enter may *see* the light. ¹⁷ For nothing is *hidden* that will not be made *manifest* (*phanēron*), nor is anything *secret* (*apokryphon*) that will not be known and *come to light*. ¹⁸ Take care then how *you hear*, for to the one who has, more will be *given*, and from the one who has not, even what he thinks that he has will be taken away."

While the parable and its interpretation obviously correspond, Luke 8:8b–10 and 16–18 correspond in less obvious but substantial ways. First, Jesus directs his teaching in both vv 8b–10 and vv 16–18 to "you" (the disciples), while the Parable of the Soils and its interpretation are for "he who has ears" (8). Second, to understand "the secrets of the kingdom of God" is to be "given" that understanding (10, 18). Third, recipients of this gift will understand what was otherwise veiled: they will "know the secrets (*mystēria*) of the kingdom of God" (10) and Jesus' teaching will not be "hidden," but "made manifest," not be "secret," but be "known and come to light" (17).

Joel Green points out that *mystēria* (secrets) occurs only at v 10 in Luke's Gospel.[20] When we scan v 16–18 for possibilities of restricted vocabulary that would correspond with *mystērion* in v 10, we do not find exactly that, but we do find two other words that also occur only once in the Third Gospel. What is "secret" (*apokryphon*, 17) will come "to light" or be made "manifest" (*phanēron*, 17).[21] Both of these unique Lukan terms correspond in their uniqueness, and partially in their meaning (synonym and antonym), to *mystēria* in v 11. Next, the "seeing and hearing" metaphors in both places (10c; 16c, 17b–18a) stand for knowing or understanding.

Thus v 9–10 and v 16–18 correspond in multiple ways, and we identify them as corresponding units. Further, we can schematize Section E as a simple, or symmetrical, parallelism having the form a-b-a′-b′. The seed falling on various "soils" parallels Jesus' explanations (units *a* and *a′*), while his teaching on knowing the secrets parallels what he says about seeing the light (units *b* and *b′*). Unit *a′* explains unit *a*, and unit *b′* supplements unit *b*. Section E grounds the entire concentric form as its axis of organization and hub of meaning. We must seek from those verses information or clues about Luke's theological intent for the entire structure.

Interpreting the Form

We now come to the question of meaning, both the meaning of the center section, and through it the meaning of the entire concentric parallelism of Luke 7:1–8:56. It is hermeneutically crucial to begin from the center section, the literary and theological core of the concentric parallelism. Since the entire structure is made up of narrative episodes, outer episodes may

---

20. Green, *Luke*, 326.

21. The verbal form of this root does occur at 9:8 ("appeared") and 24:11 ("seemed"), but in meanings different than the adjectival form in 8:17 ("manifest"). Even the word "hidden" (*krypton*) in 8:17 makes only one other appearance in Luke's Gospel (12:2).

not transparently offer the interpretive thread that the author intends a reader/listener to catch hold of. We begin in the center.

Receiving the Word (Section E, 8:4–18)

Section E is generally about receiving the word of God. The interpreted parable details four responses of people after they hear the word of God. This parable and its given interpretation put forward the following communication pattern:

- God initiates communication.
- God speaks his word so that people can hear it. He distributes his word randomly like seed being broadcast and falling indiscriminately upon the ground.
- People hear the word and, in the best case scenario, take it to heart in such a way that it achieves God's intended effect: belief, salvation, and flourishing. In the worst case scenario the devil intervenes, removing the word from hearts so people will not experience belief, salvation, and flourishing from the planted word. In other instances people hear the word and accept it, but they fail to let it have God's intended place in their hearts.
- The parable's communication pattern centers on varieties of audience response to random but purposeful communication from God.

The teaching in units *b* and *b′* adds more detail to the communication pattern. Indeed, augmentation of the parable appears to be one of Luke's compositional purposes in Section E. Units *b* and *b′* have significant themes in common in addition to the restricted synonyms described above. Deliberate hearing in v 8b resembles careful hearing in v 18. Having knowledge of the kingdom by gift (10) grows to having even more light by gift (18). Jesus speaks of "seeing" metaphorically in v 10 and includes the same word *blepein* as the point of a parable on seeing in v 16. Finally, as mentioned, knowing secrets (active verb) in v 10 parallels the secret becoming manifest (passive verb) in v 17. These units cohere by densely clustered shared thematic material as well as by restricted vocabulary.

Luke 8:8b As he said these things, he called out, "He who has (*echōn*) ears to hear (*akouein*), let him hear (*akoueto*)."

Luke 8:16 "No one after lighting a lamp covers it with a jar or puts it under a bed, but puts it on a stand, so that those who enter may see (*blepōsin*) the light.

⁹ And when his disciples asked him what this parable meant, ¹⁰ he said, "To you it has been given (*dedotai*) to know (*gnōnai*) the secrets (*mystēria*) of the kingdom of God,

¹⁷ For nothing is hidden (*krypton*, 8:17, 12:2) that will not be made manifest (*phaneron*), nor is anything secret (*apokryphon*) that will not be known (*gnōsthē*) and come to light (*phaneron*).

but for others they are in parables, so that 'seeing (*blepontes*) they may not see (*mē blepōsin*), and hearing (*akouontes*) they may not understand (*syniōsin*).

¹⁸ Take care then how you hear (*akouete*), for to the one who has (*echē*), more will be given (*dothēsetai*), and from the one who has not (*mē echē*), even what he thinks that he has (*echein*) will be taken away."

These units also augment the communication pattern established by the Parable of the Soils as follows:

- Hearing the word with understanding is not automatic: people must choose to attend to the word Jesus is speaking (8:8b).
- Coming to know the meaning of Jesus' word is a gift to those who attend to this word expectantly (10).
- Such people can be said to have the word of Jesus (10, 18).
- Having the word of Jesus does not amount to a *fait accompli*, but it either increases in extent by continued attentiveness and care or decreases in extent by neglect and carelessness toward the word of Jesus (18).
- Those who do not attend expectantly or who do not take care how they hear Jesus perceive only riddles, dark sayings, parables, mere words (10b–d, 18c–d).
- Jesus' word is about the kingdom of God (10).
- His words communicate mysteries about the kingdom of God (10, 17a).
- For those attending expectantly to Jesus' words, these mysteries become known and manifest (10, 17).

By placing units *b* and *b'* after units *a* and *a'* respectively, Luke adds perspective to the communication pattern above that arises from the interpreted Parable of the Soils.²² The word of God comes by hearing what

22. Luke gathers and deploys additional words of Jesus to expand on the Parable of the Soils, showing that the seed-soil metaphor truly but incompletely expresses what it means to know and follow Jesus. Other New Testament writers teach Christian discipleship and growth by a number of additional metaphors (abide in the vine, living sacrifice, members of the body, clay jars, temple of God, new clothing, fragrant offering, armor, death and resurrection, servant, good soldier, adorn the doctrine, run the race). Each of these metaphors calls for our careful attention and faithful response, but none

Jesus says and by seeing what Jesus does. Second, the word may be rejected because hearers/seers are unwilling to seek the word's meaning. Next, those who have previously received the word will find the word is continuously planted in their lives, if they live with expectant openness to it. Finally, bearing fruit includes coming to understand and know truths about the kingdom of God.

The communication pattern the Evangelist urges is open-ended. The main point that Luke puts forward by his editorial work here is that the sowing of the word and its reception *are broadly varied, more so than the Parable of the Soils alone would indicate* if one were to take it as a paradigm of how God's word is communicated. Luke 8:4–14, as the center section of a large concentrically structured discourse about Jesus, establishes the theme of Luke's selection and organization. The verses describe the many ways the word of God's kingdom is seen and heard in the actions and words of Jesus, and consequently the many ways people must respond (or will fail to respond) to this word.[23]

Jesus' Word in Narrative Context

Luke's authorial/editorial logic for arranging a discourse on hearing and doing the word (chapters seven and eight), becomes apparent when reviewing the preceding Gospel text from Luke 4:14 to 6:49. Jesus speaks for God, proclaiming the purposes of God's kingdom (4:14–5:3). His call to discipleship and apostleship resounds with power, holiness, and forgiveness (4:40—6:19). Jesus teaches authoritatively about justice, mercy, and love as God's kingdom ways (6:20–49). But what of human weakness, selfishness, and moral intransigence? Not everybody submits to God's purposes in Jesus. Some reject his call to repentance. Many may protest the wisdom of his teaching. These earlier Third Gospel accounts of Jesus speaking for God all reach their epitome in the expanded Parable of the Soils.

Therefore, we find that episodes in Luke 7 and 8, organized thematically in concentric units around their axis in 8:4–18, expand the range of both word-sowing and fruit-bearing provided to the listener/reader by the narrative in 4:14–6:49 or even by the Parable of the Soils. Luke draws attention particularly to one's continuing reception of the word after the first time: *sectional texts in the concentric form presume that the word was*

---

of them should be seen as the exhaustive image for following Christ.

23. The power and spread of the word continues as a motif in Luke and Acts. See especially Acts 6:7, 12:24, and 19:20 for language arising from Jesus' seed/soil/garden imagery.

previously planted and now, upon receiving additional seed, these individuals and groups are expected to bear additional fruit (see 8:18).

We now move on to interpret details of the episodes in Luke 7 and 8.

Jesus' Powerful Word (Sections A, 7:1–17, and A′, 8:40–56)

Section A (Luke 7:1–17) includes two episodes that Luke blends thematically into one section of the concentric discourse. Together they identify Jesus, this sower of the word, as a prophet of God, and even more than a prophet. Through parallel, imitation, and inference Luke shows that Jesus wields prophetic power and healing authority in the same ministries as did Elijah (1 Kg 17:17–24) and Elisha (2 Kg 4:11–37, 5:1–14), including healing both from a physical distance and across a cultural barrier. Thus those who see Jesus raise the widow's son from the dead say, "A great prophet has arisen among us!" (Luke 7:16). Jesus' authority and power exceeds Elijah's and even Elisha's: Jesus simply commands the dead to rise (14). Consonant with his exceptional capacities, the onlookers add, "God has visited his people" (v 16), a statement bearing both eschatological meaning (the hoped-for time has come) and existential meaning (the identity of Jesus).

Section A features "the word" of God (7:7).[24] In the story about the centurion and his sick servant (1–10), the officer's exceptional faith in the healing command of Jesus arises from some previous experience of hearing or seeing the word in action. In the second story of the section (11–17), the widow seems at first unexpectant and resigned, lacking the sown word in her life. But the crowd accompanying Jesus, with whom the episode begins and ends, manifests a curiosity or expectation about Jesus that arises from some unstated previous planting of the word. The crowd's fruit-bearing here stems from readiness to accept the theological implication of Jesus' actions: they recognize him as "a great prophet of God" (16).

The theme of Jesus' powerful prophetic word continues in Section A′ (8:40–56), with emphasis on an appropriate response of faith to the dynamic word of Jesus. These stories continue to echo certain details of 1 Kg 17:17–24 and 2 Kg 4:8–37, although both stories in Luke 8:40–56 refer to a female needing Jesus' healing, and although a father implores Jesus to intervene in the impending death of his child. In the OT passages the reverse has happened: sons have died and their mothers seek the prophet's help. Thus, in Section A′ Jesus continues to heal as the prophet of God, not by calling

---

24. This interpretation of Sections A and A′ borrows from insights of Green, *Luke*, 281–293, 342–351.

out for God to act as did the prophet, but by his own word of command ("arise," 7:14, 8:54).

Further, in the two accounts in Section A′ Jesus presses individuals who seek his healing power to have public faith in him regardless of censure that may come from bystanders. The healed woman, who was culturally marginalized as a woman, who had been medically and ritually unclean, who was probably destitute from years of trying to hire effective medical help, and who now dares touch and therefore pollute the rabbi, realizes ("saw that she was not hidden," 8:47) that she must step out of this obscurity and admit openly ("in the presence of all the people") her covert, desperate effort to commandeer healing from Jesus—this is fruit-bearing faith.

Likewise, in the related Section A′ episode, Jesus pressed the dead girl's parents not to grieve the dead and instead to ignore the crowd's derision toward Jesus for describing the girl as sleeping rather than dead. (52). Her parents must decide between two views of reality; they must decide whom to trust, the opinion of the crowd or the word of Jesus. The life-giving acts of Jesus in Section A′ require the beneficiaries to bear fruit by trusting his power to heal while ignoring popular opinion to the contrary.

Trampled on the Path (Sections B, 7:18–35, and B′, 8:26–39)

Section B (Luke 7:18–35) shifts the sower-seed-soil focus to illustrate that hard soil resists the God's word (building on the topic of soil quality in Section A′, 8:45, 53). For some, the word coming through Jesus looks wrong, just as for others the word coming through John is unacceptable. "This generation" dislikes John's ascetic style and consequently rejects his prophetic word. By so doing, they (Pharisees and lawyers in particular) reject "the purpose of God for themselves" (30). The same hardened generation dislikes Jesus' social and friendly style, consequently rejecting his word (34), even though the word about the coming one (the seed) has been sown in the preaching of John. Even John expects something different in "the one who is to come" (19, 20) than what has been reported to him by eyewitnesses. So Jesus concludes his reply to John's question with an exhortation for John to be receptive soil (23).

Section B′ (8:26–39) adds further perspective on soil that is hardened to the word of God. Crossing the lake to Gentile territory, Jesus encounters new resistance to his powerful word. Demons know his identity and fear such power, so they beg (28, 31, 32) to be spared of impending dismissal into judgment ("the abyss") in favor of being demoted to demonizing some pigs. Jesus permits the pigs to drown themselves, a fate that may also send the demons to the abyss. Likewise, the Gerasenes, who come out to see for themselves the reported spirit-cleansing of their town madman, see the cleansed man and consequently fear what Jesus can do.[25] The Gerasenes ask Jesus to spare them from any indeterminate future disruptions of normal life that he might cause; they ask him to depart, to go away. Jesus respects their wishes, but he leaves a back-door witness to the powerful word: the former town madman, now a restored citizen in his right mind is intent on bearing witness to "how much Jesus had done for him" (39). The former madman bears the fruit of thankfulness yielding acts of proclamation.

Roots Among Rocks (Sections C, 7:36–50, and C′, 8:22–25)

The Pharisee and the "woman of the city, who was a sinner" (37) have previous contact with Jesus and thus have been "seeded" by his word. Jesus knows Simon's name and Simon extends him an invitation to dinner at home. The woman's unusual and risky behavior honors Jesus, and makes it clear that she knows him well. As becomes explicit later, Jesus forgives her of unspecified sins. Both Simon and the woman are good soil upon which the word has fallen.

Simon had previously joined the ranks of those who believe that "a great prophet has arisen among us" (7:16), but now questions his own perceptions about Jesus when the Teacher allows himself to be ritually polluted by the woman's actions. Consequently, Jesus' further "word" for Simon (40), becomes a word of rebuke. The dinner host gives mixed honor to his guest. On one hand, Jesus is indeed an invited guest; on the other, Simon fails to follow significant conventions of hospitality that also show honor. The revelation that "Jesus is a prophet of God," for Simon, amounts to curiosity and table fellowship (which are indeed fruit of the planted word), but it does not amount to infusing his hospitality with personal acts that honor Jesus.

The nameless woman, however, boldly honors Jesus with an outward act, because she knows him as the one who provides forgiveness for sins and thanks him for forgiveness already given: her gratitude overflows. In her the word of forgiveness bears the fruit of faith expressed in intrepid thanksgiving and honor (50).

Luke's narrative remains provocatively silent about whether Simon eventually sees his own sin so that he might enjoy God's forgiveness. Perhaps this is intended to invite the reader to consider which story, Simon's or the woman's, best describes the reader's own fruit-bearing.

---

25. The sown word here is the word about Jesus spoken by the eyewitnesses (34, 36).

A soaking of a different kind, however, an unexpected and dangerous soaking, stirs complaint and rebuke in Section C′ (8:22–25). "Disciples" of Jesus (at least the fishermen of the Twelve) are, more than any others, recipients of the word of God, both in his call to them to follow Jesus and as observers of his varied ministry. They see and hear as did John the Baptist: "the blind receive their sight, the lame walk, lepers are cleansed, and the deaf hear, the dead are raised up, the poor have the good news preached to them" (7:22). All of the healings they see exhibit divine power over nature, some healings in emergency situations. Yet they are faithless when a crisis involving them arises.

The disciples' boat faces an overwhelming maritime emergency, but Jesus appears oblivious to it all. Scripture says, "As they sailed, he fell asleep. A windstorm came down on the lake, and they were filling with water and were in danger" (7:23). Luke also reports that, after having been awakened, Jesus speaks a word of rebuke to the storm, with immediate and dramatic effect.

He questions the crew about their lack of faith, faith that should have made the step from knowing that "the dead are raised up" to knowing that their lives are safe in his care, even in a storm with such demonic suddenness and intensity. By now they should have formed a view of their "master" adequate to any need, even more so since in the present circumstance he is with them in the boat. Are the disciples plants that "have no root; [who] believe for a while, and in time of testing fall away" (8:13)? Fruit-bearing for the band of disciples is portrayed as an uneven, sometimes regressive growth process. Under Jesus' authority, they must steward the word given them, moving toward greater faith in him.

Maturing Among Thorns (Sections D, 8:1–3, and D′, 8:19–21)

Section D shows a summary quality appropriate to nearing the inner end of a concentric parallelism: the seed represents the word of God in Jesus' proclamation; the outgrowth is changed lives of people who find opportunities to flourish in the kingdom of God. This brief section identifies both men (the twelve) and women who are "with" Jesus, but the textual emphasis is predominately on the women, not on the men.

The women listed are all recipients of the powerful word of God: they "had been healed" (8:2). Luke mentions them here and later in the passion and resurrection accounts (23:27, 49, 55; 24:1–11, see also Acts 1:14). While these women persist in faith during the crises of Jesus' crucifixion and burial, the main emphasis here is that they bear appropriate kingdom fruit by "providing for them [Jesus and the disciples] out of their own means." In this they bear a similarity to the "woman of the city" (7:37–38, 48) whose healing was from crippling sin and who lavished aromatic oil from her own means on Jesus' feet.

All of these women ignore the probable sharp thorns of family and friends who would frown on wasting wealth. The women find their pleasure not in rituals of wealth and status, but in pouring their wealth out for Jesus and his band. Good life-soils graced by God's word hold the word "fast in an honest and good heart, and bear fruit with patience" (8:15): such were these women.

Section D' (8:19–21) also displays a summary quality, ending, as we said above, with a sweeping pronouncement that temporarily brings one's reading of these episodes to a halt. The expression "My mother and my brothers are those who hear the word of God and do it" (21) moves the governing metaphor of relationship from living as citizens in the kingdom of God (8:1) to dwelling in the family of Jesus. In either case, however, flourishing life arises from doing what the word of God calls forth in the hearer (bearing fruit). The brothers of Jesus make their only appearance in the Third Gospel in these verses, reappearing in the Lukan corpus with all of the other characters of Sections D and D' in Acts 1:14.

In Luke's account, his brothers' history of receiving the word of God can only be imagined, whereas Luke highlights occasions when Jesus' mother Mary responds to the word. When Gabriel announces to Mary that she will bear a child known as the "Son of the Most High" (1:26–37), Mary affirms "let it be to me according to your word" (38). Having heard another angel's words after Jesus was born, words repeated to her by wondering shepherds, "Mary treasured up all these things, pondering them in her heart" (2:8–18, 19). Several years later the youngster Jesus, who unexpectedly stays in Jerusalem at the temple to discuss the scriptures with the rabbis (49), answers his distressed parents in words with dual meaning, "Why were you looking for me? Did you not know that I must be in my Father's house?" Then, as before, his mother "treasured up all these things in her heart" (51). It is also possible that Mary was present in the Nazareth synagogue, in the town "where he had been brought up" (4:16) when Jesus announced the beginning of his public ministry (4:16–19). Clearly, "the word" both spoken and exhibited by Jesus, was planted in her life-soil.

Mother and brothers come to "see" Jesus. Though the word "see" is capable of various interpretations, the context seems to eliminate the specific purpose of coming to hear Jesus— sitting at his feet for instruction. The verb "see" in the center section always appears as a metaphor for knowing, not as optical vision. Yet when the family wants to see Jesus, they seem to have something more in mind than just knowing him. His family might want to assert a culturally approved right of access to one from their own household: they own cultural capital in him and want to use it.

Possibly relevant to our understanding here, is that those gathered around Jesus who hinder access are described as "the crowd" (19), not as "disciples." Can it be that the word "crowd" represents Mary's and her accompanying sons' point of view? Jesus uses the occasion afforded by his family's request for his sweeping statement about hearing and doing the word of God, but he stops short of identifying his family as negative examples. At least Jesus cautions them. Interestingly, in the continuing story Mary and Jesus' brothers appear following the resurrection (Acts 1:14) as people closely associated in heart and mind with the Eleven, with the healed and serving women, and with their risen Lord.

Summary

With this pronouncement that true mothers and brothers of Jesus hear the word of God and do it, Luke ends the center of episodes that form an ABCDED′C′B′A′ structure. Because Luke concentrically aligned and edited episodes from Jesus' ministry for a defined didactic purpose, the whole portion of the Gospel from 7:1 to 8:56 can be called a *concentric theological discourse* as well as a *linear narrative* about Jesus. As we have shown, strong textual correspondences indicate a concentric form at work in chapters seven and eight of Luke. At the same time, or concurrently, these chapters display familiar, linear story-telling propelled forward by connectives such as "soon afterward" (7:11, 8:1), "all these things" (7:18), "then" (8:19, 26), "when Jesus returned" (40), "as Jesus went" (42), and "while he was still speaking" (49). The concentric discourse in Luke 7:1—8:56 is the second such discourse in the Third Gospel: in chapter 1 we described a similar chiastic structure that Luke crafted in 4:40—6:19, and more are to come.

So we have seen that Luke places Jesus' exhortation to "take care how you hear" in 8:18 at a position of prominence and theological significance. Jesus speaks the word of God (5:1) as teaching, as training, and as power. "Hearing" on the other hand stands for receiving any form of the word coming into one's life. According to Luke, Jesus expects stewardship of that word. In other words, hearing him should never yield a static condition of discipleship, idle curious inquiry, or satisfaction with one's mere healing. "To the one who has, more will be given, and from the one who has not, even what he has will be taken away." Care must be given that hearing the word of God yields appropriate fruit for the kingdom of God.

3

Apostolic Non-Leadership

Luke 9:1–50

JESUS IS READY, BUT the twelve are not ready. Luke 9 reveals that Jesus' apostles still lack adequate vision and spirit for leading others in God's kingdom. Jesus, on the other hand, knows God's purpose for himself in the kingdom because he is "the Christ of God" (Luke 9:20). He sees the required path and resolutely steps out on it. Luke 9:1–50 empasizes key Christological themes: Jesus' suffering, death, and resurrection become explicit teaching and testimony in the chapter, because Luke confronts readers with the identity and destiny of Jesus.

Traditional commentaries and other literature have much to say about Luke 9 and its themes, but we are studying concentric parallelisms in Luke's Gospel, so we focus particularly on one that appears in Luke 9. The chapter serves both as a third discourse on following Jesus and serves as an introduction to the next ten chapters making up the journey narrative and indeed an introduction to the rest of the Gospel.

Twelve Unready Men

Before chapter 9 Luke clarifies that men called to be Jesus' apostles (6:12–16) simply accompany Jesus (6:17; 7:11; 8:1, 22, 51), as do "a great crowd" of other disciples (6:17). They listen and ask questions, they watch and wonder. Luke 9 leaves aside the larger throng of disciples for a few episodes, for now featuring particularly the twelve apostles in their relation to Jesus. Elsewhere in the Gospel, the twelve sometimes blend into the undifferentiated "crowds" of curious and critics who follow Jesus. At times the twelve disappear from the narrative for multiple episodes, although it seems reasonable to think that they still observe and overhear others' interactions with Jesus. In 9:1–50, however, the twelve prominently participate in events that also highlight the destiny of Jesus.[1] The twelve apostles appear in or connect with every episode in 9:1–50 in some important way.[2]

Luke heavily edits accounts from Mark and organizes them as Luke 9:1–50 in a concentric pattern of paired episodes. Luke 9, however, consists not only of a third discourse on discipleship but also of a theological introduction the the journey narrative. Thus Luke 9:1–50 works like a transitional paragraph to highlight Jesus as the coming King as described in chapter 1 ("The Lord God will give to him the throne of his father David, and he will reign over the house of Jacob forever, and of his kingdom there will be no end", 1:32–33), but on a grander scale.

Documenting the form

In our usual manner we document a suspected concentric parallelism by identifying textual features that draw our attention and by searching for below-the-surface features that may confirm (or not) what we see when reading the text. Review a description of method in the Introduction. Our repeated reading of Luke 9:1–50 exposes a concentric parallelism having twelve sections, six sections at the beginning that parallel in various ways six

---

1. David Moessner ("Luke 9:1–50," 575–605; *Lord of the Banquet*, 45–70) points out that v 28–36 are also replete with Moses-Deuteronomic typology. From that vantage point Moessner develops a concentric outline for Luke 9 and characterizes Jesus' journey to Jerusalem as the new Moses leading a new exodus. I find his outline unsatisfactory for three reasons. First, moving bits of Luke's text out of the received textual order in the last half of the concentric outline implies that Luke partially failed at organizing or thinking through his own point, an implication that falls short of Luke's evident ability. Second, the Greek manuscripts of 9:28–50 show only consistency and stability; there is no evidence that the text once was organized differently and that it could be shuffled into a better order. Finally, Moessner overlooks important exegetical factors: (1) While Moses-typology clearly comes to the fore in 9:28–30, Elijah shares equally in the episode and Elijah's story thematically dominates the remainder of the chapter. (2) Structural hints point to a parallel between verses 18 and 28 and thus between their respective episodes. Jesus prominently prays in the presence of disciples in both v 18 and 28, and the two verses are linked by the Greek *kai egeneto* in v18 and then *egeneto de* in v 28. The *de* stands for a response to something similar that precedes. Moessner's outline does not recognize the prayer parallel or account for this significant feature of Greek discourse.

2. I depend heavily on Green's exegesis of Luke 9:1–50 (Green, *Luke*, 351–99, especially 351–55), but Green does not propose a concentric outline for these episodes.

at the end. Luke deliberately organized a concentric discourse among twelve episodes about Jesus and the disciples.

9:1–2 Sharing Jesus' Ministry	A
9:3–5 Status Borrowed from Jesus	B
9:6–10a Scandalized by Jesus	C
9:10b–17 Ministry with Jesus	D
9:18–20 Identifying Jesus	E
9:21–22 Dying and Rising	F
9:23–27 Dying and Rising	F'
9:28–36 Identifying Jesus	E'
9:37–42 Ministry without Jesus	D'
9:43–45 Scandalized by Jesus	C'
9:46–48 Status Borrowed from Jesus	B'
9:49–50 Sharing Jesus' Ministry?	A'

Sharing Jesus' Ministry (Section A, 9:1–2, and A', 9:49–50)

Casting out demons by the authority of Jesus' name specifies ministry acts in the first and last episodes of Luke 9:1–50. Section A includes additional kinds of ministry assigned to the twelve ("cure," "proclaim," "heal"), but the connection to Section A' singles out the ministry of exorcism for comparison. In Luke 9:1 the narrator states that Jesus "gave [the twelve] power and authority" for these ministries, and in practice they would wield Jesus' power and authority over demons "in the name of Jesus" (see 10:17–18). In Section A' (9:49), John informs Jesus that someone else casts out demons by that name. An outsider uses the authority of Jesus' name to cast out demons, and John wants Jesus to approve stopping the man.

Luke 9:1 And he called *the twelve* together and gave *them power and authority over all demons* and to cure diseases, ² and he sent *them* out to proclaim the kingdom of God and to heal.

Luke 9:49 John answered, "Master, we saw someone *casting out demons in your name*, and we tried to stop him, because he does not follow with *us*." ⁵⁰ But Jesus said to him, "Do not stop him, for the one who is not against *you* is for *you*."

Jesus (9:1–2) takes a new step by delegating to the twelve the role of assisting his work in preaching the kingdom of God, healing, and casting out demons. Jesus at first commissions only twelve apostles, although in Luke 10:1–20 he sends out seventy-two, likewise empowered and authorized to use his name to extend the kingdom of God. But now only twelve.

Section A' emphasizes Jesus' group of authorized agents in two ways. First, John worries that a stranger should not exorcise demons in Jesus' name (49). John's statement to Jesus about the man places the words "with us" in the final (emphatic) position, highlighting that his concern is that the unidentified man boasts no membership in the authorized body. The man is not one of the twelve, therefore he retains no right to do this, implies John.

Second, Jesus answers John (50) only in social terms ("you" and "him") and does not give a theological or strategic explanation. To develop a parallel between the sections, Luke edits his source in Mark. The second Gospel reads "The one who is not against *us* (*hēmōn*) is for *us* (*hēmōn*)" (Mark 9:40), but Luke edits Mark to give "the one who is not against *you* (*hymōn*) is for *you* (*hymōn*)" (Luke 9:50).[3] Thus, Section A parallels Section A' by thematic language and by Luke's edits of Mark in appropriating text for v 49–50, edits that build parallels. Jesus' name carries power and authority, and the name also lends Jesus' social status to otherwise socially marginal disciples of Jesus.

Status Borrowed from Jesus
(Section B, 9:3–5, and B', 9:46–48)

The theme of social status offers offers a unique basis for confirming Sections B and B' as parallel sections. The sections contain no particular lexical, literary, or editorial features pointing to purposeful parallel organization by Luke. Instead the sections share an important Greek word and thus share that word's cultural context: *dechomai*, "receive."[4] Luke 9:3–5 and 9:46–48 thus have conceptual roots in the Greco-Roman and Hellenized culture of hospitality. Joel Green explains that to receive people "would be to extend them the honor of hospitality, to regard them as guests, but one would only [receive] a social equal or one whose honor was above one's own."[5]

Luke 9:3 And he said to them, "Take nothing for your journey, no staff, nor bag, nor bread, nor money; and do not have two tunics. [4] And whatever house you enter, stay there, and from there depart. [5] And wherever *they do not receive you*, when you leave that town shake off the dust from your feet as a testimony against them."	Luke 9:46 An argument arose among them as to which of them was the greatest. [47] But Jesus, knowing the reasoning of their hearts, took a child and put him by his side [48] and said to them, "*Whoever receives this child in my name receives me, and whoever receives me receives him who sent me. For he who is least among you all is the one who is great.*"

    3. In Mark's account, John addresses Jesus as "Teacher" (*didaskale*, 9:38). Luke interposes "Master" (*epistata*, Luke 9:49) instead. While "teacher" in Mark evokes instruction and training, "master" in Luke evokes delegation and accountability. "Teacher" is the rabbi; "master" is the supervisor, the foreman.

    4. The following heavily depends on Green, *Luke*, 359–60, 391–92.

    5. Green, *Luke*, 391.

Since the disciples carry out their assignment (9:1–3) without any status-giving garments or luggage, their welcome in village homes depends directly on the status of Jesus whom they represent. When received, their welcome is a welcome for Jesus by proxy, a borrowed status.

In 9:46 of the opposite section disciples argue about their relative "greatness," meaning their social status. Which of them, they debate, merits a readier entrée from a host? But Jesus intervenes by teaching the way of welcome in the kingdom of God, a way that overturns deeply ingrained cultural practices. He draws in a child to the cluster of apostles and places the child in a position of honor at his side, perhaps with a hand on the child's shoulder.

Jesus teaches his apostles that honoring a child honors Jesus by proxy, just as honoring Jesus amounts to honoring God. Green explains: "Children, whose place of social residence was defined as the bottom of the ladder of esteem, might be called upon to perform acts of hospitality, e.g., washing the feet of a guest, but normally would not themselves be the recipients of honorable behavior."[6] The kingdom of God subverts a system of social hierarchy and replaces it with social parity for all, particularly for traditionally marginalized people, such as children.

Returning to our consideration of a parallel welcome theme, if any villagers receive the apostles (9:4, Section A), they in effect receive Jesus. If any disciples receive a child of the kingdom (47–48, Section A′), they also receive Jesus and God. Both texts we are comparing depend on the social dynamics of their respective societies, Luke 9:4 on Greco-Roman culture and 9:48 on the kingdom of God. The parallel feature of the texts is their conceptual basis.[7]

The kingdom of God manifest in Jesus introduces new modes of hospitality, but it also introduces unsettling questions about Jesus.

Scandalized by Jesus (Section C, 9:6–10a, and C′, 9:43–45)

The twelve, close followers of Jesus, know him, but in some ways they don't know him—Jesus baffles them. Another powerful person, Herod the tetrarch, finds rumors about Jesus perplexing. Herod too is scandalized.

---

6. Ibid., 391.

7. In terms of the tests we laid out in chapter 1 for documenting literary parallels, this proposal to counterpoise 9:4–5 and 46–48 clearly falls short. Yet I still propose that the reader consider the possibility described above. Luke paints parallels from a more diverse palette than a purely linguistic one. Further, Sections B and B′ stand between other sections (A/A′; C/C′) that do meet literary tests, giving our proposal for Sections B and B′ an additional leg up.

Section C (9:6–10a) shifts focus from apostles and villages to halls of political power, where the reader learns of Herod's perplexity about Jesus. Persistent rumors ("all that was happening," 7) are going around about healings done under the authority of Jesus. Not the apostles as agents, but Jesus as the source of "such things" (9) attracts Herod's attention. The wording "everywhere" (6), "all that was happening" (7), and "about whom I hear such things" (9) is uniquely Lukan, not appropriated from the Marcan source. Herod is perplexed (*diēporei*, 7), a word supplied here by Luke from his other resources, not from Mark.

Luke 9:6 And they departed and went through the villages, preaching the gospel and healing *everywhere*.⁷ Now *Herod* the tetrarch *heard about all that was happening*, and *he was perplexed*, because it was said by some that John had been raised from the dead, ⁸ by some that Elijah had appeared, and by others that one of the prophets of old had risen. ⁹ Herod said, "John I beheaded, but who is this *about whom I hear such things*?" And he sought to see him. ¹⁰ On their return the apostles told him all that they had done.	Luke 9:43 And *all were astonished* at the majesty of God. But while they were *all marveling at everything he was doing*, Jesus said to his disciples, ⁴⁴ "Let these words sink into your ears: The Son of Man is about to be delivered into the hands of men." ⁴⁵ But they did not understand this saying, and it was concealed from them, so that they might not perceive it. And *they were afraid* to ask him about this saying.

Section C' (9:43–45) contains similar Luke-specific wording: "all," "all," "everything he was doing" (43). In contrast to general amazement about the acts of Jesus and God, Jesus subverts the disciples' enthusiasm by announcing, for the second time, a looming crisis. "The Son of Man is about to be delivered into the hands of men" (44).⁸ For the disciples, gloom replaces joy.

And more than gloom: confusion and fear. Intellectually they can't take in Jesus' caveat. How can such majesty, power, and authority be trumped by anyone? It doesn't add up, they don't understand. But they really don't want an explanation—dark imaginings creep in that are too fearsome to think about.

Section C, 9:6–10a, parallels Section C', 9:43–45, by similar clusters of Lukan summary language (6–7, 9; 43). Further, Luke provides "perplexed" (7) in Section C to counterbalance fearful incomprehension in Section C' (45). The Evangelist counterbalances two sections by an inability of key leaders to grasp the truth about Jesus. Because the apostles in particular resist truly seeing what Jesus does and truly hearing what Jesus says, the twelve remain unprepared for certain ministry opportunities presented to them.

---

8. This announcement warns only that someone will surrender ("hand over," *paradidosthai*) Jesus to unidentified men; Jesus mentions no crucifixion or resurrection as he did in 9:22.

Ministry With and Without Jesus
(Section D, 9:10b–17, and D′, 9:37–42)

The apostles fail to fulfill two calls for kingdom action, one in the presence of Jesus and the other apart from him. The twelve do not at first call on Jesus himself or on the power of his name (apparently) for doing what was asked of them.

Luke 9:10b–17 drips with ironies about the twelve, ironies in relation to their just-completed mission. These ironies stand out particularly in the Third Gospel due to Luke's added language for the section in comparison to Mark's Gospel. Unique Lucan words in the episode enhance a parallel to Jesus' lament in Section D′. Such ironies reveal Jesus' critical stance toward the twelve about feeding the hungry people, but Jesus remains patient with them. After all, multiplying food supplies in Jesus' name was not part of their recent commission. Jesus' critical but patient treatment of the twelve, in this instance, parallels and contrasts with Jesus' lament over "faithless and twisted" disciples in Section D′.

Luke 9:10b And he took them and withdrew apart to a town called Bethsaida. ¹¹ When the crowds learned it, they followed him, and he welcomed them and spoke to them of the kingdom of God and cured those who had need of healing. ¹² Now the day began to wear away (*klinein* [decline]),	Luke 9:37 On the next day, *when they had come down* from the mountain,
and the twelve came and said to him, "Send the *crowd* away to go into the surrounding villages and countryside to find lodging and get provisions, for we are here in a desolate place."	*a great crowd* met him. ³⁸ And behold, a man from the *crowd* cried out, "Teacher, I beg you to look at my son, for he is my only child. ³⁹ And behold, a spirit seizes him, and he suddenly cries out. It convulses him so that he foams at the mouth, and shatters him, and will hardly leave him.
¹³ But he said to them, "*You give them something to eat.*" They said, "We have no more than five loaves and two fish—unless we are to go and buy food for all these people." ¹⁴ For there were about five thousand men.	⁴⁰ And *I begged your disciples to cast it out*, but they could not." ⁴¹ Jesus answered, "O faithless and twisted generation, how long am I to be with you and bear with you?
And he said to his disciples, "*Have them sit down* in groups of about fifty each." ¹⁵ And they did so, and *had them all sit down*.	Bring your son here." ⁴² While he was coming, the demon *threw him to the ground* and convulsed him.

¹⁶ And taking the five loaves and the two fish, he looked up to heaven and said a blessing over them.	But Jesus rebuked the unclean spirit
Then he broke the loaves and gave them to the disciples to set before the crowd. ¹⁷ And they all ate and were satisfied.	and healed the boy,
And what was left over was picked up, twelve baskets of broken pieces.	and gave him back to his father.

Further, in these sections the Evangelist arranges a parallel thematic development. He replaces "when it grew late" of Mark 6:35 with "when the day began to wear away (declined, *klinein*) in Luke 9:12. The change is unneeded, except that the metaphor of slope or descent that he thus provides resonates closely with Luke's narration of the beginning circumstance in the other section. Sloping down and descending of Section D links to "when they had come down from the mountain" of Section D' (9:37).

Such a connection between 9:12a and 37 launches further parallel thematic development of the sections. Next comes evident need of help in 12b–14a (hunger) and in 37b–39 (demonization), followed by the twelve's inability to help (13–14a; 40–41). Those needing help sit or fall on the ground (14b–15; 42). In the fifth parallel units Jesus addresses God (16) or the unclean spirit (42b), speaking to unseen but active powers in the respective episodes. Then Jesus resolves each crisis by God's power (16b–17a, multiplies loaves and fish; 42c, heals) and confirms his exercise power to those who sought help (17b, great quantity of leftovers; 42d, returns only child to his father). Themes in these sections appear in seven parallel units.

To summarize, Sections D and D' qualify as parallel sections in three ways. First, in counterbalanced locations Luke provides unique and significant thematic wording that was not in Mark. Second, the sections have multiple shared themes. And finally, Luke organizes those themes in the same order. Although the twelve had just returned from a mission characterized by receiving hospitality and by healing of demonized people, the apostles ironically fall short when called upon to give hospitality or heal another demonized person. They need to know deeply whom they are following and act accordingly.

Identifying Jesus (Section E, 9:18–20, and E', 9:28–36)

True knowledge of Jesus is revealed knowledge. Even then, words revealing the identity of Jesus must take root in ready soil in order for the apostles to bear appropriate fruit for God. Sections E and E′ describe moments of revelation regarding the identity of Jesus.[9]

These sections cohere in parallel based on their eye-catching similar beginnings, on their shared themes organized in the same order, and based on Luke's deliberate editing to organize their first and the last parallel units. Prominent themes tie 9:18–20 with 9:28–36, most visibly in the narrated setting for each section: Jesus prays in the presence of the disciples, but he prays alone (18; 28–29). These narrations catch one's eye all the more because they appear at the front of both sections. Further, the narrations capture attention of Greek readers and listeners through the serial discourse development that they present. Section E begins *kai egeneto* ("Now it happened," 18) and Section E′ starts out *egeneto de* ("Now it also happened," my translation, 28). The *de* signals a sequential follow-up to something that precedes.[10] *Egeneto de* and its sentence sequentially follow up *kai egeneto* and its sentence.

Luke 9:18 Now it happened (*kai egeneto*) that as *he was praying alone, the disciples were with him.*

Luke 9:28 Now (*egeneto de*) about eight days after these sayings *he took with him Peter and John and James and went up on the mountain to pray.* [29] And as he was praying,

The parallel theme of Jesus' private, but observed prayer stands out also when one examines Luke's supplementation of his source text in Mark for Luke 9:18 and 28–29a. Luke appropriates wording from a non-Marcan source for both "Now it happened that as he was praying" (18) and for ". . . to pray. And he was praying" (28–29). These expressions are unique to Luke's Gospel and together serve as evidence that Luke purposefully develops a parallel between the two episodes.

Our current sections display other themes occurring in the same order.[11] After Jesus' private prayer times, the disciples converse with Jesus. The conversations both express mistaken associations of Jesus with key Old Testament prophets. In Luke 9:18b–19 the crowds reportedly confuse Jesus with John the Baptist, Elijah, or with another ancient, but risen prophet. In 9:29b–33 the disciples represented by Peter, stupid with sleep, want to honor Moses, Elijah, and Jesus as peers. Then a voice (Peter's in Section E, a heavenly one in Section E′) asserts that Jesus' identity far surpasses any prophetic role (20; 34–36a). Finally, silence is commanded or kept (21; 36b). In sum, four thematic segments in Section E parallel four thematic segments in Section E′.

9. The issue of soil ready to take in this "word" occupies Sections F and F′.

10. There are no intervening occurrences of *egeneto*.

11. The *themes* appear in the same order, but not necessarily the *plots*. No plot element in Luke 9:18–19 parallels the Transfiguration of vv 29b–32.

Luke 9:18b And he asked them, "Who do the crowds say that I am?" ¹⁹ And they answered, "John the Baptist. But others say, *Elijah,* and others, that *one of the prophets of old* has risen."	Luke 9:29b the appearance of his face was altered, and his clothing became dazzling white. ³⁰ And behold, two men were talking with him, *Moses and Elijah,* ³¹ who appeared in glory and spoke of his departure, which he was about to accomplish at Jerusalem. ³² Now Peter and those who were with him were heavy with sleep, but when they became fully awake they saw his glory and the two men who stood with him. ³³ And as the men were parting from him, *Peter* said to Jesus, "Master, it is good that we are here. Let us make three tents, one for you and *one for Moses and one for Elijah*"—not knowing what he said.
²⁰ Then he said to them, "But who do you say that I am?" And *Peter* answered, "The Christ of God."	³⁴ As he was saying these things, a cloud came and overshadowed them, and they were afraid as they entered the cloud. ³⁵ And a voice came out of the cloud, saying, "*This is my Son, my Chosen One;* listen to him!" ³⁶ And when the voice had spoken, Jesus was found alone.
²¹ And he strictly charged and commanded them to *tell this to no one,*	And *they kept silent and told no one* in those days anything of what they had seen.

Corresponding themes offer moderate confirmation of parallelism between the sections. Their parallel order strengthens the liklihood of Luke's deliberate arranging. And the Evangelist's edits of his Marcan source, bringing in unique material at the beginnings and ends of the sections, confirm his literary/theological intent even more. Sections E and E′ offer quite strong evidence of literary parallelism.[12]

In high Lukan drama, Peter, James, and John receive astonishing disclosures about the identity of Jesus, who is both the Christ of God and the Son of God. One can imagine the disciples's racing minds as they try to process the implications of Jesus' identity. What does this mean for Jesus, and what does it mean for followers of Jesus? But Jesus cuts short any possible speculation or misunderstanding when he teaches that, for himself and for disciples, it means dying and rising.

---

12. As a reminder to pastor-exegetes and other Bible students, both our chapter introduction above, the sectional titles in the concentric outline, and our chapter subtitles were added only at the end of the study process, as aids for the reader. The compulsion to add titles to textual sections early in the study process should be resisted, coming to titles instead only as the end of the exegesis.

Dying and Rising (Section F, 9:22, and F′, 9:23–27)

Jesus *will* die and rise; Jesus' followers *must* die and rise. Israelite religious authorities will spurn Jesus and arrange to have him slain on a Roman cross, but God will raise Jesus from the dead (9:22). Analogously, a disciple "must deny himself, take up his cross daily" (23). Such a follower must "lose his life" to save it, and must be proud, not "ashamed," of Jesus and his words (23–26). Whoever loses his life by following Jesus will receive life again (24). Sections F and F′ cohere as parallel sections due to their shared and prominent dying and rising theme.

Luke 9:22 saying, "The Son of Man must suffer many things and be rejected by the elders and chief priests and scribes, and be killed, and on the third day be raised."	Luke 9:23 And he said to all, "If anyone would come after me, let him deny himself and take up his cross daily and follow me. 24 For whoever would save his life will lose it, but whoever loses his life for my sake will save it. 25 For what does it profit a man if he gains the whole world and loses or forfeits himself? 26 For whoever is ashamed of me and of my words, of him will the Son of Man be ashamed when he comes in his glory and the glory of the Father and of the holy angels. 27 But I tell you truly, there are some standing here who will not taste death until they see the kingdom of God."

One could readily describe Luke 9:22–27 as a single unified section conspicuously marked by one theme. It seems best to me, however, to separate the verses into two parallel sections, the first exposing the vocation of "the Son of Man" and the second clarifying the vocation of "all," "anyone," whoever," or "a man." In the end, however, such a distinction may have little influence on how we interpret the sections making up the concentric parallelism in 9:22–27. The central sections (9:23–27), paired or unpaired, provide the interpretive key for the whole structure, although we already see some suggestions of its theological shape.[13]

Interpreting the form

We now turn to interpretation of Luke 9:22–27. The ways disciples die and rise "for Jesus' sake" (24) are not new to readers of the Third Gospel. Jesus taught all of these commitments, or faithful disciples modelled them, within Luke's first two discourses on discipleship. We see "denying self and taking up the cross" (embracing a new Jesus-centered identity) in Peter, James, John, and Levi, who abandon their livlihoods (5:9–11, 28) for life with Jesus. The men

---

13. We will take up the connection of 9:1–50 to the journey narrative at the end of this chapter.

"follow" or "come after" Jesus (5:11, 28), as do women freed from demons (8:1–3). A man freed from demons also craves to be with Jesus (8:38–39).

Coming after Jesus means "losing life" (giving up familiar expectations and practices) for Peter (5:5), for John the Baptist (7:18–23), for the woman healed of bleeding (8:46–48), and for Jairus and his wife (8:49–56). A settled positive regard toward Jesus and his words, never giving in to shame about him, characterizes the centurion in 7:6–9 and the woman of the city in 7:37–38. We have encountered these examples of "coming after Jesus" in Luke 5–8.[14]

Luke does not build in further general examples of discipleship in 9:1–50. Instead, the Evangelist highlights instances of denying oneself and taking up one's cross daily to follow Jesus *as they apply to the twelve apostles*. Sections in the first half of the parallelism portray the twelve generally in a positive light as disciples, or at least a neutral one. Sections following the center portray the disciples negatively. We turn now to interpret the outside sections of of the concentric form.

Sharing Jesus' Ministry

Can anyone pursue legitimate apostolic ministry apart from the twelve or without participating in the Jesus community? Sections A and A′ clarify that Jesus extends his work both through those directly assigned to outreach and through those who act independently of the twelve, yet act in Jesus' name.

The apostles have become fixtures in second-level leadership of the band of Jesus-followers. Peter, James, John, and Levi become the first disciples of Jesus (5:9–11; 27–28). They accompany Jesus in the countryside, in towns and villages, in homes and synagogues, in both solitude and in crowds. As the apostles follow Jesus, they intimately know him in his prayer, his teaching, healing, and casting out demons. Then Jesus "chose from [the band of disciples] twelve" (6:13), and then "he called the twelve together and gave them . . . , and sent them . . ." (9:1–2). They know ministry with and for Jesus.

But others follow Jesus without accompanying him, making the social boundaries of being "disciples" larger and less clearly defined. Most main characters in Luke 7–8 already trust Jesus. Those who see the widow's son raised from the dead proclaim the glorious prophet Jesus to all the surrounding country (7:15–17). In their proclamation, they can be said to be

---

14. See similar in Luke 14:25–33. Green provides a thorough explanation of commitments of "coming after Jesus" in *Luke*, 371–76. Our definition of terms for interpreting 9:23–27 depends heavily on Green's explanations.

following Jesus, but separately from the apostles. The formerly demonized man goes about gentile Gerasa "proclaiming throughout the whole city how much Jesus had done for him" (8:39). Surely in his zeal to proclaim Jesus, he is a follower, but not in concert with the twelve. And now John in Section A′ asks Jesus about another man acting independently and without evident sanction (9:49). Shouldn't the twelve ("we") stop him?

In terms of the chiastic center of 9:1–50, that is, vv 21–27, John and the twelve need to give up an expectation that Jesus only authorizes mission done under his explicit command and that the apostles are his only chosen agents. The twelve must *lose their lives* for Jesus. Even though Jesus commands and approves their ministry, even though his power and authority becomes manifest through them, even though Jesus calls only them to be apostles, the purposes and ways of Jesus extend beyond what the apostles perceive to others. The twelve must put to death their insider presumption.

Status Borrowed from Jesus

Sections B and B′ clarify further what it means for apostles of Jesus to lose their lives for him. "Life" in these episodes of apostleship boasts itself as an expectation of public respect. Section B anticipated that the men would be welcomed into some homes as they preached and healed in Jesus' name. In 9:46, however, the disciples argue about who rates hospitality at more honorable homes, about which of them is greatest. A consequent "death" that Jesus calls them to has the trait of "receiving" children, a manner of giving hospitality (and receiving it) without reference to honor in the culture.

Jesus bases this culturally shocking principle on the exigency attached to his name ("receives this child in my name," 48). The phrase "in his name" draws together the range of Jesus' purposes, teaching, example, and his actions into a received way of living under his lordship and grace. It means "as I do." The apostles heard, saw, and received Jesus' ministry so far: he welcomed everybody, particularly the despised and marginalized.[15]

Moreover, and just beyond the horizon of the twelve's readiness to see, Jesus himself will be shamed and marginalized as he suffers crucifixion (9:22–23) and abuse (44). Consequently pursuing apostolic mission *in Jesus' name* must include for them an expectation of possible rejection,

---

15. As he already demonstrated with Simon's mother-in-law (4:38–39), a leper (5:12–13), a paralytic (5:19–24), a tax collector (5:27–28), a widow and a dead man (7:12–15), (possibly) a prostitute (7:37–38), a demonized man (8:27–29), a hemorrhagic woman (8:43–48), and a dead twelve-year-old girl (8:52–56); and as Jesus taught in the Sermon on the Plain (6:20–26, 35–36).

disparagement, death.[16] "Following Jesus" necessarily includes, as Green summarizes, performing "in a way consistent with Jesus' own commitments and commission."[17] The way of Jesus displaces a culture of status and honor among his followers. In Section B′ the disciples do not yet comprehend that they must die to such a way of discerning importance among people. And, scandalous as it may seem, their Lord himself must be disgraced, dishonored.

Scandalized by Jesus

Section C′ poses a contrast between the marvelous demonstration of God's majesty in "everything [Jesus] was doing" (43b) and, on the other hand, Jesus' announcement of his coming public humiliation. Deliverance of Jesus "into the hands of men" (44) points to dishonor and shaming that necessarily dogs his future (see similar wording in 18:31–34).[18] Green summarizes, "Together, then, vv 43-44 again demonstrate the necessity of the integration in the disciples' conceptualization of Jesus' messianic identity of his elevated status vis-à-vis the divine purpose and his rejection at the hands of human beings."[19] The disciples, however, cannot allow themselves to think (45) that the Christ, the Son of God, the marvelous worker of God-like wonders, must and would be treated shamefully.

But the apostles must put to death an expectation that their Master must maintain his glorious public esteem. Even though disgrace looms for Jesus, he tells the twelve and others that "whoever is ashamed of me and my words, of him will the Son of Man be ashamed when he comes in his glory and the glory of the Father and of the holy angels" (9:26). Verse 26 connects to v 44 with particular clarity arising from concern for Jesus' "words" in both places. Jesus forcefully claims the apostles's attention by exhorting, "Let these words sink into your ears . . . ." (44), an exhortation that by intensity surpasses "hear this" or "know this" or "I tell you." Jesus will be shamed, but the twelve must not be scandalized by word that their glorious Master will be shamed. God's purpose for Jesus includes the shame of death on a Roman cross.

Rome nurtured a comprehensive honor/shame culture throughout the Empire. When notables were slighted in public, much more, when they were mocked and treated with contempt, grievous shame came upon

---

16. See also Acts 9:16.

17. Green, *Luke*, 392.

18. The acts of shaming that Jesus foretold in 9:44 and 18:31–33 are fulfilled by Pilate in 23:11, 16.

19. Green, *Luke*, 390

them. Israelite culture participated in this culture of honor and shame. Luke 14:16–24 provides a parabolic example of shaming, where three invitees choose to distance themselves from a banquet host for some unstated reason. In another feast parable (14:7–11), Jesus illustrates humility and exaltation in the kingdom of God through familiar honor/shame considerations when picking a seat at a banquet. Herod the tetrarch (Section C) necessarily lives and rules within the same honor/shame culture.

Section C features Herod's perplexity over reports (9:7–8) that could imply Herod's impotence before the Israelite prophets. These rumors could have people believe that the tetrarch of Galilee and Perea ultimately failed to stamp out John the Baptist. Herod doesn't believe it (9:9), but some do. In perplexity, the tetrarch wants to see the supposed prophet for himself and dispel the rumors.

Luke 9:7–9 and the turn to Herod's concerns forms a break in the story of apostolic ministry by the authoritative name of Jesus, a break that also makes up a section of text to balance the theme of Section C′. Luke then shifts back to the apostles, to their new assignments from Jesus, and the question of their readiness to trust him.

Ministry With and Without Jesus

Jesus takes his apostles aside (9:10b–17) to a barren zone in the environs of Bethsaida, amid thronging crowds. The narrator says that Jesus "welcomed" them (11), a word that means he extended hospitality to them. It is early evening. The twelve, recent recipients of meals served to them after long hours walking and healing, feel compassion for the many hungry travelers who seek the Master. Jesus will have mercy on them too, they think, so they urge him to disperse the crowd into the hands of whatever hospitable neighbors can be found, or send people to buy their food.

No, he says, "you give them something to eat" (13)! In effect, he specifies the twelve as the neighbors whose hospitality the crowds will enjoy. Jesus unexpectedly requires the men to provide food for five thousand people, a kingdom ministry that Jesus has not demonstrated to them nor previously required of them. There are a few loaves of bread and some fish available, and maybe a little money (13), but how do they proceed? Casting out demons and healing diseases in Jesus' name was a sending away, a restoration, and breaking of Satan's hold on people.[20] But to assuage human hunger on a massive scale? Or to provide bread and table-ready fish, also on a massive

---

20. Asking Jesus to "send the crowd away" may have seemed somewhat consistent with recent ministry.

scale? The apostles had commanded demons and diseases in Jesus' name, but how does one command stomachs or loaves of bread or dry fish?

This would be awkward for the twelve, standing there in public between Jesus' expectation and the needs of thousands. Embarrassing, mortifying. Would Jesus multiply the money if some of them started toward the nearest market to buy the needed food? Jesus then relents, he takes his requirement away, giving hospitality himself by multiplying these few loaves and fish into thousands of servings. And the twelve see Jesus provide the thing he commanded them to do.

The interpretive link between Section D and the theologial center of the structure may reside in Jesus' warning about shame toward himself and toward his word (9:26). Jesus' command to apostles to feed the crowd is awkward for them and unreasonable. Jesus sees embarrassment looming in their hearts. But the Master intervenes, calling the blessing of heaven upon the bread and fish, feeding the crowd. Embarrassment about Jesus means, in terms of the theological enter of the structure, to be ashamed of him.

The theological center ties to Section D′ most obviously by the thematic parallel between 9:26 ("the Son of Man [will] be ashamed") and Jesus' lament in v 41 ("O faithless and twisted generation"). Section D′ (9:37–42) reveals the twelve's fickle faith in a critical moment. In the context, Jesus, Peter, James, and John have been away from the rest of the disciples. The three followed Jesus to a local summit where they witnessed glorious things about the Chosen One. The nine apostles remaining below the mountain tried to cast out a demon as they had been authorized to do (9:1), but it seems that this fierce spirit somehow intimidated them to stunned inaction. Joel Green traces the ups and downs of the disciples's trust in Jesus:

> The incorrigibleness of the disciples is exacerbated by the inconsistency, even deterioration, of their faith—present but not manifest in the boat scene of 8:22-25, on display in their ministry activity in 9:6 but again hidden in the episode of the feeding miracle of 9:12-17, and now altogether absent. Jesus is already anticipating his execution (9:22, 44), after which his followers will share responsibility in the divine mission, and they are in a deplorable state of readiness.[21]

Jesus then laments, "O faithless and twisted generation, how long am I to be with you and bear with you?" (9:41)[22] Borrowing Moses' disparag-

---

21. Green, *Luke*, 389.

22. Jesus' inclusive lament over their faithlessness takes in all twelve disciples (9:41). The lament, however, does not apply to the boy's father, who, even after not getting relief through the disciples, still presses his request in faith to the disciples' Master.

ing words and tone about Israel's faithlessness to God (Deut 32:5), Jesus laments unbelief among his disciples. Even when not physically next to him, disciples still have power and authority from Jesus, to be exercised by faith in Jesus. He continues to provide the power that he entrusts them to wield.

In terms of Section F' in the chiastic center, obedient faith connects in a most basic way to "coming after" Jesus, to "following" him. It is no wonder that Jesus answered with words of Moses, lamenting Israel's incorrigible trust in God, applying the lament in this case to his own disciples.

Identifying Jesus

Sections E and E' develop another aspect of "following" Jesus: that of truly knowing him. Disciples who do not comprehend their master's identity may well misconstrue his teaching, commands, character, choices, plans, and purposes. Living "for his sake" must be informed by knowing who he is. Sections E and E' describe Peter (and other disciples) receiving new truth about Jesus, and the parallel between the sections (see above) provides an explanation for how Peter came to his statement in 9:20 that Jesus is "the Christ of God."

In Luke's Gospel, encountering Jesus both raises misgivings by some about his identity and elicits claims about him by others. Pharisees protest what forgiving sins implies about Jesus (5:21, 7:49) and astonished disciples struggle to name who it is that forced a storm to cower in a sudden calm (8:25). Demonized voices (of questionable veracity for those within earshot, but nonetheless opening a line of inquiry) assert that Jesus is the Son of God (4:41, 8:28).[23]

Peter no doubt hears all of these questions and claims, and further, he has his own history with Jesus to evaluate. Normally in the Third Gospel up to chapter 9, Peter calls Jesus "Master," a title of respect for a group leader (5:5; 8:24, 45). In shock at a huge catch of fish taken at Jesus' implausible command, and sensing the holy, Peter utters "Lord" (5:8) to address Jesus. But seeing the power, wisdom, or compassion of Jesus does not prepare him for Jesus' direct question "who do you say that I am" (9:20). Neither Jesus, Peter, nor Luke provide an explicit answer for *how* Peter arrives at his answer.[24]

But a clearly implied answer to that question comes from the concentrically parallel episode, 9:28–36. As Peter, James and John drowsily wait

---

23. From Luke's point of view, and for any Theophilus reading the narrative, demonized voices speak the truth.

24. Readers should keep in mind that we are studying only Luke's Gospel and not comparing or harmonizing with other Gospels.

on a mountain while Jesus prays, suddenly Jesus dazzles them. His face and garments blaze with glory, and the disciples see and hear Jesus in conversation with two men who are somehow identifiable to the disciples as Moses and Elijah. In an effort to prolong this conference among the great prophets, Peter proposes building three tents for their comfort.[25]

A voice booms from a suddenly-forming cloud, interrupting Peter. A cloud envelops terrain, screens Jesus and the prophets from the disciples, and brings fear to the men's hearts. The transfiguration with the appearance of the prophets happens for the benefit of the disciples, as does the cloud and voice: "This is my Son, my Chosen One; listen to him" (9:35). God speaks audibly and purposefully. As Green states, "The importance of this divine intrusion into the narrative lies in the fact that Jesus' apostles have not heretofore been privy to information of this kind."[26] The disciples must know and follow this Jesus. His words are words from God, his purposes are God's purposes. Knowing Jesus' identity comes from God's revelation.

Thematic parallel of Sections E and E' imply that Peter's confession of Jesus as "the Christ of God" is given to Peter following Jesus' request to God for revelation to the apostle. So we find both sections contain multiple parallels that portray Peter as receiving grand disclosures about Jesus' identity, disclosures that must shape the ways the disciples know and follow Jesus.

The sections of Luke 9 above, aligned in pairs of textual units, portray the spiritual weakness and unreadiness of the twelve. Peter and the rest do not yet reliably "come after" Jesus as those who know, intuit, and exhibit how Jesus intends them to follow him. The first half of the parallelism portrays the disciples positively (but having ironic blind spots); the second half of the parallelism shows multiple weaknesses in their formation as apostles of Jesus. But the time has come anyway for Jesus to set out to Jerusalem to fulfill his destiny there. The disciples' training continues.

Luke 9:1–50 as Introduction to the Journey Narrative in 9:51—19:46

Commentary authors on Luke's Gospel broadly agree that Luke 9:1–50 constitutes transitions in Jesus' ministry and life. The chapter completes his mission in Galilee and foreshadows future events in Jerusalem, necessitating Jesus' journey to the capitol city. Jesus continues, however, to train the apostles and the rest of his followers as the band moves toward the capitol. Growing disciples need to have their roots sent deeper, and newly sprouted

---

25. I depend heavily on Green's insights on Luke 9:28–36 (*Luke*, 376–85).
26 Green, *Luke*, 384.

disciples must give heed to birds, rocks, thorns, and fruit-bearing (see our chapter 2). Even though several episodes of Luke 9:51—19:46 do not mention the disciples, they probably listen from nearby. Some of this training especially prepares followers for persecution and loss they will face "taking up their cross" to faithfully follow Jesus.[27]

Opposition to Jesus grows during his journey to Jerusalem, notably opposition from Pharisees and their lawyers, but also from other elites. In Luke 9:7–9 the ominous curiosity of Herod, who had killed John the Baptist, portends both the Jeruslem events and a reported death threat against Jesus on the way to the city (13:31–33).[28] Indeed Jesus forewarns his followers of coming betrayal, shaming, abuse, crucifixion, and vindication: 9:22, 44; 17:25; 18:31–34.

Grand disclosures of Jesus as God's Messiah-king in Luke 9, followed by a journey narrative replete with Jesus' teaching on the kingdom of God, make up the central theological focus both of the journey and its introduction in Luke 9.[29] Following Luke 9:35 ("this is my Son, my Chosen One"), emphasis on Jesus' identity as "Son of God" recedes.[30]

On one hand, Luke 9:1–50 makes up round three of Jesus' training for his disciples on "coming after" him. On the other hand, it anticipates Jesus' journey to Jerusalem as its approaching king, a savior and ruler that some reject and others embrace.

---

27. Jesus directly trains his disciples in Luke 9:57–62, 10:1–24, 11:1–36, 12:1–12, 12:22–48, 14:25–33, 16:1–13, 17:1–10, 17:22—18:8, 18:15–17, 18:31–34, and 19:11–27.

28. Opposition against Jesus brews during his journey to Jerusalem: Luke 10:25, 11:15–23, 12:1–12, 13:17, 13:31–35, 15:2, 16:14, 17:25, 18:31–34.

29. The theme of Jesus as God's Messiah-king and teacher of the kingdom of God begins early in the third Gospel (1:33; 4:43; 8:1, 10). In a prominent return of the theme after the journey, all interrogations, challenges, and shaming in Luke 23 concern whether Jesus is the Messiah of God.

30. Receding to come forward only once more at Luke 22:70.

Part 2

The Journey Narrative

The "journey narrative" or "central section" or "Jerusalem journey" is one large literary and theological unit of the Second Gospel. Luke arranged a unique and memorable journey narrative (as I prefer to call these chapters). In the Second Gospel the journey takes up only one and a half chapters (Mark 10:1–11:19); in Luke it takes up nine or ten chapters. Some of our most memorable Gospel stories appear only here (Mary and Martha, Zacchaeus), as do favorite parables such as the Parable of the Prodigal Son.

Authors differ when identifying the exact end of Luke's journey narrative. Some say that the journey narrative ends at one or another point in chapter 18, including some who put it where Luke's text rejoins the order of the Gospel of Mark (Luke 18:15) after having strayed from it for many chapters. Others insist from a literary standpoint that the journey motif requires an end somewhere in chapter 19, but they disagree as to where the motif closes.[1]

I find the literary approach much more likely since journeying *to Jerusalem* is the announced goal of Jesus' journey (9:51), and Luke reminds readers of this from time to time by progress reports in the narrative. The literary unit does not end until at least 19:44, because in 19:41-44 the journey continues, since Jesus is still arriving ("he came near and saw the city," 9:41) toward his previously announced destination. Luke 19:45–46 no longer describes movement toward the city, but narrates Jesus' arrival in the temple and confrontation with temple vendors there. In these two verses, the narrative transitions from arriving into Jerusalem to Jesus' presence in

---

1. For a listing of proposals from various authors, see Bock, *Luke 9:51–24:53*, 957–64.

the temple, and the verses make up a literary transition.[2] For this reason I include 19:45–46 as the final verses of the journey narrative.

Our study is comprehensive, that is, it engages the complete text of Luke 9:51—19:46 as found in the Nestle-Aland Greek New Testament[28]. We do not set aside any of the text as a parenthesis or a later addition, nor do we "cut and paste" any portion of text to "make it work." The literary symmetry we discover in Luke's full narrative as received is elegant and beautiful.[3]

The shape of this journey narrative differs from structures within the Gospel's first third. Most obvious is its massive scale, taking up more than the entire second third of Luke's Gospel (426 verses). Second, Luke develops this concentric form in twenty-six sections, thirteen of them arrayed opposite another thirteen, rather than the nine or eleven sections of the earlier structures.[4]

---

2. For a description of and examples of literary transitions in the New Testament, see Longenecker, *Rhetoric at the Boundaries*.

3. Nestle-Aland provides a composite text of Luke, assembled from the oldest and best manuscripts. In reality, we do not have Luke's narrative, but we have scholarship's best effort at reconstructing it from evidence. There is now a movement urging the legitimacy of studying a Gospel exclusively from the oldest extant and complete manuscript. I choose instead to use the composite text of Luke in Nestle-Aland.

4. Sectional titles in the tables and in the following chapters were added only at the very end of our study/writing process for the convenience of the reader. During your analysis of concentric forms, deriving sectional titles should be avoided (see the Introduction).

A	9:51-55	Leaving
B	9:56-62	Kingdom Regimen
C	10:1-24	He Comes
D	10:25-37	Signs of Life
E	10:38-42	Nearing the Life-giver
F	11:1-13	Petition the Giver
G	11:14-36	Signs of the Kingdom
H	11:37-54	Censure
J	12:1-12	Shelter
K	12:13-48	Wealth
L	12:49-13:9	Line in the Sand
M	13:10-30	Guest List
N	13:31-33	Killers
N′	13:34-35	Killers
M′	14:1-24	Guest List
L′	14:25-35	Line in the Sand
K′	15:1-32	Wealth
J′	16:1-13	Shelter
H′	16:14-17:10	Censure
G′	17:11-37	Signs of the Kingdom
F′	18:1-8	Petition the Giver
E′	18:9-17	Nearing the Life-giver
D′	18:18-30	Signs of Life
C′	18:31-19:10	He Comes
B′	19:11-27	Kingdom Regimen
A′	19:28-46	Arriving

Threads of evidence that tie some sections together suggest a more general outline as well. Continuing themes tie groups of two or three consecutive sections into larger units. In this book we will call the larger units "bands" of sections, as in a band of various greens or a band of various reds in a many-colored rainbow.[5] Thematic bands with appropriate general titles include:

A–C, A′–C′	Go Follow
D–E, D′–E′	Simply Saved
F–F′	Petition the Giver
G–H, G′–H′	Kingdom Come
J–K, J′–K′	Stuff and Money
L–M, L′–M′	Alignment

Chapters 4 through 9 in Part 2 of our book take up these bands in sequence.

---

5. Strong evidence, however, requires maintaining distinctions between 26 sections and prohibits combining the 26 into fewer sections.

Both Here and There puts forward an analysis of Luke's journey narrative as a large-scale concentric parallelism, or macro-chiasmus, validating parallels by the same method as before.[6] Similarly, we derive a hermeneutic for the entire structure out of the center sections (N, N'), especially as they relate to the outside sections (A, A'). Our interpretation connects Luke's journey narrative to the Old Testament account of David's path to the throne of Israel, connecting many chapters of Luke to many chapters of 1–2 Samuel. Rather than tracing ties of all of Jesus' journey to all of David's journey, in our book we draw a more limited sampling of the connections. Chapters 10, 11, and 12 explain the interpretive approach taken, and chapter 13 examines connections of Sections A, N, N', and A' in the Lukan journey to key portions of David's story. God willing, a future book will examine more of these connections.

---

6. Other approaches, such as the narrative criticism done by Joel Green, *The Gospel of Luke*, explore other fabrics of meaning in the same material.

4

Go Follow

JESUS AND HIS DISCIPLES set out for Jerusalem and eventually arrive. Sections A–C give an account of early events in their slow progress toward Israel's cultic, political, and cultural center. Jesus sends messengers ahead to stimulate popular anticipation and to arrange hospitality. He then enlarges his advance party and details their instructions, later receiving back their enthusiastic report.

At the other end of the journey, Section A' reports their approach and arrival in the city, with Jesus once again sending disciples ahead on assignment. In Sections B' and C' themes of discipleship prevail as they do in Sections B and C: beginning to follow, failing to follow, and faithful following.

Leaving and Arriving
(Section A, Luke 9:51–56, and A', Luke 18:28–46)

The theme of going to Jerusalem, both departing toward it and arriving at it, sets Sections A (Luke 9:51–56) and A' (Luke 18:28–46) as geographical and narrative limits of Jesus' journey. The sections also have parallels of topic and wording. For one, in both sections Jesus sends messengers into a village (9:52; 19:29–30). Further, the Samaritan village of Section A does not receive him because his face is set toward Jerusalem (9:53); likewise, in Section A' he weeps over the unresponsiveness of Jerusalem because "you did not know the time of your visitation from God" (19:44).

88   PART 2: THE JOURNEY NARRATIVE

Luke 9:51 When the days drew near for him to be taken up, he set his face *to go to Jerusalem.* ⁵² And *he sent messengers* ahead of him, who went and entered *a village of the Samaritans*, to *make preparations* for him. ⁵³ But the people did not receive him, because his face was set toward Jerusalem. ⁵⁴ And when his disciples James and John saw it, they said, "Lord, do you want us to *tell fire to come down from heaven and consume them?*" ⁵⁵ But he turned and *rebuked* them. ⁵⁶ And they went on to another village.

Luke 19:28 And when he had said these things, he went on ahead, *going up to Jerusalem.* ²⁹ When he drew near to Bethphage and Bethany, at the mount that is called Olivet *he sent two of the disciples,* ³⁰ saying, "*Go into the village* in front of you, where on entering you will find a colt tied, on which no one has ever yet sat. Untie it and bring it here. ³¹ If anyone asks you, 'Why are you untying it?' you shall say this: '*The Lord has need of it.*'" ³² So those who were sent went away and found it just as he had told them. ³³ And as they were untying the colt, its owners said to them, "Why are you untying the colt?" ³⁴ And they said, "*The Lord has need of it.*" ³⁵ And they brought it to Jesus, and throwing their cloaks on the colt, they set Jesus on it. ³⁶ And as he rode along, they spread their cloaks on the road. ³⁷ As he was drawing near—already on the way down the Mount of Olives—the whole multitude of his disciples began to rejoice and praise God with a loud voice for all the mighty works that they had seen, ³⁸ saying, "Blessed is the King who comes in the name of the Lord! Peace in heaven and glory in the highest!" ³⁹ And some of the Pharisees in the crowd said to him, "Teacher, *rebuke your disciples.*" ⁴⁰ He answered, "I tell you, if these were silent, the very stones would cry out." ⁴¹ And when he drew near and saw the city, he wept over it, ⁴² saying, "Would that you, even you, had known on this day the things that make for peace! But now they are hidden from your eyes. ⁴³ *For the days will come upon you, when your enemies will set up a barricade around you and surround you and hem you in on every side* ⁴⁴ *and tear you down to the ground, you and your children within you. And they will not leave one stone upon another in you,* because you did not know the time of your visitation." ⁴⁵ And he entered the temple and began to drive out those who sold, ⁴⁶ saying to them, "It is written, 'My house shall be a house of prayer,' but you have made it a den of robbers."

The disciples in Luke 9 urge a judgment of fire from heaven on the Samaritan village for its disregard of Jesus (54), and Jesus himself in Luke 19 laments the catastrophic attack coming to the city of Jerusalem because it refuses to "know" the person and meaning of Jesus (19:41-44). Finally, in both sections the disciples are rebuked (9:55) or rebukes are sought (19:39). The sections prove to be parallel because Luke reports the termini of the journey and because multiple shared themes generally occur in the same order. In the remaining verses following Jesus' lament over Jerusalem (19:45–46), Luke transitions his larger narrative to the next major development in the story of Jesus.

Kingdom regimen
(Section B, Luke 9:57–62, and B′, Luke 19:11–27)

This second ring of the journey narrative contains one episode in each section, but these episodes differ substantially in length. Critics of a concentric approach to analysis sometimes object, claiming that quantitative balance is essential to any legitimate proposal of chiastic form. Such a claim arises from the pattern of typical ancient poems where concentric lines of poetry matched one another in length.[1] According to the claim, even in narrative, the number of words in one section ought to approximate the number in a parallel section. Their criticism might apply not only to uneven quantities of words in two sections of narrative, but also to uneven quantities of episodes the respective sections, one episode versus four, for example.

If we were looking only at poetry arranged in chiasmus, we would expect to find an approximate balance of word counts. Luke's journey narrative, however, is prose, and few poetry conventions apply to concentrically parallel prose. Word-count is not one of them.[2] Nor is episode-count. In some concentric parallels, a short episode might align with a long episode, and in other parallels, multiple episodes on one side might align with a single episode on the other. Such is the case with Luke 9:57–62 and 19:11–27.

---

1. Chiastic balance in *poetry* may be seen in the Greek of our earlier example, 1 John 3:9: "No one born of God makes a practice of sinning [nine words in sections a and b], for God's seed abides in him, and he cannot keep on sinning because he has been born of God [nine words in sections b′ and a′]."

2. An example of deliberate imbalance between tightly structured parallel *prose* units in Luke occurs in the beatitudes and woes of Luke 6. The fourth beatitude needs fifty-one Greek words (v 22–23), but the fourth woe requires only eighteen Greek words (v 26), making the woe only a third as long as its parallel beatitude. Review chapter 1 of *Both Here and There* for textual features that *do* reveal narrative texts to be parallel.

Luke 9:57 As they were going along the road, someone said to him, "I will *follow you wherever you go*." ⁵⁸ And Jesus said to him, "Foxes have holes, and birds of the air have nests, but the *Son of Man* has nowhere to lay his head." ⁵⁹ To another he said, "*Follow me*." But he said, "*Lord, let me first go and bury my father*." ⁶⁰ And Jesus said to him, "Leave the dead to bury their own dead. But as for you, go and *proclaim the kingdom of God*." ⁶¹ Yet another said, "*I will follow you, Lord*, but let me first say farewell to those at my home." ⁶² Jesus said to him, "No one who puts his hand to the plow and looks back is *fit for the kingdom of God*."

Luke 19:11 As they heard these things, he proceeded to tell a parable, because *he was near to Jerusalem*, and because they supposed that the *kingdom of God* was to appear immediately. ¹² He said therefore, "A nobleman went into a far country to *receive for himself a kingdom* and then return. ¹³ Calling ten of his *servants*, he gave them ten minas, and said to them, 'Engage in business until I come.' ¹⁴ But his *citizens* hated him and sent a delegation after him, saying, 'We do not want this man to *reign over us*.' ¹⁵ When he returned, *having received the kingdom*, he *ordered* these *servants* to whom he had given the money to be called to him, that he might know what they had gained by doing business. ¹⁶ The first came before him, saying, 'Lord, your mina has made ten minas more.' ¹⁷ And he said to him, 'Well done, *good servant*! Because you have been *faithful* in a very little, you shall have *authority over* ten cities.' ¹⁸ And the second came, saying, 'Lord, your mina has made five minas.' ¹⁹ And he said to him, 'And you are to *be over* five cities.' ²⁰ Then another came, saying, 'Lord, here is your mina, which I kept laid away in a handkerchief; ²¹ for I was afraid of you, because you are a severe man. You take what you did not deposit, and reap what you did not sow.' ²² He said to him, 'I will condemn you with your own words, you wicked *servant*! You knew that I was a severe man, taking what I did not deposit and reaping what I did not sow? ²³ Why then did you not put my money in the bank, and at my coming I might have collected it with interest?' ²⁴ And he said to those who stood by, 'Take the mina from him, and give it to the one who has the ten minas.' ²⁵ And they said to him, 'Lord, he has ten minas!' ²⁶ 'I tell you that to everyone who has, more will be given, but from the one who has not, even what he has will be taken away. ²⁷ But as for these enemies of mine, who did not want me to *reign over them*, bring them here and slaughter them before me.'"

Sections B and B′ exhibit parallel features. Three potential followers in 9:57–62 try, but fail, to negotiate with the Son of Man. A travel-ready newcomer hears that going with Jesus means hardship. A second asks for an immediate leave of absence to bury a dead family member. Jesus commands him instead to go and proclaim the kingdom. The Son of Man cautions a third newcomer that any diversion from kingdom work renders one unfit for the kingdom.[3]

In the parable of Section B′ (Luke 19:11–27), one of three servants of a newly ascendant king fails to meet the demands the lord sets out for them. Those who wait for the king must submit to his authority and responsibly do his bidding. Jesus' words to potential followers in Section B and his parabolic teaching in Section B′ have to do with followers' fitness for the kingdom of God.

---

3. There are similar sayings of Jesus about discipleship in Luke 14:26, 27, and 33.

Shared themes of kingship, authority, and obedience literarily connect Sections B and B'. But shared themes alone do not build a strong case for parallelism. Nor does it help when we note sets of three adherents in both sections. The quantity of three examples is so common in Greco-Roman literature (and in the Bible) that we cannot claim this as a significant feature confirming parallelism. The case for parallelism between Sections B and B' resides in the shared themes noted above and in the strength of parallel sections that surround Section B (Sections A and C) and and that surround Section B' (Sections A' and C').

He Comes (Sections C and C')

Jesus comes near in Section C'; the kingdom comes near in Section C. Luke 10:1–24, the lengthy Section C, contains multiple internal connections that show its overall unity.[4] Jesus sends seventy-two disciples and then they return; they go to labor, they return in joy (1–2; 17). The Lord's assignment for the seventy-two highlights cultural-spiritual challenges that his emissaries will face in the towns just ahead (3–11), and the "debriefing" stresses the cosmic-spiritual dynamics of ministry accomplished in Jesus' name (17–20). While sending out laborers, Jesus personally rebukes cultural-spiritual power centers that are tacitly listening (12–15, using *sy* "you," as one in power would speak to a child). While welcoming the seventy-two back, he speaks familiarly (*sy*, "you") to the cosmic "Lord of heaven and earth" (21), his heavenly Father. To the towns he speaks in rebuke (for cultures of obstinate unbelief, 13, and dire warning, 12, 14–15). To his Father he speaks thanksgiving and praise that the Father reveals heavenly truths to unsophisticated people, but hides these things from the cultural cognoscenti (21).

In Section C' (18:31–19:10) Jesus again announces his impending violent death (this time at the hands of Gentiles, 18:31–34), then he heals a blind man at the approach to Jericho (18:35–43), and finally Jesus seeks out and saves the tax collector Zacchaeus (19:1–10). All three episodes have to do with the theme of seeing, either in the sense of seeing as understanding (the disciples do not understand about Jesus' violent death and the resurrection to follow, 18:34), in the sense of the physical ability to see (the blind man healed, 18:41–43), or in the sense of having a clear field of vision (short Zacchaeus up a tree, 19:3–4).

Luke places all of 10:1–24 in thematic parallel with the three episodes of 18:31–19:10, *but only in their reverse order of the latter*. In other words,

---

4. For the textual unity of Luke 10:1–24, see Green, *Luke*, 420, or Talbert, *Reading Luke*, 114.

10:1–7 locates its thematic parallel in 19:1–10 (the third episode of Section C′), 10:8–16 echoes themes in 18:35–43, and 10:17–24 thematically coordinates with 18:31–34 (the first episode of Section C′). For the three tables below, the left-hand column follows the narrative order of Luke 10, and the right-hand column reverses the order of episodes from 18:31–19:10.[5]

Hospitality (Luke 10:1–7 and 19:1–10)

Jesus and his disciples receive hospitality in homes, bringing release and salvation to their hosts. We identify correspondence between Luke 10:1–7 and 19:1–10 through shared vocabulary and two shared themes. *Ēmellen erchesthai* ("about to go") occurs only at 10:1 and 19:4 in Luke, and one finds *ēmellen* used with other verbs only two additional times in the Third Gospel (7:2, 9:31). *Ēmellen erchesthai* as a phrase, then, has a distribution restricted to Sections C and C′ in Luke's Gospel. Turning to themes in common, first, Jesus' instructions to the seventy-two about honoring Israelite conventions of hospitality in Section C (10:7) are fulfilled and nuanced as Jesus enjoys hospitality in the home of Zachaeus (19:5d–9).[6] Second, the "peace" that disciples pronounce upon "a son of peace" and his house in 10:5 parallels the "salvation" that Jesus pronounces regarding "this house" and its "son of Abraham" in 19:9.[7] These themes in common and the unique phrase in common indicate that 10:1–7 and 19:1–10 indeed correspond.

---

5. This is an interpretive strategy that does not involve dislocating Lukan text from from its given location in the ancient manuscripts.

6. On conventions of hospitality, see Green, *Luke*, 359–60.

7. Green notes that in Luke 10:5 "peace" is a metonym for "salvation." Ibid., 413–14.

Luke 10:1 After this the Lord appointed seventy-two others and *sent them on ahead of him,* two by two, *into every town and place where he himself was about to go* (*ēmellen autos erchesthai*). ² And he said to them, "The harvest is plentiful, but the laborers are few. Therefore pray earnestly to the Lord of the harvest to send out laborers into his harvest. ³ Go your way; behold, I am sending you out as lambs in the midst of wolves. ⁴ Carry no moneybag, no knapsack, no sandals, and greet no one on the road. ⁵ Whatever house you enter, first *say, 'Peace be to this house!'* ⁶ *And if a son of peace is there, your peace will rest upon him.* But if not, it will return to you. ⁷ *And remain in the same house, eating and drinking what they provide*, for the laborer deserves his wages. Do not go from house to house.

Luke 19:1 *He entered Jericho and was passing through.* ² And there was a man named Zacchaeus. He was a chief tax collector and was rich. ³ And he was seeking to see who Jesus was, but on account of the crowd he could not, because he was small in stature. ⁴ *So he ran on ahead* and climbed up into a sycamore tree to see him, for he was about to pass that way (*ekeinēs ēmellen dierchesthai*). ⁵ And when Jesus came to the place, he looked up and said to him, "Zacchaeus, hurry and come down, for *I must stay at your house* today." ⁶ So he hurried and came down and *received him joyfully.* ⁷ And when they saw it, they all grumbled, "*He has gone in to be the guest of a man who is a sinner.*" ⁸ And Zacchaeus stood and said to the Lord, "Behold, Lord, the half of my goods I give to the poor. And if I have defrauded anyone of anything, I restore it fourfold." ⁹ And Jesus said to him, "Today *salvation has come to this house*, since *he also is a son of Abraham.* ¹⁰ For the Son of Man came to seek and to save the lost."

Blockade (Luke 10:8–16 and 18:35–43)

Some towns and crowds resent and resist the kingdom of God. For the middle unit of Section C (10:8–16), Luke heavily edits his source material (Matthew or "Q") to select teaching of Jesus about the rule of the kingdom of God over towns. The Evangelist selects and deselects portions from Matt 10 and interjects a portion of Matt 11 to do this. In Section C′, Luke keeps the integrity of his source (Mark 10:46–52), adding only a few words of narration (Luke 18:36).

So doing, in 10:8–16 Luke assembles words of Jesus primarily about unresponsive towns. Jesus both teaches a public rejoinder for such a town and he rebukes certain towns (in a cosmic rejoinder to unresponsive towns) with words of judgment. Thus, 10:10–15 thematically parallels a scenario in Jericho, but with contrasting details: along the roadway, Jericho townsfolk rebuke a blind man for wanting Jesus to act in mercy (18:36–39). The sections have in common town populations that do not want Jesus to do a mighty work. Then words of rebuke follow.

Luke 10:8 *Whenever you enter a town* and they receive you, eat what is set before you. ⁹ *Heal the sick in it* and say to them, '*The kingdom of God has come near to you.*' ¹⁰ But *whenever you enter a town* and they do not receive you, go into its streets and say, ¹¹'Even the dust of your town that clings to our feet we wipe off against you. Nevertheless know this, that *the kingdom of God has come near.*' ¹² I tell you, it will be more bearable on that day for Sodom than for that town. ¹³ "Woe to you, Chorazin! Woe to you, Bethsaida! *For if the mighty works done in you had been done in Tyre and Sidon, they would have repented* long ago, *sitting in sackcloth and ashes.* ¹⁴ But it will be more bearable in the judgment for Tyre and Sidon than for you. ¹⁵ And you, Capernaum, will you be exalted to heaven? You shall be brought down to Hades. ¹⁶ "The *one who hears you hears me,* and the one who rejects you rejects me, and the one who rejects me rejects *him who sent me.*"

Luke 18:35 As *he drew near to Jericho,* a blind man was sitting *by the roadside* begging. ³⁶ And hearing a crowd going by, he inquired what this meant. ³⁷ They told him, "*Jesus of Nazareth is passing by.*" ³⁸ And *he cried out, "Jesus, Son of David,* have mercy on me!" ³⁹ And those who were in front rebuked him, telling him to be silent. But he cried out all the more, "*Son of David,* have mercy on me!" ⁴⁰ And Jesus stopped and *commanded* him to be brought to him. And *when he came near,* he asked him, ⁴¹ "What do you want me to *do* for you?" He said, "*Lord, let me recover my sight.*" ⁴² And Jesus said to him, "*Recover your sight*; your faith has made you well." ⁴³ And immediately *he recovered his sight and followed him, glorifying God. And all the people, when they saw it, gave praise to God.*

The units also correspond in another shared theme. "The kingdom of God has come near" (10:9, 11) takes personal form in 18:37, "Jesus of Nazareth is passing by," and in v 40, "when he came near." Bearing in mind the approach of the kingdom of God in the arrival of Jesus, certain words in 18:35–43 indicate that Jesus is indeed a royal personage: "Son of David" (twice in 38–39); "commanded him" (40); and "Lord" (41). Thus, by thematic parallels and by evidence of Luke's purposeful editing we find the middle units of Section C and C′ corresponding to one another.

Grasp (Luke 10:17–24 and 18:31–34)

Some towns and crowds remain in the dark about Jesus and the kingdom of God. In some ways the disciples do as well. When they do come to grasp kingdom truths, their discoveries come by revelation from God. The remaining episodes of Sections C and C′ (10:17–24 and 18:31–34) correspond by shared limited vocabulary and by multiple parallel themes appearing in the same order. First, the verb root in both *apekrypsas* (10:21) and *kekrymmenon* (18:34) occurs only one other time in the Gospel.[8] In 10:21, God the Father hides (*apekrypsas*) certain truths from those who claim to be in the know, while in 18:34, those in the best position to understand about the

---

8. Luke 19:42.

coming suffering, death, and resurrection of Jesus, that is, the twelve, do not grasp it because it was "hidden" (*kekrymmenon*) from them. This highly limited distribution of the verb *krypt*— helps confirm a correspondence of Sections C and C'.

Luke 10:17 The *seventy-two* returned with joy, saying, "Lord, even the demons are subject to us in your name!" ²⁸ And he said to them, "I saw Satan fall like lightning from heaven. ¹⁹ *Behold, I have given you authority* to tread on serpents and scorpions, and over all the power of the enemy, and nothing shall hurt you. ²⁰ Nevertheless, do not rejoice in this, that the spirits are subject to you, but rejoice that your names are written in heaven." ²¹ In that same hour he rejoiced in the Holy Spirit and said, "I thank you, Father, Lord of heaven and earth, that you have *hidden (apekrypsas) these things* from the *wise (sophōn)* and *understanding (synetōn)* and revealed (*apekalypsas*) them to little children; yes, Father, for such was your gracious will. ²² All things have been handed over to me by my Father, and *no one knows (ginōskei)* who the Son is except the Father, or who the Father is except the Son and anyone to whom the Son chooses *to reveal (apokalypsai) him*." ²³ Then turning to the disciples he said privately, "*Blessed are the eyes that see what you see!* ²⁴ For I tell you that *many prophets and kings desired to see what you see, and did not see it, and to hear what you hear, and did not hear it.*"

Luke 18:31 And taking the *twelve*, he said to them, "See, we are going up to Jerusalem, and *everything that is written about the Son of Man by the prophets will be accomplished.* ³² For he will be delivered over to the Gentiles and will be mocked and shamefully treated and spit upon. ³³ And after flogging him, they will kill him, and on the third day he will rise." ³⁴ But they *understood (synēkan)* none of these things. *This saying was hidden (kekrymmenon)* from them, and *they did not grasp (eginōskon) what was said.*

Second, the units have at least three themes in common. "Authority . . . over all the power of the enemy" that Jesus invested in the seventy-two missionaries (10:17b–19b) finds a parallel in the authority of God (18:31), whose prophetic word about the Son of Man "will be accomplished." Next in order in both units comes the theme of injury, as a contrast. "Nothing shall hurt you" (10:19c), Jesus promised the seventy-two regarding their mission, but the opposite would be true of Jesus' own mission. In five dramatic verbs (18:32–33), injury after injury will fall upon Jesus, the final deadly one to be reversed by his resurrection on the third day.

And third, Section C and Section C' each have the theme of knowing/not knowing, expressed in multiple terms, so that a cluster of eight words in Section C ("hidden," "wise," "understanding," "revealed," 21; "knows," "reveal," 22; "see," 23–24; "hear," 24) thematically match "understood," "hidden," and "grasp" in 18:34. Three themes above not only mark both units, but the thematic material occurs in the same order, adding to the probability that 10:17–24 and 18:31–34 correspond as the last of three paired units of Sections C and C'.

Overview of Sections A–C and A′–C′

Sections C and C′ complete a narrative *focus* on the journey's progress. In Section A Jesus strikes out with his disciples on their pivotal journey to Jerusalem, while in Section A′ they dramatically arrive in the city, to the very temple of God. Jesus teaches in Section B and B′ that progress toward Jerusalem (and into the rule of God) must take place according to the ways of the kingdom of God, both in its urgency and in its authority.

Jesus comes near in Section C′; the kingdom comes near in Section C. Its coming and his coming bring both triumph and loss. In the episodes of Sections C and C′, Jesus' closest followers experience intimate, emotionally charged moments with their Lord. Jesus in prayer addresses his Father as "Lord." The disciples, the blind man, and Zacchaeus devote the title "Lord" to Jesus. In the same vein, the narrator twice calls Jesus "Lord" (10:1, 19:8). Receptive and unreceptive cities and towns dot the landscapes. Sections C and C′ round off an outer band of three concentric rings that concentrate on the movement of Jesus with his disciples from Galilee to Jerusalem.

5

Simply Saved

PROGRESS AS A JOURNEY now slows and almost disappears from the narrative. Emphasis shifts to Jesus' teaching (10:25, 39; 18:9, 18), especially to his teaching on salvation—how to enter into the life of God's kingdom.

Signs of Life
(Section D, Luke 10:25–37, and D′, 18:18–30)

Luke 10:25–37 and 18:18–30 contain conversations between priveleged leaders and Jesus about gaining eternal life. A lawyer asks his question as a test for Jesus, hoping to discredit him among at least some of those listening (10:25). In the other section a wealthy ruler asks the same question about eternal life (18:18), not combatively but apparently with more than idle curiosity. It remains unclear whether the lawyer or the ruler ultimately takes Jesus' teaching to heart, and thus Luke's narrative emphasis is on the teaching itself, not on the inquirers or on their relationship to Jesus.

Luke 10:25 And behold, a lawyer stood up to put him to the test, saying, *"Teacher, what shall I do to inherit eternal life?"*	Luke 18:18 And a ruler asked him, *"Good Teacher, what must I do to inherit eternal life?"*
[26] He said to him, *"What is written in the Law? How do you read it?"*	[19] And Jesus said to him, *"Why do you call me good? No one is good except God alone.* [20] *You know the commandments: 'Do not commit adultery, Do not murder, Do not steal, Do not bear false witness, Honor your father and mother.'"*

²⁷ And he answered, "You shall love the Lord your God with all your heart and with all your soul and with all your strength and with all your mind, and your neighbor as yourself." ²⁸ And he said to him, "You have answered correctly; *do this, and you will live.*"

²¹ And he said, "All these I have kept from my youth." ²² When Jesus heard this, he said to him, "One thing you still lack. *Sell all that you have and distribute to the poor, and you will have treasure in heaven; and come, follow me.*"

A question put to Jesus at the beginning of both of these texts is "What shall I do to inherit eternal life?" (10:25; 18:18).[1] In both places Jesus counters with his own question about the law of God, with an implication that a needed basis for eternal life can be found there (10:26; 18:20). The lawyer readily gives an accurate answer from the law; Jesus affirms the man's precision, but prods his integrity: "do this and you will live" (10:27–28). The ruler, on the other hand, avows that he indeed followed the commandments (18:21). Jesus accepts his answer as far as it goes, but presses to the heart of the matter. The ruler must do only "one thing," best summarized as living in the spirit of the *first* tablet of the law, the way of life epitomized by following Jesus (18:22).

---

1. Robert Tannehill, not accrediting such correspondences as possibly pointing to concentrically parallel passages, sees them as indicators of "type-scenes" that have "special interest for the narrator" in that they "help readers to note quickly the connection between scenes so that additional similarities and differences may come to mind as the scenes develop." *Narrative Unity*, 170–71. Another possibility is that such passages might "help readers to note quickly the connection" between concentrically parallel scenes.

Luke 10:29 *But he, desiring to justify himself*, said to Jesus, "And who is my neighbor?" [30] Jesus replied, "*A man was going down from Jerusalem to Jericho, and he fell among robbers, who stripped him and beat him and departed, leaving him half dead.* [31] *Now by chance a priest was going down that road, and when he saw him he passed by on the other side.* [32] *So likewise a Levite, when he came to the place and saw him, passed by on the other side.* [33] *But a Samaritan, as he journeyed, came to where he was, and when he saw him, he had compassion.* [34] *He went to him and bound up his wounds, pouring on oil and wine. Then he set him on his own animal and brought him to an inn and took care of him.* [35] *And the next day he took out two denarii and gave them to the innkeeper, saying, 'Take care of him, and whatever more you spend, I will repay you when I come back.'* [36] *Which of these three, do you think, proved to be a neighbor to the man who fell among the robbers?"* [37] He said, "The one who showed him mercy." And Jesus said to him, "*You go, and do likewise.*"

Luke 18:23 But when he heard these things, he became very sad, *for he was extremely rich.*[24] Jesus, seeing that he had become sad, said, "*How difficult it is for those who have wealth to enter the kingdom of God!* [25] For it is easier for a camel to go through the eye of a needle than for *a rich person* to enter the kingdom of God." [26] Those who heard it said, *"Then who can be saved?"* [27] But he said, "What is impossible with man is possible with God." [28] And Peter said, "See, *we have left our homes and followed you.*" [29] And he said to them, "Truly, I say to you, there is no one who has left house or wife or brothers or parents or children, for the sake of the kingdom of God, [30] who will not receive many times more in this time, and in the age to come eternal life."

Both men, recognizing the personal implication of Jesus' teaching about the basis of eternal life, become guarded in their response (10:29; 18:23). From here on, the two sections cease to correspond *in plot development* but continue to correspond *thematically*: losing and using wealth (10:30, 34-35) corresponds to having wealth and disposing of it (18:22–25). Compassion moves both the Samaritan (10:33–35) and Jesus (18:24–25), and in both sections Jesus teaches about actions that conform to eternal life (10:37b; 18:29–30).

We confirm correspondence between Sections D and D′ on three bases. First, they correspond by a conspicuous parallel question to Jesus in each text. Second, the sections have multiple thematic parallels throughout. Finally, some of them occur in the same sequence. Luke arranged parallel texts to provide Jesus' answers to identical inquiries. As Green summarizes about 18:18-30 (but equally appropriate to 10:25–37), "Those who would inherit life in the future must enter the kingdom of God in the present—following Jesus . . . ."[2]

---

2. Green, *Luke*, 659.

Nearing the Life-giver (Sections E and E′)

Compared to the obvious correspondence in the beginnings of Sections D and D′, these episodes begin with somewhat less striking similarity, but nonetheless they have clear thematic resemblance and shared movements of plot. Both sections proclaim the need for expectant receptiveness to God's mercies. A single episode in Section E (Luke 10:38–42) looks across at its counterpart in two episodes of Section E' (18: 9–17).

The Women and the Men (Luke 10:38–42 and 18:9–14)

First, comparing 10:38-42 to 18:9-14, two women respond to Jesus in their home and two men approach God in prayer in the house of God.[3] The women differ significantly in their response to Jesus' visit in their home. Apparently Martha heads the home, with wealth enough to offer hospitality to Jesus and his disciples (38). Mary may be a dependent and possibly younger sister. While hosting "the Lord," Martha pursues frenetic hospitality arrangements ("you are anxious and troubled about many things," 41), but Mary receptively sits at his feet listening to his teaching (39).[4] Jesus gently admonishes Martha's overly tight grip on conventions of hospitality, and he approves Mary's posture of discipleship (41–42), calling Mary's response simply "the good portion, which will not be taken away from her" (42).[5]

---

3. Luke tends to balance the genders of participants, either within an episode or between corresponding episodes.

4. Esteem toward Jesus communicated in posture is significant here: Martha "went up to him" to complain (40) while Mary "sat at the Lord's feet and listened to his teaching" (39).

5. Jesus becomes master of every feast he attends, lord of every house he enters. This is a truth that Martha needs to comprehend and embrace. Three repetitions of "Lord" in five verses (10:38–42) draw this to the attention of the reader. I rely heavily on Green's analysis of three episodes making up Sections E and E' (*Luke*, 433–37, 643–52).

Luke 10:38 Now as they went on their way, Jesus entered a village. And *a woman* named Martha welcomed him into her house. ³⁹ And she had *a sister* called Mary, who *sat at the Lord's feet and listened to his teaching.* ⁴⁰ But Martha was distracted with much serving. And she went up to him and said, "Lord, do you not care that my sister has left me to serve alone? Tell her then to help me." ⁴¹ But the Lord answered her, "Martha, Martha, you are *anxious and troubled about many things,* ⁴² but one thing is necessary. Mary has chosen the good portion, which will not be taken away from her."

Luke 18:9 He also told this parable to some who trusted in themselves that they were righteous, and treated others with contempt: ¹⁰ "*Two men* went up into the temple to pray, one a Pharisee and the other a tax collector. ¹¹ The Pharisee, standing by himself, prayed thus: 'God, I thank you that I am not like *other men, extortioners, unjust, adulterers, or even like this tax collector.* ¹² I fast twice a week; I give tithes of all that I get.' ¹³ But the tax collector, *standing far off, would not even lift up his eyes to heaven, but beat his breast, saying, 'God, be merciful to me, a sinner!'* ¹⁴ I tell you, this man went down to his house justified, rather than the other. For everyone who exalts himself will be humbled, but the one who humbles himself will be exalted."

¹⁵ Now they were *bringing even infants to him* that he might *touch them. And when the disciples saw it, they rebuked them.* ¹⁶ But Jesus called them to him, saying, "*Let the children come to me,* and do not hinder them, for to such belongs the kingdom of God. ¹⁷ Truly, I say to you, whoever does not receive the kingdom of God like a child shall not enter it."

Jesus' parable in Section E' (18:9–14) describes two significantly different men from the family of Israel who pray in the Lord's house (temple). A Pharisee claims to live on moral high ground as practiced by his community (11–12) and apparently as honored in the prayer culture of the temple. He claims God's attention to his many upstanding qualities and pious behaviors, in comparison to those of this tax collector and of "other men." He, however, asks nothing of God. In that position vis à vis God, he parallels Martha's relationship to Jesus.

The other man, a tax collector, bows his head and humbly pleads for mercy. The tax collector's deliberate marginal location in the temple, his lowered eyes, and breast-beating indicate an attitude of unworthiness and an ache for God's mercy (13). Both the tax collector's body language and prayer for mercy match Mary's receptive attentiveness.

The Sisters and the Censure (Luke 10:38–42 and 18:15–17)

As in the first episode of Section E', so also in the second episode the section (18:15–17), Luke presents two contrasting characters: "infants" and "little children" for one, and disciples for the other.[6] Infants and little

---

6. At 18:15 Luke resumes using Markan material. The transition is unceremonious in terms of compiling and editing, leaving a reader no textual sign that such a shift

children in this section parallel "a sister called Mary" in Section E. Mary sits at the Lord's feet and listens (10:39), and the infants or children are carried or escorted to Jesus for his touch (18:15). Likewise, cranky disciples (16) who do not want their master to be bothered by mere nursery coddling connects to Martha who wants Mary to stop lounging next to Jesus and start helping. Section E and the second episode of Section E' have parallel sets of characters.

The episodes also progress in parallel steps: (1) some draw near to Jesus (10:39; 18:15a); (2) privileged persons, convinced that there are more important things to be done right now, complain of such behavior (10:40; 18:15b); and (3) Jesus commends seekers and admonishes the officious by affirming the importance of access to himself, his word, and his touch (10:41–42; 18:16–17). The commended attitude in each case may be seen as a form of humble receptivity that puts the person(s) in touch with Jesus the Lord or under the blessing of God's kingdom.

Overview of Sections D–E and D'–E'

We have been documenting the correspondences between Luke 10:38-42 and 18:9–17. Based on our tests, the documentation above boasts moderate strength. Parallel characters, parallel plots, and parallel meekness connect Section E with Section E'. An uncomplicated and relational salvation featured Sections E and E' could well include prayer as one of its dynamics. Prayer, however, analytically merits a separate pairing of sections, as follows.

---

occurred. Neither is there any temporal clause or other sign of an intended break in the topic of the narrative.

6

Petition the Giver

IN SECTIONS F (11:1–13) and F' (18:1–8) we encounter another instance of transparently parallel texts, this time ones that teach about petitionary prayer. The sections have less thematic continuity with the preceeding and the following text in both halves of the concentric form, so we do not group them in a band with nearby sections of Luke's Gospel.

Restricted vocabulary indicates literary correspondence between Section F and Section F'. The expression "bother me" in both sections (11:7, 18:5) is a three-word Greek phrase made up of the verb *parechein*, the noun *kopos*, and the pronoun *moi*. The noun *kopos* occurs in Luke's Gospel only in these two places. This observation, along with the parallel themes described below, confirms that Sections F and F' correspond.[1]

Luke 11:1 Now Jesus was praying in a certain place, and when he finished, one of his disciples said to him, "Lord, teach us *to pray*, as John taught his disciples."	Luke 18:1 And he told them a parable to the effect that they ought always *to pray* and not lose heart.

Quite prominently, "teach us to pray" (11:1) parallels "told them a parable that they ought always to pray" (18:1).[2] Further, both texts include a

---

1. Fitzmyer allows that "To [a certain] extent the parable [18:1–8] carries the same message as that of the parable of the persistent friend (11:5–8)." *Luke X–XXIV*, 1177. See also Tannehill, *Luke*, 263.

2. The material in Luke immediately following 18:8 seems at first glance to continue prayer as the focus: "Two men went up into the temple to pray . . ." (10). But the narrator informs us, to the contrary, that the subject has now changed to surprises in store for self-righteous persons: "He also told this parable to some who trusted in themselves that they were righteous" (9). Further, the Pharisee asks for nothing at all even though he speaks aloud in the temple.

parable of Jesus about a persistent petitioner whose legitimate request is at first denied (11:5–7, 18:2–4a), and then the seeker's tenacity prevails (explained by Jesus in 11:8; explained by the judge's thoughts in 18:4b-5).

Luke 11:2 And he said to them, "When you pray, say: "Father, hallowed be your name. Your kingdom come. ³ Give us each day our daily bread, ⁴ and forgive us our sins, for we ourselves forgive everyone who is indebted to us. And lead us not into temptation." ⁵ And he said to them, "Which of you who has a friend will go to him at midnight and say to him, 'Friend, lend me three loaves, ⁶ for a friend of mine has arrived on a journey, and I have nothing to set before him'; ⁷ and he will answer from within, *'Do not bother me;* the door is now shut, and my children are with me in bed. I cannot get up and give you anything'? ⁸ I tell you, though he will not get up and give him anything because he is his friend, yet because of his *impudence* he *will rise and give him* whatever he needs.

Luke 18:2 He said, "In a certain city there was a judge who neither feared God nor respected man. ³ And there was a widow in that city who kept coming to him and saying, 'Give me justice against my adversary.' ⁴ For a while he refused, but afterward he said to himself, 'Though I neither fear God nor respect man, ⁵ yet because this widow *keeps bothering me*, I *will give her* justice, so that she will not beat me down by her continual coming.'"

Jesus concludes each section with further teaching on prayer to the Father. In Luke 11 he applies the parable, urging the disciples to persist in asking of the Father (9–10). Jesus clarifies that God the Father's answers are always good, even to the ultimate good (11–13). In Luke 18 Jesus also applies the parable to his disciples. If an unrighteous judge will cave in and give justice to one persistent widow, will not the holy God readily give justice in response to the cries of his people (7–8)?

Luke 11:9 *And I tell you, ask, and it will be given to you; seek, and you will find; knock, and it will be opened to you.* ¹⁰ For everyone who asks receives, and the one who seeks finds, and to the one who knocks it will be opened. ¹¹ What father among you, if his son asks for a fish, will instead of a fish give him a serpent; ¹² or if he asks for an egg, will give him a scorpion? ¹³ If you then, who are evil, know how to give good gifts to your children, how much more will the heavenly Father give the Holy Spirit to those who ask him!"

Luke 18:6 And the Lord said, "Hear what the unrighteous judge says. ⁷ And will not God give justice to *his elect, who cry to him day and night?* Will he delay long over them? ⁸ *I tell you*, he will give justice to them speedily. Nevertheless, when the Son of Man comes, will he find faith on earth?"

We show that Sections F and F′ stand in parallel, then, by shared restricted vocabulary, by their attention-getting beginnings, and by parallel themes given in the same order. Two episodes of teaching on petitioning God, episodes separated widely in Luke, manifestly parallel one another. And they parallel one another adjacent to additional bands of parallel text that emphasize the coming of God's kingdom.

7

Kingdom Come

SECTIONS G–H AND G′–H′ especially proclaim the coming of the kingdom: what to expect and how to prepare. Other Lukan themes pepper these sections as well, familiar themes such as healing, gratitude, opposition, and judgment.

Signs of the Kingdom (Sections G and G′)

Can Sections G and G′ seriously be considered as parallel? Indeed, they should! Section G contains five short episodes and Section G′ two longer ones, amounting to twenty three and twenty four verses respectively, that deal primarily with signs of the kingdom. Multiple themes arrayed through six tandem subsections confirm that the sections correspond.[1]

Gifted Voices (Luke 11:14 and 17:11–19)

Sections G and G′ begin with healings, with more detail in G′. Ironically, after "the mute man spoke" (11:14) he offers nothing more, or nothing notable, to say; in particular, he apparently does not offer gratitude to Jesus for the healing. One of the ten healed lepers, however, "turned back, praising

---

1. Section G′ begins with a travel notice that prohibits finding geographically sequential signposts for Jesus' journey to Jerusalem. "On the way to Jerusalem he was passing along between Samaria and Galilee" (17:11). In a linear journey beginning at 9:51 and ending at 19:46, by chapter 17 Jesus should be in territory relatively close to Jerusalem, rather than less than half-way to the capitol. In a literarily concentric journey, however, having 17:11–37 paired with 11:14–36, passing now "between Samaria and Galilee" is less problematic at this point in the literary structure. Further, such an unusual travel notice may be a Lukan prompt for readers to pay special attention to the ordering of the whole travel narrative.

God with a loud voice" (17:15). Themes of healing and having/not having a thankful voice appear in parallel.

Luke 11:14 Now he was casting out a demon that was mute. *When the demon had gone out*, the *mute man spoke*, and the people marveled.	Luke 17:11 On the way to Jerusalem he was passing along between Samaria and Galilee. [12] And as he entered a village, he was met by ten lepers, who stood at a distance [13] and lifted up their voices, saying, "Jesus, Master, have mercy on us." [14] When he saw them he said to them, "Go and show yourselves to the priests." And as they went they were cleansed. [15] Then one of them, *when he saw that he was healed*, turned back, *praising God with a loud voice*; [16] and he fell on his face at Jesus' feet, giving him thanks. Now he was a Samaritan. [17] Then Jesus answered, "Were not ten cleansed? Where are the nine? [18] Was no one found to return and give praise to God except this foreigner?" [19] And he said to him, "Rise and go your way; your faith has made you well."

Reign (Luke 11:15–23 and 17:20–21)

In Luke 11:15–23 observers of the exorcism fill the formerly demonized man's ungrateful silence with their own critical clamor toward Jesus. Some of them insist that Jesus cast out the demon by demonic power (15).[2] Thus they style Jesus as evil for doing a good deed. Jesus counters his critics' illogic by reminding them that a divided demonic kingdom would be a failed demonic kingdom. Satan doesn't oppose himself (17–18). And on a pragmatic level, Jesus counters that their criticism claims too much, for their charge against Jesus would apply to other popular Israelite exorcists as well (19).

Luke 11:15 But some of them said, "He casts out demons by Beelzebul, the prince of demons," [16] while others, to test him, kept seeking from him a *sign* from heaven. [17] But he, knowing their thoughts, said to them, "Every *kingdom* divided against itself is laid waste, and a divided household falls. [18] And if Satan also is divided against himself, how will his *kingdom* stand? For you say that I cast out demons by Beelzebul. [19] And if I cast out demons by Beelzebul, by whom do your sons cast them out? Therefore they will be your judges. [20] But if it is by the finger of God that I cast out demons, then the *kingdom of God has come upon you* (*ephthasen eph hymas*). [21] When a strong man, fully armed, guards his own palace, his goods are safe; [22] but when one stronger than he attacks him and overcomes him, he takes away his armor in which he trusted and divides his spoil. [23] Whoever is not with me is against me, and whoever does not gather with me scatters.	Luke 17:20 Being asked by the Pharisees when the *kingdom of God* would come, he answered them, "The *kingdom of God* is not coming in *ways* that can be observed, [21] nor will they say, 'Look, here it is!' or 'There!' for behold, *the kingdom of God is in the midst of you* (*entos hymōn estin*)".

---

2. See traditional commentaries or a Bible dictionary for information on "Beelzebul."

Other observers of the event, apparently insisting on clearer credentials for Jesus' authority, want heaven to show some other irrefutable sign (16). You already have what you ask for, Jesus counters: Satan was not able to defend his own "goods" against the transcendant power that Jesus wields among spirits (21–22). And further, he implies, the real issue is not more evidence of authority over Satan, but one's readiness to be personally "overcome" by Jesus' authority. He calls listeners who oppose and hinder him to instead join with him (23).

In Luke 11:15–23 and 17:20–21 Jesus teaches the kingdom of God intensively. To his critics Jesus clarifies that two cosmic kingdoms wage war. God's kingdom overcomes and "has come upon" them in the person of Jesus (11:20). To inquirers the Master explains that the kingdom comes sooner than they imagine, in fact, "the kingdom of God is in the midst of you" (17:21). When Jesus arrives in power and wisdom, God's kingdom comes visibly and asserts its claims over all who see and hear.

Return (Luke 11:24–26 and 17:22–24)

In both texts Jesus describes a climactic return. An unclean spirit checks its former host looking for a place of rest. The "house" appears ready for guests, so the spirit gathers a gang of associates and moves back in, causing more havoc than before (11:24–26). Jesus also speaks of his own return to earth as the victorious Son of Man. His coming will not be one of a physical person to a locality, but a spiritual body coming through the skies to rule over the entire terrain (17:22–26). In both texts Jesus teaches his listeners to envision a rampant spirit-being returning to rule. The evil spirit of 11:26 enjoys his last state (*ta eschata*), while the Son of Man of Luke 17 arrives in his eschaton.

Luke 11:24 "When the unclean spirit has gone out of a person, it passes through waterless places *seeking* rest, and *finding none* it says, 'I will return to my house from which I came.' 25 And when it comes, it finds the house swept and put in order. 26 Then it goes and brings seven other spirits more evil than itself, and they enter and dwell there. And *the last state* (*eschata*) of that person is worse than the first."

Luke 17:22 And he said to the disciples, "The days are coming when you will *desire* to see one of the days of the Son of Man, and you will *not see it*. 23 And they will say to you, 'Look, there!' or 'Look, here!' Do not go out or follow them. 24 For as the lightning flashes and lights up the sky from one side to the other, *so will the Son of Man be in his day.*

Life and Passion (Luke 11:27–28 and 17:25)

Luke 11:27–28 parallels 17:25 by thematic contrasts: birth vs death, joy vs suffering. A woman from the crowd, thrilled by what Jesus says, bursts out a blessing—not on Jesus, for that would assume too much intimacy and social position—but a blessing on his mother. In the woman's enthusiasm this is an expression of hope and joy; in the Lukan narrative, her words allude to 1:39–49, where Elizabeth exudes blessing on Mary. Elizabeth exalts in Mary's unique role, exalts in the unique child Mary will bear, and (with particular relevance to 11:28 in Section G) exalts in Mary's trust of the word that God spoke to her (1:38, 45). Section G highlights a welcomed and celebrated birth in a nurturing family (epitomized by his mother's role).

Luke 11:27 As he said these things, a woman in the crowd raised her voice and said to him, "Blessed is the womb that bore you, and the breasts at which you nursed!" 28 But he said, "Blessed rather are those who hear the word of God and keep it!"

Luke 17:25 But first he must suffer many things and be rejected by this generation.

In Section G' (17:25), on the other hand, Jesus once again explains his future shameful suffering perpetrated by a spurning society. His choice of words to say this particularly echoes the words Jesus used after Peter's confession that Jesus is "the Christ of God" (9:20), namely, "The Son of Man will suffer many things and be rejected by the elders and chief priests and scribes, and be killed, and on the third day be raised" (9:22).[3] Jesus' partial quotation alludes to the whole earlier text, thus implying in 17:25 that death and resurrection follow the Son of Man's suffering and rejection. Crowds and officials will demand his death as a criminal (22:47—23:43).

Our current subsections of Sections G and G' differ dramatically. But the themes line up on opposite ends of the same continuum: birth-life-death, joy-passion-suffering.

Judgment, Luke 11:29–32 and 17:26–33

Luke 11:29–32 shows striking and numerous parallels to 17:26–33 by the theme of judgement.

---

3. Luke 9:44 and 18:32–33 have the verb "be delivered." The particular wording "suffer many things and be rejected by" appears only at 9:22 and 17:25.

Luke 11:29 When the crowds were increasing, he began to say, "This generation is *an evil generation*. It seeks for a sign, but no sign will be given to it except the sign of Jonah. ³⁰ For as (*kathōs gar egeneto*) Jonah became a sign to the people of *Nineveh*, so will (*houtōs estai kai*) the *Son of Man* be to *this generation*. ³¹ The queen of the South will rise up at the judgment with the men of *this generation* and *condemn them*, for she came from the ends of the earth to hear the wisdom of Solomon, and behold, something greater than Solomon *is here*. ³² The men of Nineveh will rise up at the judgment with *this generation* and *condemn it*, for they repented at the preaching of Jonah, and behold, something greater than Jonah *is here*.

Luke 17:26 Just as (*kai kathōs egeneto*) it was in the days of Noah, so will it be (*houtōs estai kai*) in *the days of the Son of Man*. ²⁷ *They were eating and drinking* and marrying and being given in marriage, until the *day when* Noah entered the ark, and the flood came and *destroyed* them all. ²⁸ Likewise, just as it was (*homoiōs kathōs egeneto*) in the days of Lot—they were eating and drinking, buying and selling, planting and building, ²⁹ but on the day when Lot went out from *Sodom*, fire and sulfur rained from heaven and *destroyed* them all— ³⁰ so will it be (*kata ta auta estai*) on the day when the *Son of Man is revealed*. ³¹ On that day, let the one who is on *the housetop*, with his goods in the house, not come down to take them away, and likewise let the one who is in the field not turn back. ³² Remember Lot's wife. ³³ Whoever seeks to preserve his life will lose it, but whoever loses his life will keep it.

For the sake of brevity in a long chapter, I summarize by columns of comparisons:

evil generation	(11:29–32)	*generation; days of the Son of Man*	(17:25, 26)
the judgment	(31, 32)	*the day of the Son of Man*	(30)
just as . . . so will	(30)	*just as . . . so will*	(26, 28–30)
Son of Man	(30)	*Son of Man*	(26)
condemn	(31, 32)	*destroyed*	(27, 29)
(first OT figure)	(30, 32)	(first OT figure)	(26–27)
(second OT figure)	(31)	(second OT figure)	(28–29)
Nineveh	(32)	*Sodom*	(29)
is here	(31, 32)	*is revealed*	(30)

The texts differ with regard to *when* the judicial encounter with the Son of Man takes place. In Luke 11, response to the *current presence* of the Son of Man forms the basis for judgment. He "is here" (31, 32), therefore judgment comes. The queen of the south and the men of Nineveh stand ready to condemn those who fail to respond *now* to a greater sign from God: Jesus, the Son of Man. In Luke 17, the *future* coming of the Son of Man leads to destruction (27, 29) of those who ignore all warnings of imminent judgment. Timing of judgment differs between the texts, but the fact of judgment remains a constant. Similarities of vocabulary, theme, syntax, and structure in these texts regarding judgment confirm that they are parallel subunits within the larger parallel of Sections G and G'.

Readiness (Luke 11:33–36 and 17:34–37)

Finally, in the remaining verses of both sections, Jesus again warns his hearers to maintain diligent readiness for God's kingdom, whether by truly "seeing" Jesus as he heals and teaches or when he comes in the day of the Son of Man.[4] These subunits have in common the theme of readiness for the kingdom.

Luke 11:33 "No one after lighting a lamp puts it in a cellar or under a basket, but on a stand, so that those who enter may see the light. [34] Your eye is the lamp of your body. When your eye is healthy, your whole body is full of light, but when it is bad, your body is full of darkness. [35] *Therefore be careful lest* the light in you be darkness. [36] If then your whole body is full of light, having no part dark, it will be wholly bright, as when a lamp with its rays gives you light."	Luke 17:34 I tell you, in that night there will be two in one bed. *One will be taken and the other left.* [35] There will be two women grinding together. *One will be taken and the other left.*" [37] And they said to him, "Where, Lord?" He said to them, "Where the corpse is, there the vultures will gather."

Review of Parallels between Sections G and G′

Returning now to the entire structure of Sections G and G′, in what appears as an unlikely parallel of texts, we have shown that the sections correspond by multiple shared themes. Further, these shared themes appear in the same order in six parallel subunits in both sections. Accumulated tandem themes, especially when they occur in the same order in both sections, meets two of the tests for validating parallelism.

Censure (Sections H and H′)

In Sections H and H′ Jesus castigates Pharisees, lawyers, and leaders who misguide others and misrepresent the ways of the kingdom. Sections H and H′ seem to have little else in common on first inspection. In a single episode making up Luke 11:37–54, or Section H, we encounter an introduction, a highly structured and repetitive body, and a conclusion. Section H′ (16:14–17:10), on the other hand, includes multiple episodes touching on a variety of themes, episodes having little obvious inner cohesion among them, episodes having only one transitional phrase between any of them.[5] Diver-

---

4. Some manuscripts add 17:36 as a third example of a surprising disappearance in the eschaton ("Two men will be in the field; one will be taken and the other left"), building further urgency to this teaching on the need for kingdom preparedness.

5. Of many distinctions in content between the sections, Luke 11:37–54 includes

sity of content seems to disconnect the episodes of Section H', but a general lack of transitions among them seems to call for holding them together.[6] We hold them together, and doing so, we discover multiple parallels between diverse episodes of Section H' and a shorter, cohesive Section H.

Affront and Exposure (Luke 11:37–41 and 16:14–15)

In these subsections Pharisees and scribes feel affronted (insulted) by the Lord or give affront (ridicule) to him. The Lord knows and exposes their true motives. A Pharisee invites Jesus home to dine with the host's friends (11:37–41), both Pharisees and lawyers.[7] The Lukan narrator locates Jesus within the gathered company as "Lord" (11:39) rather than as a recipient of patronage (a friend). The Lord quickly launches into stern criticism of Pharisee attitudes and practices, authoritatively representing the creator God (40), the law-giver (41), the covenanting God (42), the merciful God (46), and the Judge (49–51). Naturally enough, an offended lawyer speaks for the whole company when he objects to being insulted by Jesus (45): this is no way for Jesus to behave as a dinner guest! Jesus, however, is the Lord, speaking his mind.

Luke 11:37 While Jesus was speaking, a Pharisee asked him to dine with him, *so he went in and reclined at table.* [38] The Pharisee was astonished to see that he did not *first* wash before dinner. [39] And the Lord said to him, "Now you Pharisees cleanse the outside of the cup and of the dish, but inside you are full of greed and wickedness. [40] You fools! Did not he who made the outside make the inside also? [41] But give as alms those things that are within, and behold, everything is clean for you.	Luke 16:14 *The Pharisees, who were lovers of money, heard all these things, and they ridiculed him.* [15] And he said to them, "You are those who justify yourselves before men, but God knows your hearts. For what is exalted among men is an abomination in the sight of God.

Section H, then, exposes a combative tone from beginning to end. The opposite section (H') begins with a similar tone: Pharisees "ridicule" Jesus (16:14) because they are offended by what Jesus says about God and wealth (16:10–13). And similar to Section H, Jesus' authority throughout 16:14–17:10 is that of "Lord" (note "Lord" in 17:5–6). As Lord he proclaims what God knows and hates (15), he knows God's purpose (16),

---

six statements of "woe" (42, 43, 44, 46, 47, 52) upon Pharisees and scribes for their typical behaviors, but 16:16–17:10 offers only one "woe" (17:1) cautioning Jesus' disciples about future relationships.

6. Primary manuscript traditions do not reveal any particular instability in Luke 16:16–17:10 or ambiguity regarding keeping the episodes side by side.

7. On conventions of hospitality, see Green, *Luke*, 468–69.

he perceives familial unbelief (31), and as Lord he affirms God's judgment and mercy (17:1–4). But more specifically regarding a parallel of the subsections above, God knows these Pharisee "hearts" (16:15) and Jesus knows these Pharisees on the "inside" (11:39–41). In sum, the subsections correspond thematically by expressions of affront and by transparency of souls to before Jesus and to God.

Authority (Luke 11:42 and 16:16–18)

More short subsections display correspondence by the theme of authority. In Luke 11:42 Jesus criticizes the Pharisees for practicing hyper-purity to honor God's holiness, while they disregard other aspects of God's character: his justice and love. Regarding practices of the Pharisees, Josephus explains in *Antiquities of the Jews* (13.10.6) that they "have delivered to the people a great many observances by succession from their fathers, which are not written in the law of Moses; and for that reason it is that the Sadducees reject them and say that we are to esteem those observances to be obligatory which are in the written word, but are not to observe what are derived from the tradition of our forefathers."[8] Jesus criticizes Pharisees here not so much for embellishing the law in their zeal for purity, as for neglecting the whole revealed character of God.[9]

| Luke 11:42 But *woe to you Pharisees*! For you tithe mint and rue and every (*pan*) herb, and neglect justice and the love of God. These you ought to have done, without neglecting the others. | Luke 16:16 "The Law and the Prophets were until John; since then, the good news of the kingdom of God has been proclaimed, and everyone (*pas*) is strongly urged to enter it (*eis autēn biazetai*). [17] But it is easier for heaven and earth to pass away than for one dot of the Law to become void. 18 "Everyone who divorces his wife and marries another commits adultery, and he who marries a woman divorced from her husband commits adultery. |

Luke lines up "every (*pan*) herb" of 11:42 with "everyone" (*pas*) of 16:16. Pharisees surpass the law's statutes by including a tenth of "every" herb in their tithing. On the other hand, Jesus exceeds current views on

---

8. Tithing produce before meals in this way exceeds even then-current views (Green, *Luke*, 472, n.75). Reliable contemporaneous documentation on the Pharisees continues to be unavailable. Josephus' first-century commentary on them is considered by critics unsubstantiated. Yet, apart from the Gospels, Josephus provides most of the commentary that we have.

9. The English text of Luke 16:16 quoted here is from the *Holman Christian Standard Bible*. The rest comes as usual from the ESV. Translators differ on whether *biazetai* should be understood as a middle form or a passive.

the law and prophets when he proclaims that "everyone," not Israelites only, should enter the kingdom of God.

The theme of authority to interpret the law underlies both subsections as well as both entire sections as Jesus addresses Pharisees and lawyers. Luke presents Jesus as the authorized interpreter of the Law and Prophets. Thus, the Lord declares that they "ought . . . without neglecting" in 11:42. He clarifies that his words, "until John; since then," imply no abrogation of the law, not even of one small detail (16:17). He presses a further example of authority, this one regarding divorce and remarriage (18). Green compares Jesus' words to rabbinic teaching at the time: "Especially in prohibiting remarriage and ruling out serial monogamy, Jesus' statement distinguishes itself from contemporary rabbinic teaching by its severity."[10] Jesus does not engage Pharisees and scribes on level ground, although they may think he does. Jesus the Lord teaches the law, the prophets, and the kingdom of God in the authority of God.

Finger Work (Luke 11:43–48 and 16:19–26)

A significant validation of correspondence between Luke 11:43–48 and 16:19–26 (and between Section H and Section H' in toto) arises in that both texts contain the word "finger," a word having significantly limited distribution in the Third Gospel. *Daktylos* actually occurs three times in Luke's Gospel, first in 11:20 as "the finger of God (*en daktylō theou*)." But as the finger *of human beings*, it occurs only in 11:46 (in Section H), "one of your fingers (*heni tōn daktylōv hymōn*)", and in 16:24 (in Section H'), "to dip the end of his finger in water (*hina bapsē to akron tou daktylou autou hydatos*)." *Daktylos* as a highly limited Lukan lexeme in these sections adds significant weight to this proposal of parallelism. Further, a resulting thematic parallel in those verses also adds clout to my claim: Pharisees *do not* assist in carrying burdens with even a finger (11:46), while Lazarus *may not* lend his finger to assist the tormented rich man (16:24–26).

---

10. Green, *Luke*, 603–604.

Luke 11:43 Woe to you Pharisees! For you love the best seat in the synagogues and greetings in the marketplaces. [44] Woe to you! For you are like unmarked graves, and people walk over them without knowing it." [45] One of the lawyers answered him, "Teacher, in saying these things you insult us also." [46] And he said, "Woe to you lawyers also! For you load people with burdens hard to bear, *and you yourselves do not touch the burdens with one of your fingers.* [47] Woe to you! For you build the tombs of the prophets whom your fathers killed. [48] So you are witnesses and you consent to the deeds of your fathers, for they killed them, and you build their tombs.

Luke 16:19 "There was a rich man who was clothed in purple and fine linen and who feasted sumptuously every day. [20] And at his gate was laid a poor man named Lazarus, covered with sores, [21] who desired to be fed with what fell from the rich man's table. Moreover, even the dogs came and licked his sores. [22] The poor man died and was carried by the angels to Abraham's side. The rich man also died and was buried, [23] and in Hades, being in torment, he lifted up his eyes and saw Abraham far off and Lazarus at his side. [24] And he called out, '*Father* Abraham, have mercy on me, and *send Lazarus to dip the end of his finger in water and cool my tongue*, for I am in anguish in this flame.' [25] But Abraham said, 'Child, remember that you in your lifetime received your good things, and Lazarus in like manner bad things; but now he is comforted here, and you are in anguish. [26] And besides all this, *between* us and you a great chasm has been fixed, in order that those who would pass from here to you may not be able, and none may cross from there to us.'

Warned but Intransigent (Luke 11:49–51 and 16:27–31)

Two following subsections contribute two themes to the sustained parallel between Section H and H'. First, God sends "prophets and apostles" to warn past and present generations of Israel's elites, such as to Pharisees and their lawyers (11:49). Similarly, God gave "Moses and the Prophets" (16:29, 31) to the late rich man's "house" (27). Second, "they" (influential leaders like the Pharisees and lawyers) reject the prophetic message, assassinating the prophets (11:49c–51b). Likewise, in the other subsection, "they" (brothers of the rich man) will neither be convinced by warnings of judgment nor repent (16:30–31). The prophets of Section H indeed have gone to the "fathers" without positive impact, while the messenger of Section H' is not allowed to go to either requested destination (to the rich man or to his father's house) because of meted out judgment and because of unbelief. So we see that themes of rejecting God's messages dominate Luke 11:49–51 and 16:27–31.

Luke 11:49 Therefore also the Wisdom of God said, '*I will send them prophets and apostles*, some of whom they will kill and persecute,' ⁵⁰ so that the blood of all *the prophets*, shed from the foundation of the world, may be charged against *this generation*, ⁵¹ from the blood of Abel to the blood of Zechariah, who perished between the altar and the sanctuary. Yes, I tell you, it will be required of *this generation*.

Luke 16:27 And he said, 'Then I beg you, father, to *send him to my father's house*— ²⁸ for I have five brothers—so that he may warn them, lest they also come into this place of torment.' ²⁹ But Abraham said, 'They have *Moses and the Prophets; let them hear them*.' ³⁰ And he said, 'No, *father* Abraham, but if someone goes to them from the dead, they will repent.' ³¹ He said to him, 'If they do not hear *Moses and the Prophets*, neither will they be convinced if someone should rise from the dead.'"

Obstructors (Luke 11:52 and 17:1–6)

A further theme addressing obstruction of access to blessings in the kingdom of God connects these subsections and continues an overall parallel of Sections H and H′. In 11:52 the blessing in consideration by Jesus is knowledge of God and of his purposes, represented by the figure of a locked room. Jesus indicts lawyers listening to him: they chose to block access for others and for themselves. Therefore, "woe" awaits them.

Luke 11:52 *Woe* to you lawyers! For you have taken away the key of knowledge. *You did not enter yourselves, and you hindered those who were entering.*"

Luke 17:1 And he said to his disciples, "Temptations to sin are sure to come, but *woe to the one* through whom they come! ² It would be better for him if a millstone were hung around his neck and he were cast into the sea than that he should cause one of *these little ones* to sin. ³ Pay attention to yourselves! If *your brother* sins, rebuke him, and if he repents, forgive him, ⁴ and if he sins against you seven times in the day, and turns to you seven times, saying, 'I repent,' you must forgive him." ⁵ The *apostles* said to the Lord, "Increase our faith!" ⁶ And the Lord said, "If you had faith like a grain of mustard seed, you could say to this mulberry tree, 'Be uprooted and planted in the sea,' and it would obey you.

In 17:1–2 the Lord does not specify what blessing of the kingdom that temptation undermines and does not identify the "little ones" who may be scandalized by disciples' behavior. Nevertheless, he urgently warns his disciples against behavior that obstructs the welfare of "these." "Woe" awaits this kind of offender as well. In both subsections Jesus gives dire warning to friend or foe who trammels those who would respond gratefully to the kingdom of God.

Carefully Chosen Words (Luke 11:53–54 and 17:7–10)

The final bits of both sections differ significantly from one another in content and tone. The text in Luke 11 narrates intense efforts by scribes and Pharisees to pressure Jesus into saying something seditious or reprehensible. The scribes and Pharisees, guests with Jesus at dinner, try to strike back after Jesus' lengthy denunciation of them during the meal (11:27–52). Luke 17:7–10, however, turns one more surprising narratival corner in a seemingly random series of episodes making up Section H'. In this saying, Jesus contrasts expressions of gratitude that might be due among equals (giving preference, expressing thanks) with the hard reality of a master-servant relationship on a meagre farm holding.

Luke 11:53 As he went away from there, the scribes and the *Pharisees began to press him hard and to provoke him* to speak about many things, ⁵⁴ lying in wait for him, to catch him in something he might say.	Luke 17:7 "Will any one of you who has a servant plowing or keeping sheep say to him when he has come in from the field, *'Come at once and recline at table'*? ⁸ Will he not rather say to him, 'Prepare supper for me, and dress properly, and serve me while I eat and drink, and *afterward* you will eat and drink'? ⁹ Does he thank the servant because he did what was commanded? ¹⁰ So you also, when you have done all that you were commanded, say, 'We are unworthy servants; we have only done what was our duty.'"

These subsections have two themes in common. One theme is what happens, or what imaginatively could happen, at a meal. Section H in entirety describes what takes place at a meal and (in our current verses, 11:53–54) what takes place in response just afterwards. Luke 17:7–10 imagines a meal setting.

The second theme is that of acceptable and unacceptable speech. Jesus' words at the dinner are apparently on target and unanswerable since in 11:53 dinner guests change the subject to something more advantageous to them. They want to trap Jesus into saying some damning words. Similarly, with regard to unacceptable words, the imaginary farmer in Luke 17:7–9 will not make such a statement to his servant as the one imagined; it is outside of cultural norms. Such a scene is unthinkable, comic. So also, the imaginary servant (10b) will always say what is expected. The themes of acceptable and unacceptable speech along with conversation at a meal in Luke 11:53–54 and 17:7–10 finish out the evidence for parallelism Sections H and H'.

Review of Parallels between Sections H and H′

To review, Sections H and H′ prove parallel in three general ways. First, Luke chooses a word of highly limited distribution his Gospel for each section. The word occurs only once elsewhere in the Third Gospel, and that once in a different sense. Finding highly limited and completely restricted words in two texts suspected of being parallel lends great weight to the claim of parallelism. Second, we have shown that the sections correspond by many shared themes (affront, Lord, authority, warning, woe). And finally, themes in the two sections consistently appear in the same order.

For some the kingdom's coming means confrontation, warning, and judgment. For others who hear and heed Jesus, whether committed disciples or those drawn to him, primary concerns for God's kingdom may center on issues of daily living such as possessions and wealth.

8

Stuff and Money

Many continuing Lukan themes fill Sections J–K and J′–K′, and prominent among them resurface themes of supply and ownership. Jesus directs most of his teaching to the disciples (12:1, 4, 22; 16:1), but he tells familiar parables (lost sheep, lost coin, and prodigal) to grumbling Pharisees (15:2). Yet, because many curious people crowd in to listen to Jesus, even Peter finds it unclear to whom Jesus directs his comments (12:41). Opponents of Jesus may be coming to faith by little steps and disciples may be entertaining doubts about Jesus, so it doesn't finally matter who his immediate audience is. All need to hear and heed him.

Shelter (Sections J and J′)

Disciples of Jesus shelter under the care of God. Jesus moves down the road in Luke 12:1–12 and resumes the direct training of his disciples (with many others listening in). Jesus warns against a behavior of Pharisees (1–3), teaches on the relative importance of fears (4–7), and then prepares those who follow Jesus for possible future testimony in court (8–12). Jesus also reminds his disciples of the resources they have in God to face such difficult days (6–7, 11–12). Section J offers no action other than a circumstantial transition, it contains no conversations, but the section recounts Jesus' sustained teaching of his disciples.

Luke 16:1–13 forms Section J′ in the other half of the journey narrative, where Jesus instructs his disciples. Unlike Section J, however, in the first nine verses of the section Jesus teaches by parable. He tells a story rooted in the culture of patronage to urge his disciples toward submitting this life's resources to God' purpose, a stewardship leading to eternal shelter. Regardless of differing in genre, Sections J and J' have parallel themes in a similar order.

Exposure (Luke 12:1–3 and 16:1–2)

The first verses of each section reveal the theme of exposure of secrets. Word gets around about secrets: God and a rich man discern what is really going on behind facades.

Luke 12:1 In the meantime, when so many thousands of the people had gathered together that they were trampling one another, he *began to say to his disciples first*, "Beware of the leaven of the Pharisees, which is *hypocrisy*. ² Nothing is covered up that will not be revealed, or hidden that will not be known. ³ Therefore *whatever you have said in the dark shall be heard* (*akousthēsetai*) *in the light*, and what you have whispered in private rooms *shall be proclaimed* on the housetops.	Luke 16:1 He also *said to the disciples*, "There was a rich man who had a manager, and *charges were brought to him* that this man was wasting his possessions. ² And he called him and said to him, '*What is this that I hear* (*akouō*) *about you?* Turn in the account of your management, for you can no longer be manager.'

Eternal Welfare (Luke 12:4–7 and 16:3–9)

Next, Jesus teaches in both sections about preparing for life after death. He does so in a particularly urgent manner, calling special attention to his words by the formula "I tell you" (12:4, [5a], 5d; 16:9). How might one be confident of eternal welfare in light of threats on life?

The Master's warning to his disciples in 12:4–7 assumes that the disciples know of an afterlife with God and know of another fearful afterlife. Now that access to life with God is manifest through commitment to Jesus, physical death of his disciples means continuing life with God rather than hell (Gehenna). Jesus warns disciples to fear the wrath of God more than the murderous wrath of people. Those who may have authority to kill have no authority beyond the grave, so disciples who suffer because they commit to Jesus need not fear for their eternal welfare.

Luke 12:4 "*I tell you (legō de hymin), my friends, do not fear* those who kill the body, and after that have *nothing more that they can do (ti poiēsai).* ⁵ But *I will warn you (hypodeiksō de hymin) whom to fear: fear him* who, after he has killed, has authority to *cast into hell.* Yes, I tell you *(nai legō hymin), fear him!* ⁶ Are not five *sparrows* sold for two *pennies*? And not one of them is forgotten before God. ⁷ Why, *even the hairs of your head* are all numbered. Fear not; *you are of more value* than many sparrows.	Luke 16:3 And the manager said to himself, '*What shall I do (ti poiēsō), since my master is taking the management away from me? I am not strong enough to dig, and I am ashamed to beg.* ⁴ I have decided *what to do (ti poiēsō),* so that when I am removed from management, *people may receive me into their houses.*' ⁵ So, summoning his master's debtors one by one, he said to the first, 'How much do you owe my master?' ⁶ He said, 'A hundred measures of oil.' He said to him, 'Take your bill, and sit down quickly and write fifty.' ⁷ Then he said to another, 'And how much do you owe?' He said, 'A hundred measures of wheat.' He said to him, 'Take your bill, and write eighty.' ⁸ The master commended the dishonest manager for his shrewdness. For the sons of this world are more shrewd in dealing with their own generation than the sons of light. ⁹ And I tell you *(egō hymin legō),* make friends for yourselves by means of unrighteous wealth, so that when it fails *they may receive you into the eternal dwellings.*

The other section, 16:3–9, continues Jesus' parable about the corrupt manager. Someone betrays the manager to his master and the manager loses control over the villa. The man can no longer manage his master's wealth, and apparently can no longer live in the primary servants' quarters.[1] This former manager in Jesus' parable worries about how to generate an income for himself ("I am not strong enough to dig, and I am ashamed to beg," 3) or how to live off someone else's wealth through a debt of patronage.[2] In back-room deals, the man lines up two patronage debts (4–7) to provide for himself future shelter and ease. The man fears destitution and shame, but does not fear death at the hands of persecutors, as in Section J. In general, fear of personal catastrophic loss and appropriate safeguards connect Sections J and J' thematically.

Undivided Hearts (Luke 12:8–12 and 16:10–13)

Sections J and J' each end in a series of highly structured contrasts that deal with divided hearts. Green notes regarding both subsections that these aphorisms are not randomly gathered in either place, but follow logically from preceding context.[3] In both texts Jesus proclaims radical choices that his followers must make: to love Jesus more than life (12:8–10) and to love God, not money (or to serve God while using money) (16:10–13).

---

1. A light punishment indeed compared to those doled out in Jesus' other parables. Compare to Luke 12:42–48 and 19:11–27.
2. Green, *Luke*, 593–94.
3. Ibid., 479, 595.

Luke 12:8 "And I tell you, *everyone* who acknowledges me before men, *the Son of Man* also will acknowledge before the angels of *God*, ⁹ but *the one who denies me before men* will be denied before the angels of *God*. ¹⁰ And *everyone who* speaks a word against *the Son of Man* will be forgiven, but the *one who* blasphemes against *the Holy Spirit* will not be forgiven. ¹¹ And when they bring *you* before the synagogues and the rulers and the authorities, do not be anxious about how you should defend yourself or what you should say, ¹² for the *Holy Spirit* will teach *you* in that very hour what you ought to say."

Luke 16:10 "*One who* is faithful in a *very little* is also faithful in much, and *one who* is dishonest in a *very little* is also dishonest in much. ¹¹ If then you have not been faithful in the unrighteous wealth, who will entrust to you the true riches? ¹² And if you have not been faithful in that which is another's, who will *give you that which is your own*? ¹³ No servant can serve two masters, for either he will *hate the one* and love the other, or he will be devoted to the one and *despise the other*. You cannot serve *God* and money."

We find another detail in these subsections confirming our thesis: Luke uses in 12:9, 10 two verbs of highly limited distribution that parallel the meaning of a restricted distribution verb in 16:13. The verbs all describe ways people betray God. Luke 12 includes "one who denies me, *aparnēthēsetai*" (9) and "one who blasphemes against the Holy Spirit, *blasphēmēsetai*" (10). Both verbs occur in Luke only three times, the other times at 22:34, 61(deny) and 22:65; 23:39 (blaspheme). On the other hand Luke 16 shows "despise the other, *kataphronēsei*" (13), standing as the semantic parallel. This verb appears only here in Luke's Gospel. This parallel set of conceptually related lexemes that uncover depths of the human heart have highly limited distribution, and are features that confirm parallel structure.[4]

Review of Parallels between Sections J and J'

Luke 12:8–11 and 16:10–13 exhibit typical features of parallelism. First, the sections include shared multiple themes appearing in the identical order. Second, Luke signals a parallel arrangement by including teaching from Jesus having quite similar and at the same time quite rare language.

Wealth (Sections K and K')

Why did Luke include two scenes about dividing an inheritance? It could be that the topic came up frequently in ancient Israelite society, and Luke was merely repeating a common domestic scene. It could be that Luke

---

4. In these studies, evidence for corresponding sections derives not only from instances of shared restricted vocabulary, but from shared limited vocabulary, from shared unique phraseology, and from shared restricted or limited-use synonyms.

deliberately included two scenes of the same type, because he wrote his Gospel using formulaic patterns, modifying them in successive occurrences.[5] Or it could be that Luke was organizing a concentrically parallel narrative of the words and works of Jesus, in other words, a macro-chiasmus. The very similar questions about wealth and inheritance in Luke 12 and Luke 15 together are one of those prominent signposts in Luke pointing, along with other prominent signposts, to a concentric journey narrative.

Shares (Luke 12:13–15 and 15:11–12)

In Luke 12:13 someone asks Jesus to intervene with a brother over distributing an inheritance, and in Jesus' parable at 15:11, the second son pleads with his father for an advance distribution of the son's part of a future inheritance. Three features in common between these subsections indicate parallelism. First, the eye-catching plot parallel we just mentioned. Next, 12:13 and 15:12 each have a one-use word in the identical semantic domain. "To divide (*merisasthai*)" and "divided (*dieilen*)" occur only once each in Luke's Gospel. And third, in each request an older brother's privilege plays a role in motivating the request (12:13; 15:11; see v 25). These themes connect 12:13–15 closely with 15:11–12.[6]

---

5. For discussions of "type-scenes," see Alter, *Art of Biblical Narrative*, 47–62, and Tannehill, *Narrative Unity*, 170–71.

6. For Luke 15, the specific correspondences begin at v 11, with vv 1–10 having no specific correspondences to Section K. We do not ignore these verses, however. Luke 15 is a unitary text. First, the syntactical connectives (3, 8, 11, 17, 25) show that this is one continuous episode of teaching. Next, the narrator identifies everything from v 3 through v 32 as a single parable (2). And finally, v 1–32 exhibits a chiastic structure that connects v 1–10 the rest of the parable:

A, 15:1–3, "grumbled; this man receives sinners and eats with them; so he told . . . parable"
  B, vv 4–7, "sheep, open country; rejoice with me; calls . . . friends; found . . . lost"
    C, vv 8–10, "loses . . . finds; house; found . . . lost; joy"
      D, vv 11–16, "younger son; took a journey; reckless living; hired himself out"
      D', vv 17–21, "your son; arise and go, arose and came; sinned; hired servant"
    C', vv 22–24, "eat and celebrate; dead . . . alive; lost . . . found; celebrate"
      ["house," v 25]
  B', vv 25–28, "field; music and dancing; called . . . servants; killed . . . calf"
A', vv 29–32, Complaint; "this son of yours . . . devoured your property with prostitutes; he said to him"

Regarding the lack of correspondences of Section K to Luke 15:1–10, the factors above mean that any correspondence of Section K to Luke 15:11–32 amounts to a correspondence to all of Luke 15. For another scheme of concentric structure in Luke 15, see Bailey, *Poet & Peasant*, 142–156.

Luke 12:13 Someone in the crowd said to him, "*Teacher, tell my brother to divide the inheritance with me.*" ¹⁴ But he said to him, "Man, who made me a judge or arbitrator over you?" ¹⁵ And he said to them, "Take care, and be on your guard against all covetousness, for one's life does not consist in the abundance of his possessions."

Luke 15:11 And he said, "There was a man who had *two sons*. ¹² And the younger of them said to his father, '*Father, give me the share of property that is coming to me.*' And he divided his property between them.

Fare Well (Luke 12:16–21 and 15:13–14)

The next pair of segments correspond through ironic parallels (contrasts). Both parables imagine a man who starts out relatively rich ("rich man," 12:16; "gathered all he had," 15:13), but the men prosper in different ways. A bountiful harvest, conservation of resources, self-satisfaction, and festive plans in 12:16–19 sharply contrast with severe famine, squandering, and destitution in 15:13–14. The segments correspond thematically by the multiple opposite experiences of these two men.

Luke 12:16 And he told them a parable, saying, "The *land* of a *rich man* produced *plentifully* (*euphorēsen hē chōra*), ¹⁷ and he thought to himself, 'What shall I do, for I have nowhere to store my crops?' ¹⁸ And he said, 'I will do this: I will tear down my barns and build larger ones, and there I will store *all my grain and my goods*. ¹⁹ *And I will say to my soul, Soul, you have ample goods laid up for many years; relax, eat, drink, be merry.*' ²⁰ But God said to him, 'Fool! This night your soul is required of you, and the things you have prepared, whose will they be?' ²¹ So is the one who lays up treasure for himself and is not rich toward God."

Luke 15:13 Not many days later, the younger son gathered *all he had* and took a journey into a far *country* (*eis chōran makran*), and there he *squandered his property* in reckless living. ¹⁴ And when he had *spent everything*, a *severe famine* arose in that country, and *he began to be in need*.

Want (Luke 12:22–31 and 15:15–17)

The disciples and the younger son experience anxiety about getting food. The generic expression "what you will eat" in 12:22, 29 finds a specific and ironic parallel in 15:16: "pods that the pigs ate." Fear of want and experience of want connect these subsections. The disciples of Jesus must trust in the generous Father's awareness of their need for food (30) rather than live in anxiety and worry about it (22, 29). If God feeds his created animals (24), he will certainly feed his children (29). The younger son of Luke 15, similarly, meditates on how well his father's servants are fed, and begins to consider whether he, the prodigal son, might not after all have to perish from hunger (15:17).

Luke 12:22 And he said to his disciples, "Therefore I tell you, *do not be anxious about your life, what you will eat, nor about your body, what you will put on.* ²³ For *life is more than food*, and the body more than clothing. ²⁴ Consider the ravens: they neither sow nor reap, they have neither storehouse nor barn, and yet *God feeds them*. Of how much more value are you than the birds! ²⁵ And which of you by being anxious can add a single hour to his span of life? ²⁶ If then you are not able to do as small a thing as that, why are you anxious about the rest? ²⁷ Consider the lilies, how they grow: they neither toil nor spin, yet I tell you, even Solomon in all his glory was not arrayed like one of these. ²⁸ But if God so clothes the grass, which is alive in the field today, and tomorrow is thrown into the oven, how much more will he clothe you, O you of little faith! ²⁹ *And do not seek what you are to eat and what you are to drink, nor be worried.* ³⁰ *For all the nations of the world seek after these things, and your Father knows that you need them.* ³¹ Instead, seek his kingdom, and these things will be added to you.

Luke 15:15 So he went and hired himself out to one of the citizens of that country, who sent him into his fields *to feed pigs.* ¹⁶ And *he was longing to be fed* with the *pods that the pigs ate*, and *no one gave him anything.* ¹⁷ "But when he came to himself, he said, 'How many of *my father's hired servants have more than enough bread, but I perish here with hunger!*

Father's Pleasure (Luke 12:32–34 and 15:18–24)

A further set of segments feature the goodness of the respective fathers. The heavenly Father takes pleasure in giving the kingdom to disciples of Jesus (12:32), and the father in the parable famously runs to the son, embraces him, dresses him honorably, and orders a celebration (15:20, 22–23).[7]

---

7. See Green, *Luke*, 582–84, and Bailey, *Poet & Peasant*, 180–87, for cultural and symbolic meaning in the father's actions of welcoming his son.

Luke 12:32 "Fear not, little flock, for *it is your Father's good pleasure to give you the kingdom.* ³³ Sell your possessions, and give to the needy. Provide yourselves with moneybags that do not grow old, with a treasure in the heavens that does not fail, where no thief approaches and no moth destroys. ³⁴ For where your treasure is, there will your heart be also.

Luke 15:18 I will arise and go to my father, and I will say to him, "Father, I have sinned against heaven and before you. ¹⁹ I am no longer worthy to be called your son. Treat me as one of your hired servants." '²⁰ And he arose and came to his father. *But while he was still a long way off, his father saw him and felt compassion, and ran and embraced him and kissed him.* ²¹ And the son said to him, 'Father, I have sinned against heaven and before you. I am no longer worthy to be called your son.' ²² *But the father said to his servants, 'Bring quickly the best robe, and put it on him, and put a ring on his hand, and shoes on his feet.* ²³ *And bring the fattened calf and kill it, and let us eat and celebrate.* ²⁴ *For this my son was dead, and is alive again; he was lost, and is found.'* And they began to celebrate.

Giving Accounts (Luke 12:35–40 and 15:25–28)

The imagined master of the house in Luke 12:35–40 corresponds by multiple ironies to the parable's older brother of Luke 15. The older brother acts as foreman of his father's lands and thus as master of the servants. Both men come home, one from a feast (12:36–38), one to discover a feast (15:25); one expects to come in (12:36), the other refuses to go in (15:28). One man blesses the wakeful, attentive servants by serving them a pre-dawn breakfast (12: 37–38); the other man questions the servants about the party going on inside the house (15:26–27).⁸ One man regrets the unexpected arrival of a thief (12:39), while the other man angrily deplores the sudden return of his rapacious brother (15:28).

Luke 12:35 "Stay dressed for action and keep your lamps burning, ³⁶ and be like men who are *waiting for their master to come home from the wedding feast,* so that they may open the door to him at once *when he comes and knocks.* ³⁷ Blessed are *those servants* whom the master finds awake *when he comes.* Truly, I say to you, *he will dress himself for service and have them recline at table, and he will come and serve them.* ³⁸ *If he comes* in the second watch, or in the third, and finds them awake, blessed are those servants! ³⁹ But know this, that *if the master of the house had known at what hour the thief was coming, he would not have left his house to be broken into.* ⁴⁰ You also must be ready, for the Son of Man is coming at an hour you do not expect."

Luke 15:25 "Now his older son was in the field, and *as he came and drew near to the house, he heard music and dancing.* ²⁶ And he called one of the servants and asked what these things meant. ²⁷ And he said to him, 'Your brother has come, and your father has killed the fattened calf, because he has received him back safe and sound.' ²⁸ But he was angry and refused to go in.

---

8. For the breach of custom that 12: 37–38 imagines, see Luke 17:7–10.

Settling Accounts (Luke 12:41–48 and 15:28–32)

Thematic parallels between the segments continue to be ironic parallels (contrasts). A wise manager in Luke 12 allocates food for the other servants according to the master's instructions (42) and an unwise manager fails to do so (45). The elder son of 15:29, however, complains that his father "never gave me a young goat, that I might celebrate with my friends." The master in Luke 12 rewards a "faithful and wise" manager with promotion to general manager over "all his possessions" (44), but the older son in Luke 15 is already the heir to "all that is [the father's]" (31) and one day will inherit the whole estate.

Luke 12:41 Peter said, "Lord, are you telling this parable for us or for all?" [42] And the Lord said, "*Who then is the faithful and wise manager, whom his master will set over his household, to give them their portion of food at the proper time?* [43] Blessed is that servant whom his master will find so doing when he comes. [44] Truly, I say to you, he will set him over *all his possessions.* [45] But if that servant says to himself, 'My master is delayed in coming,' and begins to beat the male and female servants*, and to eat and drink and get drunk,* [46] the master of that servant will come on a day when he does not expect him and at an hour he does not know, and will cut him in pieces and put him with the unfaithful. [47] And that servant who knew his master's will but did not get ready or act according to his will, will receive a severe beating. [48] But the one who did not know, and did what deserved a beating, will receive a light beating. Everyone to whom much was given, of him much will be required, and from him to whom they entrusted much, they will demand the more.

Luke 15:28b His father came out and entreated him, [29] but he answered his father, '*Look, these many years I have served you, and I never disobeyed your command, yet you never gave me a young goat, that I might celebrate with my friends.* [30] But when this son of yours came, *who has devoured your property with prostitutes*, you killed the fattened calf for him!'[31] And he said to him, 'Son, you are always with me, and *all that is mine is yours.* [32] It was fitting to celebrate and be glad, for this your brother was dead, and is alive; he was lost, and is found.'"

Review of Parallels between Sections K and K′

While most thematic parallels between these sections are contrasts, they are nonetheless parallels. Luke 12:13–48 and 15:1–32 agree by disagreeing, so to speak. The roles of fathers in the two sections (God and the prodigal's father) provide the dominant positive parallel. That shared feature may be the most memorable. The restricted-use synonyms in 12:13 (*merisasthai*, divide) and in 15:12 (*dieilean*, divided), however, most effectively validate a claim of parallelism between the sections.

While Sections J and J′ emphasized faithfulness in following Jesus, Sections K and K′ featured trust in the Father's provision for his children. Luke assembled four sections of narrative where Jesus primarily teaches and encourages his disciples. In the next band of four sections, however, Jesus urgently challenges both the undecided and his critics to see the costs of their intransigence and to come into the kingdom of God. One must begin by stepping over the line.

9

Alignment

ALL FOUR SECTIONS OF this ring dwell on the particularity of God's kingdom: who is in and who is out of it. The sections ask questions: Who thinks rightly (Section L)? Who can be Jesus' disciple (Section L')? Who will be saved (Section M)? Who participates in the feast of God (Section M')? The coming of the kingdom of God manifest in Jesus necessitates decision and division.

Line in the Sand (Sections L and L')

Division and Decision (Luke 12:49–53 and 14:25–27)

The beginnings of Sections L and L' bristle with urgency and necessity to divide from the crowd and decide for Jesus. A yet-future "baptism" of Jesus (12:50, understanding the metaphor as one of Jesus dying and rising) thematically corresponds to "bear his own cross" (14:27), a metaphor from 9:23 for the life-expending commitment that Jesus expects of his followers. Such a commitment to Jesus and to the ways of his kingdom may break up family harmony when not all members of the family follow Jesus (12:53; 14:26).[1] The repentance and renunciation that Jesus calls for warrants radical social implications for any who want to follow him.

---

1. The beginning of Section L is distinctive also for its lack of transitional markers, leading Joel Green, for example, to see no major break in the narrative at this point (*Luke*, 508). The typical transitional marker at the beginning of Section L', however, along with clear parallels between 12:49–53 and the beginning of Section L', support construing a structural boundary at 12:49 anyway.

Luke 12:49 "I came to cast fire on the earth, and would that it were already kindled! ⁵⁰ *I have a baptism to be baptized with*, and how great is my distress until it is accomplished! ⁵¹ Do you think that I have come to give peace on earth? No, I tell you, but rather division. ⁵² For from now on in one house there will be five divided, three against two and two against three. ⁵³ *They will be divided, father against son and son against father, mother against daughter and daughter against mother, mother-in-law against her daughter-in-law and daughter-in-law against mother-in-law.*"

Luke 14:25 Now great crowds accompanied him, and he turned and said to them, ²⁶ *"If anyone comes to me and does not hate his own father and mother and wife and children and brothers and sisters*, yes, and even his own life, he cannot be my disciple. ²⁷ Whoever does not *bear his own cross* and come after me cannot be my disciple.

Discernment (Luke 12:54—13:5 and 14:28–33)

Here, Jesus accents the demands of discipleship, beginning with his requirement that volunteers discern and carefully assess of their readiness for the rigors of discipleship. They must "interpret the present time" (12:56), "judge for [themselves] what is right" (57), and "repent" (13:3, 5). Similarly in Section L', such volunteers must "first sit down and count the cost" (14:28) or "sit down and deliberate" (31), because a person wanting to be Jesus' disciple is expected to "renounce all that he has" (33).

Luke 12:54 He also said to the crowds, "When you see a cloud rising in the west, you say at once, 'A shower is coming.' And so it happens. ⁵⁵ And when you see the south wind blowing, you say, 'There will be scorching heat,' and it happens. ⁵⁶ You hypocrites! You know *how to interpret* the appearance of earth and sky, but why do you not know *how to interpret* the present time? ⁵⁷ "And why do you not *judge for yourselves* what is right? ⁵⁸ As you go with your accuser before the magistrate, make an effort to settle with him on the way, lest he drag you to the judge, and the judge hand you over to the officer, and the officer put you in prison. ⁵⁹ I tell you, you will never get out until you have paid the very last penny." 13:1 There were some present at that very time who told him about the Galileans whose blood Pilate had mingled with their sacrifices. ² And he answered them, "Do you think that these Galileans were worse sinners than all the other Galileans, because they suffered in this way? ³ No, I tell you; but *unless you repent*, you will all likewise perish. ⁴ Or those eighteen on whom the tower in Siloam fell and killed them: do you think that they were worse offenders than all the others who lived in Jerusalem? ⁵ No, I tell you; but *unless you repent*, you will all likewise perish."

Luke 14:28 For which of you, desiring to build a tower, does not *first sit down and count the cost*, whether he has enough to complete it? ²⁹ Otherwise, when he has laid a foundation and is not able to finish, all who see it begin to mock him, ³⁰ saying, 'This man began to build and was not able to finish.' ³¹ Or what king, going out to encounter another king in war, will not *sit down first and deliberate* whether he is able with ten thousand to meet him who comes against him with twenty thousand? ³² And if not, while the other is yet a great way off, he sends a delegation and asks for terms of peace. ³³ So therefore, any one of you who does not *renounce all that he has* cannot be my disciple.

Discarded (Luke 13:6–9 and 14:34–35)

What is useless is discarded. In Jesus' parable at the end of Section L, the vinedresser advises fertilizing a recently fruitless fig tree with manure (13:8). Similarly, at the end of Section L', Jesus teaches that the remains inside a completely leeched-out salt bag should be discarded, and not even put on a manure pile (14:35). The word "manure" (*kopri-*) occurs in Luke only in these two places, qualifying the word as restricted vocabulary, and thus strongly qualifying the sections as corresponding sections.[2]

---

2. These are the only two occurrences of the word in the entire New Testament.

Luke 13:6 And he told this parable: "*A man had a fig tree planted in his vineyard, and he came seeking fruit on it* and found none. ⁷ And he said to the vinedresser, 'Look, for three years *now I have come seeking fruit on this fig tree, and I find none.* Cut it down. Why should it use up *the ground* (*gēn*)?' ⁸ And he answered him, 'Sir, let it alone this year also, until I dig around it and *put on manure* (*kopria*). ⁹ Then if it should bear fruit next year, well and good; but if not, you can cut it down.'"

Luke 14:34 "*Salt is good*, but *if salt has lost its taste*, how shall its saltiness be restored? ³⁵ It is of no use either for *the soil* (*gēn*) or for *the manure pile* (*koprian*). It is thrown away. He who has ears to hear, let him hear."

The sections also contain thematic evidence of correspondence. First, in each segment a good resource (fig tree, 13:6; salt, 14:34) goes bad, or potentially goes bad. The tree, says the fruit farmer, should not "use up the ground" (*gēn*, 13:7). Similarly, the waste minerals from the salt bag are of "no use ... for the soil" (*gēn*, 14:35) and should be discarded elsewhere. Very clear shared themes tie the sections in correspondence, as does a rare word that Luke arranged to stand opposite itself in these two passages.

Review of Parallels between Sections L and L'

As often before in these studies, so now: Luke's arrangement of two texts having a restricted-use lexeme and having multiple shared themes occurring in the same order make it clear that Sections L and L' flow in parallel. The sections form the twelfth ring of Luke's extensive concentric parallelism that structures the journey narrative.

Guest List (Sections M and M')

Our study now arrives at the final pair of literary rings surrounding the center of Luke's narrative about Jesus traveling from Galilee to Jerusalem. In both sections Jesus addresses the questions of inclusion in and exclusion from the kingdom of God. Having a place in the guest list of God's eschatological kingdom is a grace only bestowed by the king.

Luke as compiler/editor counterpoises texts of Jesus' teaching that exhibit strong confirmatory signs of parallelism. For one, the word "street" (*plateia*) in Luke 13:26 and 14:21 are two of only three occurrences of this word in Luke's narrative, the other being in 10:10 ("go into its streets"). Such a narrow distribution of this word in the Lukan journey narrative invites comparison of the three listed texts, and especially comparison of those in Luke 13 and 14, if another strong confirmatory sign of parallelism is present there. And indeed a very strong confirmation is present: a word restricted in distribution to Sections M and M′ only. The word "ox" (*bous*) occurs in Luke only three times, all three occurrences in Sections M and M′ (13:15; 14:5, 19). Neither of these words is theological in meaning, but terms from everyday life in Israel. They nevertheless indicate *literary* parallelism between Sections M and M′. Further indications of parallelism arise from thematic similarities, as follows.

Release (Luke 13:10–17 and 14:1–6)

Both segments begin with concern by Israelite authorities over appropriate behavior on the Sabbath for Jesus as healer (13:10–17; 14:1–6). More specifically, a person with a non-life-threatening illness inexplicably shows up in both venues (13:11; 14:2). Jesus heals each (13:12–13; 14:4), releasing them from their disabilities. Authorities object to Sabbath-day healing, and Jesus responds by posing questions having to do with an ox and water (13:15; 14:5), questions with obvious answers. Jesus silences his questioners because the answers to Jesus' questions subvert their arguments (13:17; 14:6). These thematic parallels accumulate in the same order in the respective texts.

Luke 13:10 Now he was teaching in one of the synagogues *on the Sabbath*. [11] *And behold, there was a woman who had had a disabling spirit for eighteen years*. She was bent over and could not fully straighten herself. [12] When Jesus saw her, he called her over and said to her, "Woman, you are freed from your disability." [13] And he laid his hands on her, and immediately she was made straight, and she glorified God. [14] But the ruler of the synagogue, indignant because Jesus had healed on the Sabbath, said to the people, "There are six days in which work ought to be done. *Come on those days and be healed, and not on the Sabbath day.*" [15] Then the Lord answered him, "You hypocrites! *Does not each of you on the Sabbath untie his ox* (boun) *or his donkey from the manger and lead it away to water it?* [16] And ought not this woman, a daughter of Abraham whom Satan bound for eighteen years, be loosed from this bond on the Sabbath day?" [17] As he said these things, *all his adversaries were put to shame*, and all the people rejoiced at all the glorious things that were done by him.

Luke 14:1 *One Sabbath*, when he went to dine at the house of a ruler of the Pharisees, they were watching him carefully. [2] *And behold, there was a man before him who had dropsy*. [3] And Jesus responded to the lawyers and Pharisees, saying, "*Is it lawful to heal on the Sabbath, or not?*" [4] But they remained silent. Then he took him and healed him and sent him away. [5] And he said to them, "*Which of you, having a son or an ox* (bous) *that has fallen into a well on a Sabbath day, will not immediately pull him out?*" [6] And they could not reply to these things.

Rise (Luke 13:18–21 and 14:7–11)

The second segments of Sections M and M' have in common only one theme, the change from inconspicuous to prominent, a theme at the theological center of both passages. In Luke 13 a little seed becomes a large shrub or tree, and a bit of leaven proliferates in a large amount of flour. In Luke 14 the wedding guest who deliberately takes a low-status seat remote from the host may be invited to move to a seat implying a rise in honor and status vis-à-vis the host. These segments share in common a theme of appropriate transition from inconspicuous to prominent.

Luke 13:18 He said therefore, "What is the kingdom of God like? And to what shall I compare it? [19] It is like a grain of mustard seed that a man took and sowed in his garden, *and it grew and became a tree*, and the birds of the air made nests in its branches." [20] And again he said, "To what shall I compare the kingdom of God? [21] It is like leaven that a woman took and hid in three measures of flour, *until it was all leavened*."

Luke 14:7 Now he told a parable to those who were invited, when he noticed how they chose the places of honor, saying to them, [8] "When you are invited by someone to a wedding feast, do not sit down in a place of honor, lest someone more distinguished than you be invited by him, [9] and he who invited you both will come and say to you, 'Give your place to this person,' and then you will begin with shame to take the lowest place. [10] But when you are invited, go and sit in the lowest place, so that when your host comes he may say to you, '*Friend, move up higher*.' Then you will be honored in the presence of all who sit at table with you. [11] For everyone who exalts himself will be humbled, and *he who humbles himself will be exalted*."

In or Out (Luke 13:22–30 and 14:12–24)

Jesus explicitly teaches about the kingdom of God in the remaining segments of both sections: who will be included in and who will be excluded from the kingdom feast.[3] Having a place at the feast (13:29; 14:15, 24) signifies those who are "saved" (13:23). Some of those excluded from the feast are locked out and left in the streets (26), but in the other section possible banqueters are sought from the streets (14:21). Eventual guests who recline at table in the kingdom feast come from unexpected places (13:29; 14:23) and include both storied guests (13:28) and culturally marginalized guests (14:21). We ultimately learn that the final guest list will be unsettling or shocking to those who are excluded (13:30; 14:24).

---

3. The theme of the kingdom of God was introduced through similes in 13:18–21.

Luke 13:22 He went on his way through towns and villages, teaching and journeying toward Jerusalem. [23] And someone said to him, "*Lord, will those who are saved be few?*" And he said to them, [24] "Strive to enter through the narrow door. For many, I tell you, will seek to enter and will not be able. [25] When once the master of the house has risen and shut the door, and you begin to stand outside and to knock at the door, saying, 'Lord, open to us,' then he will answer you, 'I do not know where you come from.' [26] Then you will begin to say, '*We ate and drank in your presence*, and you taught *in our streets (en tais plateiais hēmōn)*.' [27] But he will say, 'I tell you, I do not know where you come from. Depart from me, all you workers of evil!' [28] *In that place there will be weeping and gnashing of teeth, when you see Abraham and Isaac and Jacob and all the prophets in the kingdom of God but you yourselves cast out.* [29] *And people will come from east and west, and from north and south, and recline at table in the kingdom of God.* [30] *And behold, some are last who will be first, and some are first who will be last.*"

Luke 14:12 He said also to the man who had invited him, "When you give a dinner or a banquet, do not invite your friends or your brothers or your relatives or rich neighbors, lest they also invite you in return and you be repaid. [13] But when you give a feast, invite the poor, the crippled, the lame, the blind, [14] and you will be blessed, because they cannot repay you. For you will be repaid at the resurrection of the just." [15] When one of those who *reclined at table with him* heard these things, he said to him, "*Blessed is everyone who will eat bread in the kingdom of God!*" [16] But he said to him, "A man once gave a great banquet and invited many. [17] And at the time for the banquet he sent his servant to say to those who had been invited, 'Come, for everything is now ready.' [18] But they all alike began to make excuses. The first said to him, 'I have bought a field, and I must go out and see it. Please have me excused.' [19] And another said, 'I have bought five yoke of *oxen (boōn)*, and I go to examine them. Please have me excused.' [20] And another said, 'I have married a wife, and therefore I cannot come.' [21] So the servant came and reported these things to his master. Then the master of the house became angry and said to his servant, 'Go out quickly to *the streets (eis tas plateias) and lanes of the city*, and bring in the poor and crippled and blind and lame.' [22] And the servant said, 'Sir, what you commanded has been done, and still there is room.' [23] And the master said to the servant, '*Go out to the highways and hedges and compel people to come in, that my house may be filled.* [24] *For I tell you, none of those men who were invited shall taste my banquet.*'"

Review of Parallels between Sections M and M′

Multiple, common themes linking 13:10–30 to 14:1–24 occur in the same order in the respective texts. *Plateia*, a word in both sections having limited distribution in Luke, and *bous*, a word restricted in distribution to Sections M and M′, give strong evidence that 13:10–30 and 14:1–24 are literarily parallel. Sections M and M′ fall in place inside the boundaries of eleven other pairs of parallel journey narrative sections to form the penultimate sections of Luke's massive literary construction.[4]

---

4. We will study Section N/N′ in chapter 12.

We have shown throughout Part 2 of his book that *Luke did indeed* assemble an enormous concentrically parallel journey narrative of texts gathered from "eyewitnesses and ministers of the word" (1:2). Two questions immediately come to mind. First, why would he do this? Our next chapter sorts this out. Then, what does it mean? What theology does Luke intend his readers to grasp by attending to the way the journey is compiled, beyond attending to the episodes in linear sequence as a story about Jesus? Chapters 11 and 12 below clarify Luke's theological intention.

Chapter 10

Luke the Stylist

THE ARTICULATE HISTORIAN/BIOGRAPHER/THEOLOGIAN WHOM we know as Luke necessarily came from a privileged, wealthy, resourced class making up merely 2–5 percent of Greco-Roman (and Hellenized Jewish) society.[1] Karl Allen Kuhn, in his *The Kingdom according to Luke and Acts: A Social, Literary, and Theologial Introduction,* locates Luke's literacy within three restrictive social rings. First, "In Luke's day, literacy was restricted to a small minority of the population."[2] The ability to write was rare. The Apostle Paul often used the services of a secretary (*amanuensis*), and it is likely that other New Testament authors did so as well. Secretaries may may have achieved some literacy working as "bookkeepers or military clerks," or they, like Luke and Paul, may have been converted to Christ from elite social strata where they received systematic formal literacy training.[3]

Second, "In ancient Rome, higher levels of literacy and literary acumen were achieved only by a very select few."[4] So also in Greco-Roman and Hellenized Jewish culture. Writing according to conventions of eloquence resulted from years of reading and copying ancient masters, activities possible only for a wealthy and connected few. Last, "In Luke's world, literacy and especially advanced levels of literacy were primarily restricted to the social elite."[5] Luke's articulate Greek writing, his researched narrative, and

---

1. Kuhn, *Kingdom*, 63. In this Chapter I depend heavily on Kuhn's summaries of scholarship on ancient literacy.
2. Ibid., 56.
3. Ibid., 58.
4. Ibid., 57.
5. Ibid., 58

his purposeful structuring of the narrative carry the stamp of literary training practiced only among the cultural elite.

But by becoming a follower of Jesus, Luke's familiar literary (and medical?) life must have taken a much different direction.[6] Luke obviously did not go away sad from Jesus, like a wealthy young ruler did (Luke 18:18–30). Luke's response to Jesus must have been something akin to that of Levi, who "left everything and followed" Jesus, yet who could still make "a great feast in his house" for Jesus and for "a large company of tax collectors and others" (5:27–32). Luke began following Jesus and learning how literary artistry could serve the kingdom of God. Eventually the Lord provided an opportunity for Luke to write a narrative for Theophilus, a narrative to clarify the truth about Jesus (1:1–4), a narrative showing God's purposes being fulfilled in the words, actions, and in the person of Jesus of Nazareth.

Luke and Rhetorical Practice

We already studied Luke's literary artistry at work in the service of God's kingdom. The early narrative displays simple parallelism in the birth announcements of John and Jesus, and in the infancy and childhood of both figures. Luke's parallels between the two are meant to show differences as well as similarities: both are great ones raised up by God; John is the eschatological prophet; Jesus is the savior, Christ the Lord. Next, Luke articulates the dynamics of following Jesus by means of three lengthy concentric parallelisms covering most of Luke 5–9. The Evangelist employs additional rhetorical conventions in telling his story, but we are narrowly focused on studying only his large-scale concentric parallelisms.

Luke's teachers would have schooled young Luke in valuing, copying, and imitating the masters of literature who went before: poets, dramatists, and rhetoricians. He would imitate their good writing. Later, as God's Gospel writer, Luke's familiar mode for creating a narrative for Theophilus would be to copy and imitate the best Jesus-narratives of the past. Again, Luke's early teachers would also have insisted that Luke not only imitate his models, but adapt them and improve on them. Thomas Brodie summarizes typical Greco-Roman acts of literary adaptation this way: "At the risk of over-simplifying, these adaptations are . . . elaboration, compression, fusion, substitution of images, positivization, internalization, form-change."[7] By adding Luke's own narration to parts of the story, he could elaborate; by se-

---

6. Paul names a Luke who was a physician (Col 4:14), but it is only speculation to identify that person as the author of the Third Gospel.

7. Brodie, "Imitation," 23.

lective appropriation of texts from his sources, Luke could compress or fuse certain parts of the account.[8] By organizing large parallels and concentric parallels, Luke could adapt the story by form-change.

Later, when Luke writes his Gospel narrative for Theophilus, he adapts source material based on at least two concerns. First, the account of Jesus must be expressed in such a way to offer Theophilus a "certainty" apparently not offered by Theophilus' other sources (1:4). It is not clear on the surface what Lukan adaptations would do so. Second, Luke intends to tidy up or reorder the account in some way: he provides "an orderly account" (1:3). His word "orderly" (*katheksēs*) broadly means some kind of ordering of time, or of space, or of logic.[9] Rhetorical structuring of the Jesus-story into concentric parallelisms for theological purposes certainly falls within the semantic range of *katheksēs*.

Luke the Communicator

So one answer to the question regarding why Luke organizes complex literary structures in his narrative is that he is applying the resources of his training: it is normal for him as an author. But what about the readers, Theophilus and others? What value does Luke offer them in his grand parallelisms?

In the Preface I described my friend's answer to this question: humor! Lacking background about ancient writing and about Luke the theologian, she could only find one reason for the evident parallel structures. God and Luke must entertain readers out of a divine sense of humor! But while there certainly are ironic and humorous episodes, funny turns of language, and puns in the Bible, concentric parallelisms have serious theological purposes. They are not essentially humorous, even though various parallels between sections may be ironic in nature.

In chapter 1 we explained that generally concentric parallelisms serve a variety of purposes, including filling out a thesis with illustrations, exceptions, contrasts, alternatives, special emphases, or development; adding nuance; establishing continuity for a subdivision of text (or continuity of a whole text); and holding a listener's or reader's attention. But *why does Luke do it in his Gospel*? Luke's role as an agent of God for convincing Theophilus about the meaning of Jesus' life and ministry greatly controls how Luke organizes his narrative. He arranges concentric parallelisms to arrest a

---

8. Luke fuses 13:31–33, appropriated from an unknown source, with 34–35, which he appropriated almost word-for-word from an eschatological context in Matthew 23.

9. Limiting the meaning of the word to events consecutive in time is a possible, but not at all a necessary understanding of the word.

reader's attention, to interrupt reading of the historical story, to redirect every Theophilus from events to meaning, to expose the theology that Luke centers within curiously repetitive groups of episodes.

A web of recurring names, identities, and titles in Luke 4:40—6:19 stops a theologically curious reader from pressing on without looking for an answer. A persistent series of prosaic doublets crisscrossing the length 106 verses (7:1—8:56) draws a tenacious reader to ask whether this is a theological discourse and what it means (as in 8:9). Multiple contrasts in Luke 9 between Jesus's glory and his inept followers beg for a theological explanation.

Likewise, the massive parallel-structured journey narrative that we have documented at length resides in the Third Gospel for the same reasons. First, Luke had the training, skill, and motivation to organize it. Second, Luke placed the structure there to claim our attention to its theological meaning. However, once we have accepted Luke's prompt to look deeper, we must decide how to proceed. Two main approaches have proven value: investigate both the concentric structure's context and and investigate its center section.

11

Context of the Journey Narrative

We explained our method for interpreting concentric parallelisms in chapter 1. The center section or sections contain the key for understanding a whole concentric arrangement of texts. As a consideration in addition to interpreting from the center, two of the forms we analysed in earlier chapters attach to important contexts. First, gathering disciples (4:40—6:19) arises from Jesus' period of solo ministry (4:14–39). Second, his teaching on the word of God (7:1—8:56) has roots in the Sermon on the Plain (6:20–49). We find also that the journey (9:51—19:46) gains momentum from the Mount of Transfiguration and from the Chosen One's interactions with the twelve in Luke 9:1–50.

It stands to reason that interpreters not working from a concentric point of view would look for the key to the meaning of the journey narrative in chapter 9 of Luke. Indeed, any interpretation of 9:51—19:46, including ours, *must* take into account 9:1–50. While a linear-oriented interpreter looks in Luke 9 for the essence of the journey's meaning, those who find a concentric approach valid, as this book does, expect to find in Luke 9 a confirmation of the main idea arising from the chiastic center of the journey. Interpreters have somewhat different expectations of Luke 9 when analyzing the journey narrative.

Further, both the journey narrative and Luke 9 are woven within the fabric of Luke's entire Gospel. To interpret the journey narrative, we must understand it within the whole work, within the immediate context of Luke 9, and out from the chiastic center (13:31–35). We begin from the broadest perspective.

Aspects of the Kingdom of God in Luke

The kingdom of God theme pervades Luke's Gospel, although there are fewer explicit references to it in the concentric structures of Luke 5–8.[1] In the rest of Luke before the journey section, reliable voices apply titles and kingly authority to Jesus. As "Son of the Most High," Mary's child will sit on the throne of David reigning over God's people forever (1:32). The newborn child is Savior, Christ, and Lord (2:11). Jesus rebukes demons "because" they know him as Christ and Son of God (4:41). These titles, role, and longevity derive from biblical and popular Second Temple Period expectations of God's reign.[2]

In Luke 9, at key moments in the narrative, two more voices reliably ascribe kingly titles to Jesus. First, Peter confesses Jesus as "the Christ of God" (20), a confession that Jesus accepts yet tightly controls (21–22). The politically incendiary claim that Jesus is the Christ requires that disciples keep the news to themselves for now. Any hope of the disciples that God's Messiah will act to drive out occupying armies must be redirected. Second, on the mountain the voice of God admonishes Peter and the other disciples: "This is my Son, my Chosen One, listen to him!" (35). Ascriptions to Jesus of royal status and authority before God in Luke 9 continue and bring climax to the birth narrative announcements. The voices (except one) are supernatural. Significantly, the one human voice is that of Peter representing the disciples. In a more lucid moment he and they recognize in Jesus their Christ, their Messiah. Luke draws readers of Luke 1–9 into a dramatic discovery of Jesus' identity, power, and authority as the Chosen One who rules God's kingdom.

Aspects of the Kingdom of God in the Journey Narrative

The kingdom of God theme sets the tone for the journey narrative. Language of kingdom and lordship unite diverse journey episodes of Jesus' teaching and interactions. The Lord explains what it means to enter the kingdom. He trains disciples, potential disciples, and even opponents to follow the ways of the kingdom. Except for once during the journey, Jesus calls himself "Son of Man" in the eschatological sense of the title: "one like a son of man"

---

1. Explicitly at 4:43; 5:24; 6:5; 8:1, 10. The theme may be found implicitly in many Lukan episodes, as numerous authors explain (see, for example, Kuhn, *Kingdom*, 205–209). In *Both Here and There* I limit discussion to explicit instances of the theme as expressed by "kingdom," "king," "reign," "Son of God," "Christ," "Lord," "Savior," and "Son of Man."

2. Kuhn, *Kingdom*, 217–23.

who is "given dominion and glory and a kingdom" (Dan 7:13–14).[3] As the journey ends, his disciples exclaim "Blessed is the King who comes in the name of the Lord!" (Luke 19:38). Episodes making up the journey can be parsed in detail to exhibit yet more fully the ubiquity of the kingdom of God theme in the journey narrative. But this is not our purpose here.[4]

Kingdom of God in the Chiastic Center of the Journey Narrative

If I were biasing the boundaries of concentric sections by concern for theological tidiness, I might set the boundaries of the structure's middle as Luke 13:10—14:24, and call it all Section M/M′. That would not only make a neat twelve tandem sections, but also specify a chiastic middle having in both sections a grand metaphor for the kingdom of God: the kingdom feast. It would be theologically and poetically satisfying. But no, a close literary reading does not allow such a move. Luke 13:31–35 intrudes into the kingdom banqueting with a death threat, travel plans, a sacred city that is toxic to its prophets, and ritual lament over the city.[5] The verses must be set apart as a new section (or sections). The kingdom of God theme, however, continues in verses that make up the center of the journey narrative. The theme continues in three ways.

> Luke 13:31 At that very hour some Pharisees came and said to him, "Get away from here, for Herod *wants (thelei) to kill (apokteinai) you*." 32 And he said to them, "*Go and tell* that fox, 'Behold, I cast out demons and perform cures today and tomorrow, and the third day I finish my course. 33 Nevertheless, I *must (dei me) go on my way* today and tomorrow and the day following, for it *cannot be (ouk endechetai)* that a prophet should *perish* away from *Jerusalem*.' 34 O *Jerusalem, Jerusalem*, the city that *kills (apokteinousa) the prophets* and stones *those who are sent to it*! How often *would I have (ēthelēsa)* gathered your children together as a hen gathers her brood under her wings, and you *were not willing (ouk ēthelēsate)*! 35 Behold, your house is forsaken. And I tell you, you will not see me until you say, 'Blessed is *he who comes* in the name of the Lord!'"

---

3. Luke 11:30; 12:8, 10; 17:22, 24, 26; 18:8, 31; but not 9:58.

4. See Green, *Luke*, 394—694.

5. Darrell Bock notes that these days "most see [13:31–35] as the center of the unit" (*Luke 9:51–24:53*, 1243). See, for example, Tiede, *Prophecy and History*, 72.

First, 13:31 evokes the beginning of David's progress to the throne of the Israelite kingdom (1 Sam 19:11). Israel remembered David as its ideal king and founder of the national capitol at Jerusalem. Second, Jesus in Luke 13:32–33a proclaims his sovereignty over Herod the Tetrarch, making a pronouncement through some Pharisees to Herod that any travelling Jesus will do, he will do for his own purpose, on his own schedule, and it will indeed conclude in Jesus' death. Herod boasts no authority over Jesus' ministry or life.

Third, God sends his prophets to warn a power-wielding elite in Jerusalem of his displeasure and proclaim his call to repentance and reformation. God gives kingdom authority to his prophets.[6] But Jerusalem is a death-trap for God's prophets (13:33). It is "the city that kills the prophets and stones those who are sent to it" (34). Jerusalem resists the good kingdom news of Jesus as well, even though he "comes in the name of the Lord" (34–35; see Ps 118:26).[7]

In these ways Luke 13:31–35, the chiastic center of the journey narrative, continues and develops further the kingdom of God theme that fills 9:51—19:46 and that pervades the entire Third Gospel. We have already transitioned in our study from context to chiastic center. Let us pass on now from the center's thematic kingdom content to the center's literary function as the axis of the structure (our chapter 12). Subsequently we will consider the kingdom theology generated by Luke's long and deliberately concentric narrative of Jesus' journey from Galilee to Jerusalem (chapter 13). That theological discourse arises because the outer ends of the journey structure are tied to its center.

---

6. Kuhn, *Kingdom*, 221–22.

7. When Jesus' disciples loudly begin citing the same text from Psalm 118 upon Jesus' approach to the city (19:38), they modify its wording: not "blessed is *he* who comes," but "blessed is the *King* who comes in the name of the Lord!" For them (and for Luke), when Jesus comes comes into the city, the king comes in. Jesus' lament in section N' anticipates his own arrival in Jerusalem as king (19:27–44).

12

Inside Out

WHEN INTERPRETING CONCENTRIC PARALLELISMS, one hopes that authors of these structures provide explicit hermeneutical guidance in the central section(s). Lacking that, an interpreter must tease out implicit interpretive hints from the axis of the ring-structure. In the case of Luke 13:31–35, we must do the latter. In this chapter we study 13:31–35 from a literary point of view, and building on that, we discern significant narrative connections between the structural center and its outer ends, 9:51–56 and 19:28–46. These narrative connections have great promise for our comprehensive interpretation of the entire journey narrative.

Killers (Sections N and N')

Sections N and N' each feature an apparently offstage high-profile killer (Herod, Jerusalem) and also feature Jesus' rebuke of the respective killers. It is possible to see 13:31–35, on one hand, as continuous narrative and thus a unified center to the concentric structure. As Joel Green notes, "Jesus' reply to the Pharisees (vv 31–33) and his declaration concerning Jerusalem (vv 34-35) are joined by the representation of Jerusalem as the city that kills the prophets (vv 33-34)."[1] It is just as possible, on the other hand, to see the five verses as falling into two parts, distinguished at the surface level by genre. In vv 31-33 Jesus makes a pronouncement to some Pharisees and to Herod that any travelling Jesus will do, he will do for his own purpose, on his own schedule, and it will indeed conclude in Jesus' death. In vv 34-35 Jesus shifts abruptly to words of ritual lament,

---

1. Green, *Luke*, 534.

contrasting sharply in genre with his pronouncements in vv 31–33. Jesus' listeners during the pronouncements are some Pharisees; in the lament he addresses Jerusalem as a living being.

Luke 13:31 At that very hour some Pharisees came and said to him, "Get away from here, for Herod *wants* (*thelei*) to *kill* (*apokteinai*) *you*." ³² And he said to them, "Go and tell that fox, 'Behold, I cast out demons and perform cures today and tomorrow, and the third day I finish my course. ³³ Nevertheless, I *must* go on my way today and tomorrow and the day following, for it *cannot be* that a prophet should *perish* away from *Jerusalem*.'

Luke 13:34 O *Jerusalem, Jerusalem*, the city that *kills* (*apokteinousa*) *the prophets* and stones *those who are sent to it*! How often *would I have* (*ēthelēsa*) gathered your children together as a hen gathers her brood under her wings, and you *were not willing* (*ouk ēthelēsate*)! ³⁵ Behold, your house is forsaken. And I tell you, you will not see me until you say, 'Blessed is he who comes in the name of the Lord!'"

Further, Luke arrayed the words in such a way that their distribution between vv 31–33 and vv 34–35 is consistent with two sections of text. The "wanting" of Herod (31) balances with the "wanting" of Jesus and of Jerusalem (34). The threat of death for Jesus (31, 33) is counterpoised with the practice of Jerusalem to kill prophets (34). "Go on my way" (33) anticipates "he who comes" (35).

Luke 13:31–35 divides into two parts that I designate Sections N and N'. Two parts or sections in the chiastic center direct us first of all, as they should, to the outer ends of the concentric parallelism, in other words, to Sections A and A'. Luke 13:31–33 harbors a close affinity to 9:51–56 and 13:34–35 holds kinship with Section A', particularly with 19:41–44. Anticipating what follows below, two halves of the chiastic center serve as billboards, if I may, that urge the reader to stop and consider carefully what the beginning and end of Jesus' journey mean as the outside sections of Luke's concentric theological discourse. Luke 13:31–33 provides two motivations for Jesus to leave Galilee and 9:51–56 describes him doing so. Similarly, in 13:34–35 Jesus begins a formal lament about Jerusalem, his destination, and in 19:41–44 he completes the lament. Let us consider more closely ties between Section N and Section A and ties between Section N' and Section A'.

Setting Out (Luke 13:31–33 and 9:51–56)

A shared plot movement of setting out for Jerusalem implies that Section N (13:31–33) *belongs* to 9:51–56 and to its context. By this I mean minimally that the former belongs to the latter as a billboard advertisement belongs to the genuine item, service, or idea it proclaims. But further and more to the point, 13:31–33 belongs to 9:51–56 because the former provides a completed context for the latter. In Luke's appropriation and placement of 13:31–33 from his unidentified textual resource, Luke varied the narrative order of events for his own literary/theological purpose.[2] He put 13:31–33 in the chiastic center section so that the incongruity would draw a reader's attention to the way the journey narrative is organized.[3]

Luke 13:31–33 brings aspects of Luke 9 to a fulness that prepares Luke's reader for Jesus' departure toward Jerusalem in 9:51–56. First, Luke's intensified temporal notice at the beginning of 13:31 ("at that very hour") draws attention to the elegant timeliness of Pharisees showing up just then. Out of their character as it may seem, Pharisees warn Jesus that Herod wants to kill him (31).[4] Jesus' disciples back in Luke 9 have reason to suspect the good will of Pharisees toward Jesus and his followers, because Pharisees seem intent on criticizing those who follow the way of Jesus (5:30, 33; 6:2). What's more, Pharisees exhibit suspicion, hatred, and wrath toward Jesus, Lord of the disciples (6:7, 11).

In Luke 9:50, however, Jesus teaches John and other disciples that outsiders are not automatically to be considered as misguided, or as hindrances, or even as opponents. The unknown man casting out demons in Jesus' name (49) should be seen as supportive to the kingdom of God. It is "at that very hour" that certain Pharisees arrive to offer an urgent warning that supports Jesus (13:31). They too should be seen as "not against" Jesus but "for" him. They are not cynical or devious, but well-intentioned. Jesus' words in response to them criticize Herod, not the Pharisees giving an alarm. Thus, unlikely messengers of warning in 13:31 fit exactly in timeliness and as another example of Jesus' teaching on well-intentioned outsiders in 9:50–51. We could even say that 13:31–33 fits the plot of Luke

---

2. See Chapter 11. The journey sections in both Matthew (19:1—21:11) and Mark (10:17—11:11) lack any mention of the events in Luke 13:31–33. We have no example of 13:31–33 appearing between 9:50 and 51 in biblical manuscripts of Luke. Whatever the source of the words or their context in that material, Luke used them deliberately and provocatively in Section N of Luke.

3. I do not propose a "cut and paste" of Luke 13:31–33 into position before 9:51. Section N serves a dual purpose in 9:51—19:46: both a fuller context for the beginning of the journey, and where it stands in Luke, a necessary part of a comparison of Jesus to David. See chapter 14. Further, it is important to fully respect the literary integrity of the Third Gospel as received.

4. We would do well to note Joel Green's correction to our stereotypical estimate of Pharisees: Luke "does not lump all Pharisees together in one composite group . . . ." Instead, "Some Pharisees actually align themselves with Jesus." Jesus acts on the "hope that the Pharisees may join him in his solidarity with God's redemptive project." Green, *Luke*, 537 (also 199, 301–302, 307). Consider the example of Simon the Pharisee (Luke 7:36–50), whose final response to Jesus remains unclear at the end of the episode.

9 exactly between 9:50 and 9:51. It belongs there (except that Luke deliberately placed the episode in the center section of the concentrically organized journey narrative).[5]

Another confirmatory concurrence between 13:31–33 and Luke 9 is Herod's predatory intent. The prophet-killer who wants to see Jesus in Luke 9:9 wants to do away with Jesus in 13:31. We should recognize the Pharisees's warning as legitimate and not assume that in 9:9 Herod is only another well-intentioned outsider!

Third, Jesus' destiny to die in Jerusalem and his intent to begin traveling to the city join our two passages into a single plot (9:22, (30); 13:33; 9:51). Next, both texts highlight Jesus' movement toward fulfilling his earthly calling. He will "accomplish" his departure (*eksodos*) in Jerusalem (9:31), and on the third day Jesus will "finish" his course (13:32). And finally, authors have noted that in 9:51–56 the verb *poreuomai* (to go, to travel) occurs four times in various grammatical forms (51, 52, 53, 56; see also 57).[6] When one associates 13:31–33 with 9:51–56, the verb now accumulates three more drumbeats of "go, go, go." Such an accumulation of textual concurrences invite us to read Luke 9 and 13:31–33 together. Luke placed a rather obvious bit of the Luke 9 story into place in the concentric center section to capture readers' curiosity about the way the journey story is structured.[7]

Lamenting (Luke 13:34–35 and 19:41–44)

Section N' *belongs* to 19:41–44. The two texts certainly have similar features, as many have noted.[8] But further and more to the point, 13:34–35

---

5. Fitzmyer, following Conzelmann, states that "The tradition enshrined in [13:31–33] not only presupposes a stay in Galilee and a connection with Herod (recall 9:9; cf. 23:6–12), but it may even reflect the reason for Jesus' departure from Galilee and the journey to Jerusalem in the first place." *Luke X–XXIV*, 1029.

6. For example, Green, *Luke*, 402.

7. Reading Luke 13:31–33 between 9:50 and 51 also provides for our Theological Outline of Luke's Gospel (chapter 1) the narrative transition lacking between "Jesus and the Coming Crisis" (9:1–50) and "Jesus the King" (9:51—19:46).

8. Luke 13:34–35 highlights coming to the city, tying the verses intimately into 18:28–46 describing Jesus' arrival in Jerusalem. Jesus' lament that "you would not [be gathered under my wings]" (13:34) anticipates his lament, "Would that you, even you, had known on this day the things that make for peace" (19:42). The dirge over a "forsaken house" of 13:35 becomes a weeping vision of the destroyed city of 19:43–44. The warning that "you will not see me until . . . ." in Section N' (13:35) comes to fruition in the statements "but now they are hidden from your eyes" (19:42) and "you did know the time of your visitation" (44). And finally, Jesus' requirement that the Jerusalem religious

belongs to 19:41–44 because the the two neatly combine to form one complete ritual lament. Luke must have appropriated 13:34–35 from the same source that Matthew took his 23:37–39, but Luke subdivided the yet larger ritual lament into two parts. Luke put 13:34–35 in the chiastic center section to draw his reader's attention to literary structuring. The remainder of the lament (unused by Matthew) he stitched into the fabric of the final section of Jesus' journey to Jerusalem. Theophilus should discern the whole lament by genre sameness and discern its fragmentation by breach of a conventional form.

Neither Jesus' lament in Section N' nor those in Section A' come from idiosyncratic outbursts of passion by Jesus, although they are certainly passionate. His lament in both sections form *a single ritual lament* of a kind specifically for persons (Jerusalem personified).[9]

Luke 19:41 When He approached Jerusalem, He saw the city and wept over it, [42]saying,

Luke 13:34"O Jerusalem, Jerusalem, the city that kills the prophets and stones those sent to her! How often I wanted to gather your children together, just as a hen gathers her brood under her wings, and you would not have it! [35]"Behold, your house is left to you desolate; and I say to you, you will not see Me until the time comes when you say, 'BLESSED IS HE WHO COMES IN THE NAME OF THE LORD!'"

Luke 19:42"If you had known in this day, even you, the things which make for peace! But now they have been hidden from your eyes. [43]"For the days will come upon you when your enemies will throw up a barricade against you, and surround you and hem you in on every side, [44]and they will level you to the ground and your children within you, and they will not leave in you one stone upon another, because you did not recognize the time of your visitation."

Luke 19:41 and the first word of 42 serve as an introduction to the entire lament. With two Lukan texts as one, we see standard features of Greco-Roman ritual lament for a person. Among such features are double address of the dying or deceased, intimate second-person pronouns and verbs, reproach of the fallen/falling, citing of desolation left behind by the death, expressing unfulfilled wishes of the lamenting person, recalling "then" and regretting "now."[10]

---

leadership would confess, "Blessed is he who comes in the name of the Lord" (13:35) is fulfilled in Jerusalem not by the city's leaders (their representative says, "Teacher, rebuke your disciples," 19:39) but only by the multitude and by Jesus' disciples who exclaim, "Blessed is the king who comes in the name of the Lord. Peace in heaven and glory in the highest!" (38).

9. See Alexiou, *Ritual Lament*, 84-85. My comments on ritual lament in Luke are based heavily on Alexiou. Jesus' lament does not fit the conventional pattern for the fall or destruction of *cities*, but it shows many marks of lament for a *person*.

10. Plural "you" in Luke 14:35 arises from Jesus' quotation of scriptures containing the plural pronoun.

Beyond shared standard ritual lament features, in the aggregated texts concentric structure binds the texts poetically into one:

13:34"O Jerusalem, Jerusalem, the city that kills the prophets and stones *those sent to her*! How often I wanted to gather your children together, just as a hen gathers her brood under her wings, and *you would not have it*!

> 35"Behold, your house is left to you *desolate*;
>> and I say to you, *you will not see Me* until the time comes when you say, 'BLESSED IS HE WHO COMES IN THE NAME OF THE LORD!'"
>>
>> 19:42"If you had known in this day, even you, the things which make for peace! But *now they have been hidden from your eyes*.
>
> 43"For the days will come upon you when your enemies *will throw up a barricade* against you, and *surround you* and *hem you in* on every side, 44and *they will level you* to the ground and your children within you, and *they will not leave* in you one stone upon another,

because *you did not recognize* the time of *your visitation*."

This brief poetic lament shows an ABCC'B'A' structure. Strophes *a* and *a'* highlight the cause of God's displeasure with Jerusalem: its resolute rejection of the Sent One. Strophes *b* and *b'* identify a consequent desolation. And strophes *c* and *c'* proclaim a judicial blindness now to cover the eyes of the incorrigible city. God is named only in the quote of Psalm 118:26, but his salvific purpose for Jerusalem and Israel through the Sent One underlies the entire lament.

I am not urging a cutting and pasting of Lukan text. Luke 13:31–35 must stay where it is in the journey narrative and so must 19:41–44. Instead I urge interpreters of Luke to *read* them together, to *see* them together, as a cohesive lament that Luke divides and distributes to direct the reader's attention to the organization and purpose of a concentric journey narrative.[11]

By the textual linkages described above Luke provides interpretive guidance for Theophilus and for us. Consider this plot line: God's chosen but unrecognized king receives a death threat; he departs into multiple locations, gaining followers as he goes; they hail him king at Jerusalem; and at God's house he contemplates the institution's future. One other biblical plot line exhibits all of these turns and moments in the life of God's chosen king. That king is the unique ideal historical king of Israel, David, son of Jesse;

---

11. By his literary and poetic tie between Luke 13:34–35 and 19:41–44, Luke directs readers' attention to the last episode of the journey. And by the sequential tie between 13:31–33 and 9:51–56, Luke directs readers' attention to the beginning of the first episode of the journey. Luke 13:31–33 is the beginning of the beginning of the journey; 13:34–35 is the beginning of the end of the journey.

while the king of Luke's Gospel is the unique eschatological king that the angels announced, Jesus, son of God. The Gospel writer prompts his readers to pursue a more detailed comparison of kings' journeys, those of Jesus and David, which is the comparison we turn to in chapter 13.[12]

---

12. Luke 13:31 also evokes Jezebel's threat at Jezreel of imminent death to Elijah. Her threat and Elijah''s subsequent journey shows evident parallels to Herod's threat against Jesus and Jesus' subsequent journey. The respective journeys run in thematic parallel for several episodes, but eventually the journeys cease to be parallel. See Appendix 2.

13

Jesus' Journey and David's Progress

THE THIRD GOSPEL RARELY brings up David, who was Israel's ideal historical king. David's name appears in Luke only at 1:32–33; 2:4, 11; 18:38–39; and 20:41–44. But, as we will see, Luke brings David's *story* into comparison with Jesus' journey in a way that exalts Jesus as king.

Luke persistently puts forward the kingdom of God theme in the episodes of his narrative about Jesus. The theme pervades Jesus' journey to Jerusalem. It comes as no surprise that great King David boasts a place in Luke's continued emphasis on God's kingdom. Readers who link 13:31–33 and 9:51–56 as parts of one departure narrative of Jesus find that this departure story in Luke evokes the story of David's departure from Saul's court in 1 and 2 Samuel. The journey of King Jesus in Luke's Gospel maintains a certain kind of parallel to the progress of King David in the Old Testament, from the night the future king fled from Saul to the day of the Davidic Covenant.

Preparation

Now we will trace how Jesus' journey in Luke links to David's story as provided in the Septuagint (LXX). In Luke's time (first century), most people of the ancient world read the Bible in a Greek version. When Jesus reads from Isaiah (Luke 4:16–20), for example, he reads from the LXX, not from the Hebrew Bible. When the narrator proclaims John the Baptist's calling (Luke 3:4–6), he quotes the LXX of Isaiah, not the Hebrew of Isaiah. When Luke arranges Jesus' journey to Jerusalem in parallel with David's progress toward the throne of Israel, he envisions David's story as given in the LXX.

Our journey-to-journey linkage details given below connect Luke specifically to the LXX, but usually linkages may be clearly seen by comparing Lukan journey sections to portions of David's progress as read in the same-numbered chapters and verses of 1 and 2 Samuel. The numbering of chapters and verses in our portions of the LXX (1 and 2 Reigns) run generally the same as in the analogous portions of the Hebrew Bible (1 and 2 Samuel). Differences will be identified.

	Luke	LXX, 1 Reigns
N	13:31–33	19:11
A	9:51–56	19:12–18
B	9:57–62	19:19–24
C	10:1–24	20:1–11
D	10:25–37	20:12–23
E	10:38–42	20:24–42
F	11:1–13	21:1–9
G	11:14–36	21:10—23:6
H	11:37–54	23:7–28
J	12:1–12	23:29—24:23
K	12:13–48	25:1—26:25
L	12:49—13:9	27:1—28:25
M	13:10–30	29:1—30:31
N	13:31–33	31:1–13 and 2 Rns 1:1–16, plus 4:5—5:5

The Old Testament portions in the bottom cell of the table above extend from 1 Reigns (31:1-13) into 2 Reigns (1:1–16), across a traditional boundary. Joyce Baldwin explains that "Originally one book in the Hebrew Bible, the text was first divided by the translators who framed the Greek version, where Samuel/Kings was known as 'Basileōn A, B, C, D' (the four books of the kingdoms)."[1] The arbitrariness of breaking the LXX version between 1 Kingdoms 31:13 and 2 Kingdoms 1:1 may have been due to the length constraints of ancient Greek scroll-making. In more recent centuries, it has become standard publishing practice to divide even the Hebrew text of Samuel/Kings into four books (1, 2 Samuel; 1, 2 Kings). So it is entirely appropriate for our purposes to unify texts on both sides of this artificial boundary.

1. Baldwin, *1&2 Samuel*, 17.

Below we continue the table of links between Jesus' journey to Jerusalem and David's progress to the throne of Israel:

	Luke	LXX, 2 Reigns
N'	13:34–35	1:17–27
M'	14:1–24	2:1–11
L'	14:25–35	2:12–16
K'	15:1–32	2:17–32
J'	16:1–13	3:1–11
H'	16:14—17:10	3:12–21
G'	17:11–37	3:22–34
F'	18:1–8	3:35–39
E'	18:9–17	4:1–6a
D'	18:18–30	4:6b–12
C'	18:31—19:10	5:1–16
B'	19:11–27	5:17–25
A'	19:28–46	6:1–19
N'	13:34–35	6:20–23

Pairs of texts linking Jesus' journey and David's progress vary in literary and theological richness as paired texts. Some pairings show obvious literary parallels and pulse with theological possibilities. Other pairings offer less.

When Luke juxtaposes an episode from Jesus' journey that evokes an episode from 1–2 Reigns, he prompts us to make textual comparisons regarding kingdom, power, and authority. He prompts us to ask how David or others compare with Jesus' teaching or example of the kingdom of God. Sometimes, however, even rather often, Jesus comes into comparison, not with David, but with Saul, or Jonathan, or a military leader, or with some other person in David's story. Still, the interpretive question remains: how do this person's words or actions compare in the kingdom of God with the teaching or example of Jesus?[2] This chapter explores links of Luke's Sections A, N, N', and A' to the progress of David.

---

2. Sections of the Lukan journey narrative seem to provide commentary or midrash on sections of the Davidic progress. Sometimes the midrash has qualities of the familiar two midrash types, Halakhic and Haggadic. Often the midrash has unfamiliar qualities, but always Luke's purpose is to exalt Jesus Christ when comparing the narratives.

Luke 13:31–33, 9:51–56, and 1 Reigns 19:11–18

Reading Lukan Sections N and A together evokes David's sudden departure from home after Michal's warning, "If you do not save your own life this night, tomorrow you will be put to death." (1 Rns 19:11). The aggregated departure episodes of Luke (N and A) evoke David's departure story in 1 Rns 19:11–19 by multiple links. Most prominently this arises from the Lukan narrator's use of *aggelos* ("messenger") in the manner of the LXX translator's vocabulary in 1 Rns 19:11–19. Luke frequently uses *aggelos* to mean "angel," but quite rarely to mean a human messenger. Those who are "sent" in Luke are *aggeloi* only in three places, two of which have to do with John the Baptist (7:24, 27; 9:52). Luke's unusual use of *aggeloi* in Luke 9:52 correlates to seven occurrences of the word *aggeloi* as messengers in 1 Rns 19:11–21.

Luke 13:31 *At that very hour (en autē tē ōra)* some Pharisees came and said to him, "Get away from here, for Herod wants to kill you." ³² And he said to them, "Go and tell that fox, 'Behold, I cast out demons and perform cures *today and tomorrow, and the third day I finish my course*. ³³ Nevertheless, I must go on my way *today and tomorrow and the day following*, for it cannot be that a prophet should perish away from Jerusalem."	1 Rns 19:11 *And it happened in that night (en tē nukti ekeinē)* that Saoul sent messengers *(apesteile . . . aggelous)* to Dauid's house to keep watch over him to *put him to death* in the *morning*. And his wife Melchol told Dauid, saying, "If you do not save your own life *this night, tomorrow* you will be *put to death*." ¹² And Melchol let Dauid down through the window, and he departed and flew away and escaped. ¹³ And Melchol took and laid the cenotaph on the bed, and she put goats' liver by its head and covered them with a garment. ¹⁴ And *Saoul sent messengers (apesteile . . . aggelous)* to take Dauid, and they said he was unwell. ¹⁵ And he sent for Dauid, saying, "Bring him to me on the bed, that I may *put him to death*." ¹⁶ And *the messengers (aggeloi) come*, and behold, the cenotaph is on the bed, and goats' liver by its head. ¹⁷ And Saoul said to Melchol, "Why have you thus deceived me and sent off my enemy, and he has escaped?" And Melchol said to Saoul, "He said, 'Send me off, but if not, I will *put you to death*.'" ¹⁸ And Dauid fled and escaped and came to Samouel at Harmathaim and told him all that Saoul did to him, And Dauid and Samouel *went and settled at Nauath in Rama*. ¹⁹ And it was told to Saoul, saying, "Behold, Dauid is *at Nauath in Rama*."
Luke 9:51 When the days drew near for him to be taken up, he set his face to go to Jerusalem. ⁵² And *he sent messengers (apesteilen aggelous)* ahead of him, who went and entered a village of the Samaritans, to make preparations for him. ⁵³ But the people did not receive him, because his face was set toward Jerusalem. ⁵⁴ And when his disciples James and John saw it, they said, "Lord, do you want us to tell fire to come down from heaven *and consume them*?" ⁵⁵ But he turned and rebuked them. ⁵⁶ And *they went on to another village*.	

The departure stories have other corresponding features: similar introductory clauses, a king intent on murder (Saul and Herod), a concerned advocate of indeterminate trustworthiness (Pharisees and Michal), an urging to depart immediately, and the episodes both end with traveling on to another village.

Luke contrasts Jesus and David, and by that contrast shows David's limitations and Jesus' supremacy. While David is silent about the imminence and power of the threat against his life, Jesus is not. Jesus assures the Pharisees that no harm will come to himself at the hand of Herod and that there is no hurry to leave Galilee, because Jesus is in control, not Herod. David fails to express confidence in God's protection of his life and in God's sovereign control of events. He caves in to the threat and submits to Michal's escape plan. David is vulnerable, Jesus is not, and their journeys begin.

Luke 13:34-35, 19:28-46 and 2 Reigns 6:1—7:17

Section A' (Luke 19:28–46) records the journey's end, a triumphal entry of Jesus riding on a donkey never previously used to carry people. He enters Jerusalem as the arriving king. Once there Jesus laments the unresponsiveness of the city to its messianic visitation. Similarly, Section N' (13:34–35) is a lament over Jerusalem's unresponsiveness, which will be tested again when he "comes" (35). The lament in chapter 13 recounts Jesus' longing for an open-hearted Jerusalem, and then the lament in chapter 19 concludes in sad resignation that "Jerusalem's mind" is firmly closed to Jesus (19:42, 44d). The combination of these texts reminds the reader of an OT king who brings the Ark of the Covenant into Jerusalem on a new cart, God's special presence arriving into the center of Israelite worship.

The combined story beginning at 19:28 in Luke (A' and N') evokes by multiple links the arrival of David, the king, and of God, the king of kings, to Jerusalem in 2 Rns 6:1—7:17. Jesus the arriving king links in various ways to the arriving king David *and* to God arriving, as represented by his ark. The disciples of Jesus fill the role of both David and of David's men as those who accompany the arrival of the king of kings.[3]

The aggregated Sections A' and N' (sequenced as Luke 19:28–41, then 13:34–35, and then 19:42–44) link by plot and language to 2 Rns 6:1–23, as shown in the paired citations below. I have broken up both lengthy texts into smaller units for clarity. Observations of linking features and some interpretative comments follow each paired citation respectively.

---

3. As king of kings God calls David his "slave" (*doulos,* 2 Rns 7:8).

Luke 19:28 And when he had said these things, he went on ahead, going up to Jerusalem. ²⁹ When he drew near to Bethphage and Bethany, at the mount that is called Olivet, he sent two of the disciples, ³⁰ saying, "Go into the village in front of you, where on entering you will find *a colt tied, on which no one has ever yet sat* (*eph' hon oudeis pōpote anthrōpōn ekathisen*). Untie it and bring it here. ³¹ If anyone asks you, 'Why are you untying it?' you shall say this: 'The Lord has need of it.'" ³² So those who were sent went away and found it just as he had told them. ³³ And as they were untying the colt, its owners said to them, "Why are you untying the colt?" ³⁴ And they said, "The Lord has need of it." ³⁵ And they brought it to Jesus, and throwing their *cloaks* (*ta himatia*) on the colt, they set Jesus on it.

2 Rns 6:1 And Dauid again gathered every young man of Israel, about seventy thousand. ² And he arose and went, Dauid and all the people with him, from the rulers of Ioudas on an ascent, to bring up from there the ark of God on which the name of the Lord of hosts who is seated on the cheroubin upon it is called. ³ And he loaded the ark of the Lord on *a new (kainēn) cart* and brought it out of the house of Aminadab which was on the hill, and Oza and his brothers, sons of Aminadab, were leading the cart ⁴ with the ark, and his brothers were going in front of the ark.

The most striking link is that of Jesus mounted on an unused donkey and the ark of God mounted on a new cart. Both Jesus and God are honored for this momentous arrival by a new chariot or throne. Luke introduces the topic of garments here, as the disciples partially undress in order to provide suitable covering for their arriving king's throne (the donkey). David's state of partial undress in order to honor God becomes an issue in the following two units of 2 Rns 6.

Luke 19:36 And as he rode along, they spread their cloaks (*ta himatia*) on the road. ³⁷ As he was drawing near—already on the way down the Mount of Olives—the whole multitude of his disciples began to *rejoice and praise God with a loud voice (chairontes ainein ton theon phōnē megalē)* for all the mighty works that they had seen, ³⁸ saying, "Blessed is the King who comes in the name of the Lord! Peace in heaven and glory in the highest!"	2 Rns 6:5 And Dauid and the sons of Israel were *sporting before the Lord with tuned instruments, with strength and with songs and with cinyras and with nablas and with drums and with cymbals and with flutes.* ⁶ And they came to the threshing floor of Nodab, and Oza reached out his hand to the ark of God to steady it and took hold of it, for the bull calf caused it to swerve, to steady it. ⁷ And the Lord was angry with Oza, and God struck him there, and he died there beside the ark of the Lord before God. ⁸ And Dauid was disheartened because God breached a breach upon Oza, and that place was called the Breach of Oza to this day. ⁹ And Dauid was afraid of the Lord in that day, saying, "How will the ark of the Lord come to me?" ¹⁰ And Dauid did not want to turn aside the ark of the covenant of the Lord to him in the city of Dauid, and Dauid turned it aside into the house of Abeddara the Geththite. ¹¹ And the ark of the Lord sat in the house of Abeddara the Geththite three months, and the Lord blessed the whole house of Abeddara and all that belonged to him. ¹² And it was told King Dauid, saying, "The Lord has blessed the house of Abeddara and all that belongs to him because of the ark of God." And Dauid went and brought up the ark of the Lord from the house of Abeddara to the city of Dauid *with rejoicing (en euphrosunē).* ¹³ *And there were with them seven bands carrying the ark and a sacrifice: calf and lamb.* ¹⁴ *And Dauid struck upon tuned instruments before the Lord, and Dauid was girded with a distinguishing garment (stolēn exallon).* ¹⁵ And Dauid and all the house of Israel brought up the ark of the Lord *with shouting (meta kraugēs) and with sound (phōnēs) of trumpet.*

Jesus' disciples do not have the musical skills or instruments that David and his men have, but the disciples give full voice in their own way to honor the king as he approaches. The "peace in heaven and glory in the highest" that they shout resounds in ironic correspondence to the holiness of God that takes Oza's life and that temporarily discourages David. David's "linen ephod" (6:14), is David's state of undress that scandalizes Michal in 6:20 below.[4] The story in 2 Reigns does not imply that anyone removed outer garments to spread either for covering or for a royal pavement, but in the Lukan episode (19:35, 36) they were.

---

4. The ESV translates the garment as "linen ephod," the *New English Translation of the Septuagint* gives "distinguishing garment," and the Brenton translation of the LXX has "fine long robe." Another possibility is "jumping robe" (my translation).

Luke 19:39 And some of the Pharisees in the crowd said to him, "Teacher, *rebuke your disciples.*" ⁴⁰ He answered, "I tell you, *if these were silent, the very stones would cry out.*"	2 Rns 6:16 And it happened, as the ark of the Lord was entering the city of Dauid, that Melchol the daughter of Saoul was peeking through the window and saw King Dauid dancing and striking up before the Lord, and she despised him in her heart. ¹⁷ And they brought the ark of the Lord and set it in its place into the midst of the tent that Dauid pitched for it, and Dauid offered whole burnt offerings and peace offerings before the Lord. ¹⁸ And Dauid finished offering up the whole burnt offerings and the peace offerings and blessed the people in the name of the Lord of hosts ¹⁹ and distributed to all the people, to all the host of Israel from Dan to Bersabee, from man until woman, to each a small loaf of bread and a portion of roasted bread and a cake from a frying-pan, and all the people went back, each to his home. ²⁰ And Dauid returned to bless his household, and Melchol the daughter of Saoul came out to meet Dauid and blessed him and said, *"How the king of Israel has honored himself today, who was uncovered today in the eyes of his own slaves' maids, as one of the disrobed dancers uncovers himself!"* ²¹ And Dauid said to Melchol, "I will dance before the Lord; blessed be *the Lord who chose me over your father and over all his house to appoint me as leader for his people, for Israel*, and I will play and dance before the Lord, ²² and I will again be uncovered thus, *and I will be worthless in your eyes and with the maids with whom you said I am held in honor.*" ²³ And to Melchol daughter of Saoul there was no child to the day of her death.

David's wife Michal raises an objection to the grand arrival in 2 Samuel, as do the Pharisees in Luke 19. Michal sees David, particularly in his degree of undress, but does not "see" the ark of God in the way that David sees it or rejoice in the Lord as he does. She complains to him because she is scandalized by his behavior. The Pharisees can honor Jesus as a peer, a "teacher" (Luke 19:39), but when Jesus' disciples honor him as "the king who comes in the name of the Lord" (38), this offends their propriety and their theological plausibility structure. They want Jesus to put a halt to such liberties in his disciples' behavior. The theme of 'seeing but not seeing' as a linking feature begins in the story of Michal's reaction (2 Rns 6:16, 20, 22), continues in Luke among Pharisees who do not agree that Jesus is the blessed coming one (Luke 19:39), and concludes in Jesus' lament (13:35; 19:42, 44).[5]

---

5. I inserted Luke 13:34–35 into the Luke 19 episodes at the point where similarities to 2 Rns most abound.

Luke 19:41 And when he drew near and saw the city, he wept over it, ⁴² saying,	2 Rns 7:1 And it happened, when the king sat in *his house* (*en tō oikō autou*) and the Lord had given him an inheritance round about from all his enemies who were round about him, ² that the king said to *the prophet Nathan* (*pros Nathan ton prophētēn*), "Behold, indeed I am living in *a house* (*en oikō*) of cedar, and the ark of God stays in the midst of the tent" (*en mesō tēs skēnēs*). ³ And Nathan said to the king, "Go, and do all that is in your heart; for the Lord is with you." ⁴ And it happened on that night that a word of the Lord came to Nathan, saying: ⁵ Go, and say to my slave Dauid: This is what the Lord says: You shall not build me *a house* (*oikon*) for me to live in; ⁶ for I have not lived in *a house* (*en oikō*) from the day I brought up the sons of Israel from Egypt to this day, and I was moving about in a *temporary abode* and in *a tent* (*en katalumati kai en skēnē*). ⁷ In all places to which I have moved about among all Israel, speaking did I speak with one tribe of Israel whom I commanded to shepherd my people Israel, saying, "Why is it that you have not built me *a house* (*oikon*) of cedar?"
Luke 13:34 "O Jerusalem, Jerusalem, the city that kills *the prophets* (*tous prophētas*) and stones those who are sent to it! How often would I have gathered your children together as a hen gathers her brood under her wings, and you were not willing! ³⁵ *Behold, your house* (*ho oikos humōn*) is forsaken. And I tell you, you *will not see me* (*ou mē idēte me*) until you say, 'Blessed is he who comes in the name of the Lord!'"	

In 2 Reigns there are shifts of time, topic, and conversation partner beginning at 7:1, introducing a new but related episode of the narrative. Likewise in both Luke 13:34 and 19:41 new but related material begins: Jesus unexpectedly cries out in lament, speaking to the city Jerusalem as a dying being. Jesus claimed to be the shelter, the safe haven, for the entire Jewish leadership in Jerusalem, but they were satisfied instead with their own "house" (13:35). Jesus' word about "your house," the temple of God or perhaps the "household of Jerusalem", links to what the prophetic voice of the Lord in 2 Reigns says about "a house for me to live in" (7:5, 7).⁶ Jerusalem's house, as Jesus speaks prophetically, is "forsaken," vacant. Likewise David's creative idea for God's "house" lacks merit; it will not happen in David's lifetime.

---

6. The "house" of Jerusalem may not be a reference to the temple of God, although Luke's rhetorical moves imply as much. See Green, *Luke*, 539.

| Luke 19:42 "Would that you, even you, had known on this day the *things that make for peace* (*ta pros eirēnēn*)! But now they are *hidden from your eyes* (*ekrubē apo ophthalmōn sou*). | 2 Rns 7:8 And now this is what you shall say to my slave Dauid: This is what the Lord Almighty says: *I took you* from the sheepfold for you to be leader for my people, for Israel [9] and *was with you* in all to which you went and *destroyed all your enemies* from before you and made you renowned like the name of the great ones who are upon the earth. [10] And *I will appoint a place* for my people Israel and *will plant* them, and they will encamp by themselves, and they *will be distressed no more*, and *a son of injustice shall not add to afflict them as formerly* [11] from the days that I appointed judges over my people Israel, and *I will give you rest from all your enemies*, and the Lord will tell you that you will make *a house* (*oikon*) for him. |

The Lord gave David personal peace in terms of defeated enemies and respect from Israel's people (7:9). The peace of national stability will come from the Lord as well: definite and secure boundaries, freedom from oppression, defeat of enemies, and centralized worship of the Lord in a temple (10–11). Jesus, however, viewing the national capitol and its temple from the slope of the Mount of Olives, laments that the city as the soul of Israel turned a blind eye to the other "things that make for peace," resulting now in punitive blindness. The topic of "enemies" arising in this unit of 2 Reigns (7:9, 11) comes to the fore in the next unit of Luke (9:43).

| Luke 19:43 For the *days will come upon you* (*hēksousin hēmerai epi se*), when your enemies (*hoi echthroi sou*) will set up a barricade around you and surround you and hem you in on every side [44] and tear you down to the ground, you and your children within you. And they will not leave one stone upon another in you, because you did not know the time of your visitation" (*ton kairon tēs episkopēs sou*). | 2 Rns 7:12 And it will be *if your days are fulfilled* (*plērōthōsin hēmerai sou*) and you lie down with your fathers, that I will raise up your offspring after you who shall be from your belly, and I will prepare his kingdom; [13] he shall build me a house (*oikon*) for my name, and I will restore his throne forever. [14] I will be a father to him, and he shall be a son to me, and *if his injustice comes* (*ean elthē hē adikia autou*), then *I will punish him with a rod of men and with attacks of sons of men*, [15] but I will not remove my mercy from him, as I removed it from those whom I removed from before me. [16] And *his house* (*ho oikos*) and his kingdom shall be made sure forever before me, and his throne shall be restored forever. [17] According to all these words and according to all this vision, thus Nathan spoke to Dauid. |

The coming of Jesus as king to Jerusalem is a time of destiny (*kairos*) within the eternal Davidic dynasty (2 Rns 7:13, 16). Jerusalem refuses to know this, making the days of Jesus arrival a time of "injustice" (2 Rns 7:14) and subsequent punishment for those in power and for the place of Israel's throne (Luke 19:43–44).

The story in 1 Reigns continues as David, entering the tent and sitting before the Lord, "found his own heart to pray this prayer" (7:28), a prayer of gratitude and worship (7:18–29). In similar fashion, the Lukan story of Jesus immediately transitions to the topic of prayer in the temple (19:45–46). Jesus drives out the vendors of sacrificial animals and grains, protesting "My house shall be a house of prayer, but you have made it a den of robbers." The co-texts, however, cease to have further coordinate details. In Luke's narrative these verses serve as a transitional unit that concludes the juxtaposition of Jesus and David.

Most of the links above between Luke 19:28–46 and 13:34–35 as an aggregate and 2 Rns 6:1–7:17 are topical and/or theological in nature, and lack exact correspondences of vocabulary. There are, however, several similar expressions and numerous parallel concepts.

In the current and previous subsections of this Chapter we show how Luke's Sections N and N' can be read with Luke 9:51–56 and 19:29–46 respectively to evoke the beginning and ending of David's progress to the throne of Israel. My wording—"can be read with"—deliberately avoids any implication that Sections N and N' should be dislocated and moved to the beginning and end of Jesus' journey. On the contrary, Sections N and N' occupy their own sequential places as episodes linking to the middle parts of David's progress. To underline this point, we now turn to the linkage in Reigns of Luke 13:31–33 and afterward to the linkage in Reigns of 13:34–35.

Luke 13:31–33 and 1 Reigns 31:1—2 Reigns 1:16

First we must exlore a question regarding the 2 Reigns side of this linkage. 2 Rns 1:1–16 retains a literary twin text (2 Rns 4:5–12) and narrative completion (2 Rns 5:1–5). The literary twin and the narrative completion combine with 2 Rns 1:1–16 to round off a single story. Events narrated in 4:5–12 take place about two years later than those in 1:1–16, with the intervening narrative mostly centering on the rise and demise of Abner and Iebosthe (Ishbosheth, Mephibosthe) in the northern kingdom. The texts are fraternal twins in that they share the same plot line: in both, messengers come to David helpfully bearing news that a competitor for the throne of Israel has been killed, and bring evidence of their claim. In both, David states his verdict of death for the messengers, noting that in each case their death sentence arises from their own despicable actions. In both, David commands his men to do the executions. The similarities of 1:1–16 and 4:5 –12 invite our curiosity about their literary and theological relationship.

In addition to similarities, these texts show sequential plot development. When facing the messenger in 4:5–8, David mentions the other messenger he encountered in 1:1–16. He says, "The Lord lives, who redeemed my life out of every adversity, for the one who told me that Saoul had died—and he was as one bringing good news before me—and I seized and killed him at Sekelak, to whom I ought to have given a reward for good tidings" (9–10). This back-reference strongly ties the two texts together in plot.

Further, in terms of context, in 1:1–16 the kingship is about to fall on David's shoulders because Saul is dead. Immediately the men of Judah anoint David king over the house of Judah (2:4). Likewise, in 4:8-12 the kingship again is about to fall on David's shoulders because Ishbosheth is dead. Immediately the tribes of Israel anoint David king to reign over all Israel (5:1–3). And *only then* in 5:4–5 comes the account of David's regnal years, *including David's years as king over Judah*. This regnal refrain collects 2 Rns 1:1–16 and 4:5—5:5 into a single story.

Consequently we will pursue links between Section N of Luke to 1 Rns 31:1—2 Rns 1:16 *and* to 2 Rns 4:5—5:5.[7] Section N of Luke, 13:31–33, is very short and the combined texts in 1 and 2 Rns are quite long, so that the links between Luke and 2 Rns are general and thematic. For example, "Herod wants to kill you" (Luke 13:31b) (the references being to Herod, tetrarch of Galilee, and to Jesus, king in the kingdom of God) links doubly, first, to the Philistine lords putting King Saul to death, and second, to Rekcha and Baana killing King Mephibosthe. The kings of the north were actually killed, but Jesus in Luke 13:31–33 at this point is only under a supposed threat of death.

---

7. Second Reigns 4:5–12 and 5:1–5 have their own sequential linking roles to Sections C′ and D′ of Luke in addition to special ties to Section A. In this regard, two short portions of Reigns bear a double function just as do two portions (13:31–33; 34–35) of Luke's journey narrative.

JESUS' JOURNEY AND DAVID'S PROGRESS 163

Luke 13:31 At that very hour some Pharisees came and said to him, "Get away from here, for Herod wants to kill you."	1 Rns 31:1 And the *allophyles were fighting against Israel*, and the men of Israel *fled* from before the allophyles, and wounded fell on Mount Gelboue. [2] And allophyles engaged Saoul and his sons, and allophyles smote Ionathan and Aminadab and Melchisa, sons of Saoul. [3] And the battle pressed hard upon Saoul, and the darters, the bowmen found him, and he was wounded in the abdomen. [4] And Saoul said to the one who bore his armor, "Draw your sword, and thrust me through with it, lest these uncircumcised come and thrust me through and make sport of me." And the one who bore his armor was unwilling, for he feared greatly, and *Saoul took the sword and fell upon it*. [5] And the one who bore his armor saw that Saoul had died, and he also fell upon his sword and died with him. [6] And *Saoul and his three sons and the one who bore his armor died together in that day*. [7] And the men of Israel who were on the other side of the valley and those beyond the Jordan saw that the men of Israel fled and that Saoul had died, and his sons, and they forsook their towns and fled, and the allophyles came and settled in them. [8] And it happened on the next day that the allophyles came to strip the dead, and they found Saoul and his three sons fallen on the mountains of Gelboue. [9] And they brought him back and stripped off his armor and sent them into the land of allophyles round about, proclaiming the good news to their idols and to their people. [10] And they put his armor in the Astarteion and they fastened his body on the wall of Baithsan. [11] And the inhabitants of Iabis of Galaaditis heard what the allophyles had done to Saoul, [12] and every man of might arose and went *the whole night* and took the body of Saoul and the body of Ionathan his son from the wall of Baithsan and brought them to Iabis and burned them there. [13] And they took and buried their bones under the cultivated ground of Iabis and fasted seven days.	2 Rns 4:5 And sons of Remmon the Berothite, Rekcha and Baana, went, and about the heat of the day they entered into the house of Memphibosthe, and he was sleeping on the bed at noonday, [6] and behold, the doorkeeper of the house was cleaning wheat, and she became drowsy and slept, and Rekcha and Baana, the brothers, escaped notice [7] and entered into the house, and Memphibosthe was asleep on his couch in his bedchamber, and *they attacked him and put him to death and beheaded him* and took his head and returned by the western road *the whole night*.

Luke 13:32 links to 2 Rns 1:1–16 in two ways: by reference in each to "the third day" (1:2) and by the theme of defeated satanic opponents. In Luke Jesus casts out demons while in 1 Rns, as one link, David discerns and does away with an Amalekite who is also a thief and liar. In 2 Rns 4:8–12, as another link, David sees through the supposed enterprising loyalty of two men to discern their wickedness, and puts the men to death. David sees and acts for the kingdom of God in the moral realm; Jesus the King asserts his authority over the spiritual realm.

Luke 13:32 And he said to them, "Go and tell that fox, 'Behold, I cast out demons and perform cures today and tomorrow, and the third day (*sēmeron kai aurion kai tē tritē*) I finish my course.

2 Rns 1:1 And it happened, after Saoul died, that Dauid returned from smiting Amalek, and *Dauid settled two days in Sekelak.* [2] *And it happened on the third day* (*hēmera tē tritē*) and behold, a man came from the camp of Saoul's people, and his clothes were torn, and earth was on his head. And it happened, when he came in to Dauid, that he fell to the ground and did obeisance to him. [3] And Dauid said to him, "Where have you come from?" And he said to him, "I have come safe from the camp of Israel." [4] And Dauid said to him, "What is this word? Tell me!" And he said, "The people fled from the battle, and many of the people have fallen and died, and Saoul died, and his son Ionathan died." [5] And Dauid said to the lad who was telling him, "How do you know that Saoul and his son Ionathan died?" [6] And the lad who was telling him said, "By accident I had an encounter on Mount Gelboue, and behold, Saoul was propped up on his spear, and behold, the chariots and the horse captains drew close to him. [7] And he looked on the things behind him and saw me and called me, and I said, 'Behold, here am I.' [8] And he said to me, 'Who are you?' And I said 'I am an Amalekite.' [9] And he said to me, 'Do stand over me, and put me to death, for a terrible darkness has laid hold of me, for all my life is in me.' [10] And I stood over him and put him to death, for I knew that he could not live after he had fallen, *and I took the crown that was on his head and the armlet that was on his arm, and I have brought them here to my lord.*" [11] And Dauid took hold of his clothes and tore them, and all the men who were with him tore their clothes. [12] And they beat themselves and wept and fasted until evening for Saoul and for his son Ionathan and for the people of Ioudas and for the house of Israel, because they were smitten with a sword. [13] And Dauid said to the lad who had told him, "Where are you from?" And he said, "I am son of a man, a resident alien, an Amalekite." [14] *And Dauid said to him, "How did you not fear to bring your hand to destroy the Lord's anointed?"* [15] And Dauid called one of his lads and said, "Drawing near, fall upon him," and he struck him down, and he died. [16] And Dauid said to him, "Your blood be on your head, for your mouth answered against you, saying, 'I put to death the Lord's anointed.'"

2 Rns 4:8 And they brought the head of Memphibosthe to Dauid at Chebron and said to the king, "*Behold, the head of Memphibosthe son of Saoul your enemy, who used to seek your life, and the Lord gave the lord king vengeance on his enemies, as this day, on Saoul your enemy and on his offspring.*" [9] *And Dauid answered Rekcha and his brother Baana sons of Remmon the Berothite and said to them, "The Lord lives, who redeemed my life out of every adversity,* [10] *for the one who told me that Saoul had died—and he was as one bringing good news before me—and I seized and killed him at Sekelak, to whom I ought to have given a reward for good tidings.* [11] *And now wicked men have killed a righteous man on his bed in his own house! And now I shall require his blood at your hand and destroy you from the earth."* [12] *And Dauid commanded his lads, and they killed them and docked their hands and their feet and hung them at the well at Chebron, and the head of Memphibosthe they buried in the tomb of Abenner son of Ner.*

We turn to links of Luke 13:33 to 2 Rns 5:1–5, based on the justification above. The progress of David to be king of Israel reaches its penultimate stage in 2 Rns 5:1–5, a stage meriting an overall summary of regnal years by the narrator (4–5). The journey narrative of Jesus also arrives at half way in Luke 13:33. In his teaching there, Jesus, for the only time in Sections A–N, speaks of *dying in Jerusalem*. The Lukan narrator two other times in Sections A–N identified Jerusalem as the destination (9:51; 13:22), but never mentioned until now Jesus' death in the city.[8] Even in Luke 13:33 the connection between Jesus and death in Jerusalem is not explicit, but strongly implied: "a prophet," he says, may not "perish away from Jerusalem." The city will be the place of his death. David also, by implication, will die in Jerusalem, but after forty years of reign as king (2 Rns 5:4).[9]

The other link between Luke 13:33 and 2 Rns 5:1–5 regards process rather than climax. Jesus "must go on [his] way today and tomorrow and the day following": what he must yet do will take some time. Similarly, the elders of Israel interpret David's military leadership under Saul, happening "yesterday and the third day," as time well spent exhibiting the qualities of "shepherd" for Israel (5:2). The respective kings show their kingly authority and power in the extended course of daily life.

Luke 13:33 Nevertheless, I must go on my way today and tomorrow and the day following (*sēmeron kai aurion kai tē tritē*), for it cannot be that a prophet should perish away from Jerusalem.'	2 Rns 5:1 And all the tribes of Israel came to Dauid at Chebron and said to him, "Behold, we are your bone and your flesh, [2] and *yesterday and the third day* (*echthes kai tritēn*), while Saoul was king over us, it was you who led out and brought in Israel, and the Lord said to you: It is you who shall shepherd my people Israel, and it is you who shall become a ruler over Israel." [3] And all the elders of Israel came to the king at Chebron, and King Dauid made a covenant with them at Chebron before the Lord, and they anointed Dauid king over all Israel. [4] *Dauid was a son of thirty years when he began to reign, and he reigned forty years,* [5] *seven years and six months he reigned at Chebron over Ioudas, and thirty-three years he reigned over all Israel and Ioudas at Ierousalem.*

The links between King Jesus and King David, as they appear in Luke 13:31–33 and in our texts in 1 and 2 Rns, are links paralleling and contrasting their final destinies: Jesus and David will make their ways through various difficulties to be hailed as king in Jerusalem, but Jesus will perish there like a rejected prophet while David in the same city will die well-loved after a fruitful reign.

8. Even in Luke 9:44, just before the journey narrative, neither Jesus' death nor Jerusalem are explicitly mentioned.

9. Another, and very similar, statement of David's regnal years comes in the narrative just after his death (3 Rns 2:10–11). According to that summary, David died and was buried in the "city of David," or Jerusalem (see Acts 2:29).

Luke 13:34–35 and 2 Reigns 1:17–27

The laments of David in 2 Rns cry louder and longer than any laments for the dead in the rest of the Old Testament. The Pentateuch and 1 Reigns elsewhere record occasions of lament for the dead, but only by summary: there was mourning, grieving, and weeping, usually in public, in concert with the people; it was common to tear one's garments as an expression of grief and/or wear sackcloth (goat-hair fabric); grieving extended to thirty days, but no longer.[10] Cultural historians agree that grieving in ancient Middle Eastern cultures, including those of the Canaanites and Israelites, was highly ritualized and regimented.[11] Thus, even with minimal descriptions of grief, the scene of mourning with its familiar rituals could readily be imagined by ancient readers.

In 2 Reigns, however, the text records the very words of grief, words no doubt uttered within the well-worn rituals of grief for the dead: "Shall Abner die according to the death of Nabal? Your hands were not bound; your feet were not in fetters; he did not bring, like Nabal; before the sons of injustice you fell" (3:33–34). We also find David's complete ritual dirge for the fallen Saul and Jonathan in 2 Rns 1:17–27. This is the only complete dirge for the dead provided us in the Old Testament: it is intense, dramatic, and powerful, drawing the reader into the passion of David's loss.

---

10. Gen 23:2b; 37:34–35; Num 20:29; Deut 34:8; 1 Rns 25:1.

11. See, for example, Feldman, *Defilement and Mourning*, 8–11. The mourning practices of Philistines await accurate description.

Luke 13:34 "O Jerusalem, Jerusalem, the city that kills the prophets and stones those who are sent to it! How often would I have gathered your children together as a hen gathers her brood under her wings, and you were not willing! [35] Behold, your house is forsaken. And I tell you, you will not see me until you say, 'Blessed is he who comes in the name of the Lord!'"	2 Rns 1:17 And Dauid lamented this lamentation over Saoul and over his son Ionathan [18] and said to teach the sons of Ioudas—behold, it is written in a book of the upright— [19] Set up a monument, O Israel, for the wounded that have died upon your heights! How the mighty have fallen! [20] Tell it not in Geth, and proclaim it not in the exits of Ascalon, lest daughters of allophyles rejoice, lest daughters of the uncircumcised exult. [21] You mountains that are in Gelboue, let no dew descend, and let there be no rain upon you or fields of first fruits! For there the shield of the mighty was treated with vexation; Saoul's shield was not anointed with oil. [22] From the blood of wounded, from the fat of mighty ones, Ionathan's bow did not return empty to the rear, and Saoul's sword did not turn back empty. [23] Saoul and Ionathan, the beloved and lovely, not divided; comely in their life and in their death they were not divided; swift beyond eagles they were, and they had strength beyond lions. [24] O daughters of Israel, weep over Saoul, who clothed you with scarlet with your ornament, who brought gold ornament to your apparel. [25] How the mighty have fallen amidst the battle! Ionathan, a casualty upon your heights. [26] I grieve for you, my brother Ionathan; you were made very beautiful to me; your love to me was wonderful, beyond women's love. [27] How the mighty have fallen, and the weapons of war perished!

Jesus' Greco-Roman ritual lament (Luke 13:34–35) and David's lament in high Hebrew poetic style link, first and primarily, in that both are ritual laments appearing at the same place in the sequence of their respective stories. One could tease out further minor similarities, but detailed comparison mostly reveals contrasts of occasion, addressee, and style. In terms of a comparison of Jesus and David in the kingdom of God, David mourns the possible end of an Israelite dynasty in the deaths of both king and heir-apparent (the "house" of Saul). Jesus, however, mourns the passing of the house Israel centered in Jerusalem and the temple as the bearer of God's glory and servant of his purposes. The scope of David's grief is personal and national; the scope of Jesus' grief is personal, national, and eschatological.

Overview of the Textual Relations of Sections N and N′

The concentric center of the journey narrative points to David's story in 1 and 2 Reigns. Israelites looked back to David as their kingly ideal and virtual founder of the kingdom, so his story appropriately intersects with Jesus' story and the kingdom of God theme in Luke: the stories inform one another.[12] The journey of Jesus from Galilee to Jerusalem (Luke 9:51—19:46)

---

12. On kingly ideal and kingdom-founder, see Jones, "David," 261.

seemingly meanders over the countryside of Israel's highlands and seems to contain a random expanded collection of Jesus' teaching and a few healings. Luke, however, organizes the episodes of Jesus' journey in a deliberate way: episodes of the Lukan journey link in parallel sequence to episodes in David's life. Jesus' journey begins in Galilee and ends at the temple in Jerusalem. David's "journey" begins as he flees from Saul at Gibeah and ends in Jerusalem as he hears God's prophet promise David a familial house (unending dynasty) and a house (temple of God). David's "journey" is more properly both a spiritual "progress" from faltering faith to confident faith in God and a "progress" from fleeing as a homeless king-designate to arriving with the ark of God, as prince to God the king.

In review, Luke fashions an attention-getting beginning to Jesus' journey that recalls David's tumultuous exit from Saul's retinue. The Evangelist also deploys a lament of Jesus over the coming fall of Jerusalem to connect ironically (by thematic contrast) with rise of David under God's blessing to an everlasting throne. Literary fragments of departure and of lament found in the chiastic center of Luke's journey narrative have, nevertheless, their own coordinating role vis à vis episodes also in the center of David's progress. By consistently evoking episodes from 1 and 2 Reigns, Luke brings David's story into comparison with Jesus' journey in a way that interprets the kingdom of God and exalts Jesus as king.

Conclusion

BOTH HERE AND THERE provides to pastors and other Bible students an introduction to literary concentric parallelism in the Gospel of Luke. We explained the phenomenon of concentric parallelism, a common literary form in Greco-Roman antiquity even for historiography and biography. Luke, as a historian, biographer, theologian, and evangelist, presented large portions of the Jesus tradition in concentric form, doing so with theological intent.

We prepared readers of Luke to accept a possibility that the Evangelist presented portions of the Jesus tradition chiastically. Next we outlined tests to advance (or not advance) a possibility of concentric structure to a probability that Luke actually organized certain episodes into a concentric discourse. Further, testing large swathes of narrative, we confirmed that Luke arranged four extensive concentric discourses in the first two-thirds of his account of Jesus. And finally, we applied to them a hermeneutic that systematically exposes meaning in Luke's discourses.[1]

Luke provided a narrative to be both heard and read, but a narrative having additional riches for careful readers. Hearers of an oral performance of the journey narrative (9:51—19:46) probably could not retain an early episode's details, while hearing dozens of additional episodes over many minutes, to compare those details to a much later episode. It is more likely that a hearer could grasp connections between episodes and sections performed close together in the middle of the journey narrative or between sections of a shorter concentric discourse. It was by careful reading that Theopilus and others would perceive both structure and theology in the discourses.

---

1. We have only begun to find meaning in the journey narrative (Luke 9:51—19:46).

Theophilus, Luke's intended first reader, as a participant in literate culture, could discern this kind of complex parallel structure in a narrative about Jesus and about recent events in Israel. For him, claims of "certainty" or "truth" about reported events found legitimate expression in concentric parallelisms as well as in linear narratives.

Today's typical reader of Luke's narrative lives in a substantially different media culture where large concentric literary forms seldom appear. Certainly a modern concentric argument for a truth claim might not get much traction among readers, if any. Possibly it might not even be perceived as an argument. Instead, such a presentation might appear as a meaningless jumble of incomplete ideas. Today's reader requires training even to see concentric discourse, let alone understand what an author intends to communicate. We have provided training for students of Luke's Gospel to see and understand.

When we read Luke, his concentric discourses begin unannounced. We may eventually find them after multiple readings of the Gospel. We see "over here" one eye-catching feature that has a fraternal twin feature "over there." We pause and read the two contexts closer, finding other (perhaps less obvious) thematic, lexical, and even structural features in both contexts. We see evidence of deliberate parallel structuring. Then we may find other tandem texts that are arrayed between or beyond the previously observed "here and there." A concentric pattern emerges. But we were blind to it at the start.

When Theophilus read Luke's narrative, he faced similar challenges, except in two respects. First, of course, he read in Greek. He could more readily, for example, notice pairs of words occurring in restricted distribution. Second, and more importantly, Theophilus lived in, and likely was trained in, Greco-Roman literary culture, then dominant in Hellenized Israel. Theophilus probably also had experience reading and copying compex literary forms, including concentric presentations. He could readily "see" them, while we cannot readily "see" concentric forms due to our culture's pervasive practice of linear presentation.

Another "seeing" challenge facing today's readers of Luke is agreeing together on what we see, once we have seen something concentric. For example, numerous readers have seen evidence of a concentric structure in Luke's journey narrative and have written up schematic descriptions, sometimes with exegetical and theological commentary. But hardly any agree on the shape of the structure, on how many pairs of sections there are and where the textual boundaries between sections lie.

Using a shared analytical method would help us "see" texts together, even with expected challenges to details of method. Having no method at all commonly leads to subjective and idiosyncratic "seeing," arising from the reader's own theological concerns and sensitivities. This book borrows, modifies, practices, and offers a method that has promise for checking claims of chiastic textual structure.

One more criticism of claims for chiastic schemes is that such schemes tell more about the ingenuity of the claimant than about the biblical text. But a careful method consistently applied to biblical text undercuts that criticism. From studies in *Both Here and There*, clearly it is Luke's ingenuity, his genius, that shapes four concentric structures in the Third Gospel. Behind his ability stands the genius of the Holy Spirit to reveal in beautiful literary expression the glory of God and the glory of his Son.

Appendix 1

Glossary

Band. I use band in the literary sense only in Part 2 of *Both Here and There*. While the primary unit of analysis that we identify in Luke are its concentric sections (see below), sometimes there are enough overlapping themes among adjacent sections to justify collecting them into larger topical units called bands.

Chiasm or *Chiasmus* (*Chiastic*). I substitute chiasm or chiasmus as a synonym for concentric parallelism (see below), although other authors disagree with such a practice on definitional grounds.

Concentric Parallelism occurs in poetry and prose when an author organizes words and ideas reflectively so that the two halves of a text parallel each other in a reversed order. The first idea reflects in some way the final idea, the second idea mirrors distinctly or less distinctly the penultimate idea, and so on. Thus, large-scale prose compositions such as in Luke's narrative may have extensive sections that correspond in an ABCBA or ABCCBA fashion. This ancient and modern literary form is also variously called chiasm, chiasmus, ring-structure, inverted parallelism, introverted parallelism, reverse parallelism, step parallelism, *apantesis*, *epanodos*, and more.

Discourse or *Narrative Discourse.* As I use the terms, discourse happens when Luke organizes Jesus-stories to imply a theological message without overtly identifying it as a unified message. In Luke's Gospel, for example, the parallel accounts of Jesus' and John's origins (1:5–25 with 1:26–38; 1:39–80 with 2:1–40) prompt the reader to both compare and contrast the stories, even though Luke does not explicitly give notice to the reader about it. Luke discourses when he deliberately organizes together multiple episodes about

Jesus in an attention-arresting way (such as parallelism) that provokes in a reader consideration of an implied theology arising from the series of episodes.

Limited-Use Vocabulary describes the observation that a certain Greek word or phrase occurs only in three to five places in Luke's Gospel. We value these expressions as possible evidence that Luke intends two of the contexts to correspond literarily and theologically.

Literary (*Literary Structure, Literary Form, Literary Architecture*) refers to an author's deliberate application of artistic expression to written text, usually by application of conventions established in the historical development of the written language. Literary expression can be seen as high language while non-literary expression can be seen as low, or minimalist, language. A helpful analogy may be seen in building construction, when an architect designs a structure while a person throws up a shelter.

Narrative is Luke's term for compilations of stories about Jesus, including his own work (Luke 1:1). The term "Gospel," meaning an historical account, became attached to Matthew, Mark, Luke, and John only from the second century onwards in the writings of the early church fathers. Even in Mark 1:1, "gospel" refers to Mark's proclamation of Jesus rather than to a genre of literature. Luke calls his work a narrative.

Narrator in Luke's Gospel is the voice of Luke (see Luke 1:1–4) as he describes moments, persons, emotions, motivations, and outcomes in his narrative about Jesus. Luke assembled his narrative from various manuscript sources, sometimes borrowing their narrative voices as given, sometimes editing them, and sometimes shaping his own narrations. Behind all of these narrative choices remains Luke's posture of speaking for God, of knowing God's purposes and the ways of the kingdom, of being privy to God's knowledge of human minds and hearts.

Prime means the sections past the middle of a concentric form, distinguishing those sections from the ones before the middle. I attach the prime mark (′) to lettered designations for sections in the last half of a concentric form, as in ABCC′B′A′.

Restricted-Use Vocabulary describes an observation that a certain Greek word, phonemic series, or phrase occurs only in two places in Luke's Gospel. We value these expressions as primary evidence that Luke intends the two contexts to correspond literarily and theologically.

Rhetorical refers to formal qualities of artistically written Greek language.

Rhetorical Transition is a conventional and artistic device in Greek literature for passing from one topic to another smoothly. See Longenecker, *Rhetoric at the Boundaries*.

Section means a delineated portion of text that exhibits multiple thematic, structural, and lexical parallels to another delineated portion of text. Because of the quantity and nature of parallels to the other text, a section may be distinguished from preceding and following text. In *Both Here and There* sections sometimes divide into "parts" and sometimes may be seen grouped together as "bands." The primary unit of analysis that we identify in Luke, however, are its concentric sections.

Story. I sometimes substitute story as a synonym for narrative. Story does not imply fictional writing.

Structure (Form, Architecture) expresses the concept of deliberate large-scale artistic organization applied to compiled accounts of Jesus' life and ministry. Our particular project looks for concentrically parallel structures, but Luke also arranges structures that have simple parallels in forms such as ABAB.

Appendix 2

Jesus' Journey and Elijah's Journey

Jesus' journey toward Jerusalem Luke 9–12 also evokes and parallels the account of Elijah's flight from Jezebel in 1–2 Kings—to a certain extent. The following table of parallel journeys makes some assumptions. First, Luke could and did displace text from its relative position in his sources in order to pursue Luke's own rhetorical purpose in his narrative. Thus, the Lukan journey begins from 13:31–33, both for its parallel to David's journey and for its parallel to Elijah's journey. See Chapter 12 of *Both Here and There* for more background on common rhetorical practices of ancient authors.

Second, not every section in Kings names Elijah as the prophet in question. There is nevertheless a connective tissue of prophets, the prophetic spirit, and the voice of God that unites the story in Kings. Assuming the unity of these phenomena, we continue drawing thematic parallels between texts in sequence. Finally, in the table below for the usual reasons I try to avoid titling sections. Words in the "themes" columns are either quotes of thematic material from the texts (in italics, ESV) or titles *applied at the end of the study process* when similar textual words were unavailable (not italics).

Luke	Themes in Luke	Themes in Kings	Kings
Lk 13:31–33	Death warning	Death warning	1 Kg 19:1–3
9:51–56	the people did not receive him	The people refused	19:4–18
9:57–62	I will follow you	I will follow you	19:19–20
10:1–20	laborers	messengers	20:1–12
10:21–24	knows who the son is	know that I am the Lord	20:13–22
10:25–37	mercy	mercy	20:23–34
10:38–42	anxious and troubled	vexed and sullen	20:35–43
11:1–13	give him whatever	give it to me	21:1–29
11:14–36	word of God	word of the Lord	22:1–50
11:37–54	blood of all the prophets	Death of Elijah	22:51—2 Kg 2:25
12:1–12	leaven of the Pharisees	I am as you are	3:1–27
12:13–34	Too much food, what to eat	Not enough food	4:1–7
12:35–48	Ready for the master's return	?	?

The question marks under Kings indicate that substantial parallels do not continue beyond 2 Kg 4:7. Themes run parallel to an extent, but no further.

Luke draws some kind of a parallel between Jesus and Elijah/Elisha, yet does not round it to a conclusion. Broadly we can say that Luke compares the two biblical figures. Elijah is the great old covenant prophet, although not a writing prophet like Isaiah or Jeremiah. Even the coming of the "great and awesome Day of the Lord" (Mal 4:5; 3:1) would be marked by the presence of Elijah. Jesus, then, is the greater prophet and Son of Man who comes to establish God's kingdom. The Day of the Lord is the Day of the Son of Man (Luke 17:20–37).

From Luke 9 we learn that Jesus is the new and greater Moses. But since Elijah also appears with Jesus on the Mount of Transfiguration, perhaps we should expect Luke to develop that comparison in some way. This, then, is the way: Luke compares the journeys to an extent along shared thematic lines beginning from Luke 9.

Bibliography

Alexiou, Margaret. *The Ritual Lament in Greek Tradition*, edited by Dimitrios Yatromanolakis and Panagiotis Roilos. Lanham: Rowman and Littlefield, 2002.

Alter, Robert. *The Art of Biblical Narrative*. New York: Basic Books/Perseus, 1981.

Assis, Elie. "Chiasmus in Biblical Narrative: Rhetoric of Characterization." *Prooftexts* 22 (2002) 273–304.

Bailey, Kenneth E. *Poet & Peasant and Through Peasant Eyes*. Grand Rapids: Eerdmans, 1976.

Baldwin, Joyce G. *1 & 2 Samuel: An Introduction and Commentary*, Tyndale Old Testament Commentaries, edited by D. J. Wiseman. Leicester: InterVarsity, 1988.

Banwell, B. O., "King, Kingship," *The New Bible Dictionary*, edited by D. R. W. Wood and Ian Howard Marshall, 646–47. Downers Grove, IL: InterVarsity, 2001.

Beregovskaja, Eda Moiseevna. *Ocherki po eksperssivnomu sintaksisu* (Notes on Expressive Syntax). Moscow: Rokhos, 2004.

Blomberg, Craig. "Midrash, Chiasmus, and the Outline of Luke's Central Section." In *Gospel Perspectives: Studies in Midrash and Historiography* 3, edited by R. T. France and David Wiseman, 217–61. Sheffield: Journal for the Study of the Old Testament, 1983.

Bock, Darrell L. *Luke 1:1–9:50*. Baker Exegetical Commentary on the New Testament, edited by Moisés Silva. Grand Rapids: Baker, 1994.

———. *Luke 9:51–24:53*. Baker Exegetical Commentary on the New Testament, edited by Moisés Silva. Grand Rapids: Baker, 1996.

Borgman, Paul. *The Way according to Luke: Hearing the Whole Story of Luke-Acts*. Grand Rapids: Eerdmans, 2006.

Breck, John. *The Shape of Biblical Language: Chiasmus in the Scriptures and Beyond*. Crestwood, NY: St. Vladimir's Seminary, 1994.

Brodie, Thomas Louis. "Greco-Roman Imitation of Texts as a Partial Guide to Luke's Use of Sources." *Luke-Acts: New Perspectives from the Society of Biblical Literature Seminar*, edited by Charles H. Talbert, 17–46. New York: Crossroad, 1984.

Conzelmann, Hans. *The Theology of St. Luke*. Translated by Geoffrey Buswell. New York: Harper & Row, 1960.

Denaux, Adelbert. *Studies in the Gospel of Luke: Structure, Language and Theology* 4. Münster: LIT Verlag, 2010.

Dinkler, Michal Beth. *Silent Statements: Narrative Representations of Speech and Silence in the Gospel of Luke*. Berlin: DeGruyter, 2013.

Dorsey, David A. *The Literary Structure of the Old Testament: A Commentary on Genesis—Malachi.* Grand Rapids: Baker Academic, 1999.

Farrell, Hobert K. "The Structure and Theology of Luke's Central Section." *Trinity Journal* 2/7 (1986) 33–54.

Feldman, Emanuel. *Biblical and Post-Biblical Defilement and Mourning.* Jersey City, NJ: Yeshiva University Press/Ktav, 1977.

Fitzmyer, Joseph A. *The Gospel according to Luke I-IX: Introduction, Translation, and Notes.* New York: Anchor, 1981.

———. *The Gospel according to Luke X-XXIV: Introduction, Translation, and Notes.* New York: Anchor, 1981.

Garner, G. G. "En-gedi." *The New Bible Dictionary*, edited by D. R. W. Wood, et al., 316. Downers Grove, IL: Inter-Varsity, 1996.

Gingrich, Felix Wilbur, et al. *A Greek-English Lexicon of the New Testament and Other Early Christian Literature.* Chicago: University of Chicago Press, 1979.

Goulder, Michael D. *Luke: A New Paradigm.* Sheffield: Journal for the Study of the Old Testament, 1989.

Green, Joel B. *The Gospel of Luke.* New International Commentary on the New Testament, edited by Gordon Fee. Grand Rapids: Eerdmans, 1997.

———. *The Theology of the Gospel of Luke.* Cambridge: Cambridge University Press, 1995.

Guhrt, J. "Time," *The New International Dictionary of New Testament Theology* 3, edited by Colin Brown, 827–28. Grand Rapids: Zondervan, 1978.

Jobes, Karen H., and Moisés Silva. *Invitation to the Septuagint.* Grand Rapids: Baker Academic, 2015.

Johnson, Luke Timothy. *The Gospel of Luke.* Collegeville, MN: Liturgical, 1991.

Jones, T. H. "David." *The New Bible Dictionary*, edited by D. R. W. Wood, et al., 258–61. Downers Grove, IL: Inter-Varsity, 1996.

Josephus, Flavius. *The Works of Flavius Josephus.* Translated by G. Routledge, 1873. Repr., Nashville: Thomas Nelson, 1998.

Kennedy, George A. *New Testament Interpretation through Rhetorical Criticism.* Chapel Hill, NC: University of North Carolina Press, 1984.

Kuhn, Karl Allen. *The Kingdom according to Luke and Acts: A Social, Literary, and Theological Introduction.* Grand Rapids: Baker Academic, 2015.

Longenecker, Bruce W. *Rhetoric at the Boundaries: The Art and Theology of New Testament Chain-Link Transitions.* Waco: Baylor University Press, 2005.

Lowrie, Joyce O. *Mirrors in Texts—Texts in Mirrors.* Amsterdam, NY: Editions Rodolphi, 2008.

Lund, Nils W. *Chiasmus in the New Testament.* Chapel Hill, NC: University of North Carolina Press, 1942.

Manley, G. T. and F. F. Bruce. "Names of God, The Lord of Hosts." *The New Bible Dictionary*, edited by D. R. W. Wood, et al., 422. Downers Grove, IL: Inter-Varsity, 1996.

Marshall, I. Howard. *Luke: Historian and Theologian.* Grand Rapids: Zondervan, 1971.

———. *The Gospel of Luke.* Grand Rapids: Eerdmans, 1978.

McComiskey, Douglas. *Lukan Theology in the Light of the Gospel's Literary Structure.* Eugene, Oregon: Wipf & Stock, 2007.

Meynet, Roland. *A New Introduction to the Synoptic Gospels.* Miami: Convivium, 2010.

Milgrom, Jacob. *Numbers*. The JPS Torah Commentary 4. Philadelphia: Jewish Publication Society, 1990.

Moessner, David P. *Lord of the Banquet: The Theological and Literary Significance of the Lukan Travel Narrative*. Minneapolis: Fortress, 1989.

———. "Luke 9:1–50: Luke's Preview of the Journey of the Prophet like Moses of Deuteronomy." *Journal of Biblical Literature* 102:4 (1983) 575–605.

Motyer, J. A. "Anointing, Anointed." *The New Bible Dictionary*, edited by D. R. W. Wood, et al., 49. Downers Grove, IL: Inter-Varsity, 1996.

Neyrey, Jerome H., ed. *The Social World of Luke-Acts: Models for Interpretation*. Peabody, MA: Hendrickson, 1991.

Nolland, John. *Luke 1–9: 20*. Word Biblical Commentary. Waco, TX.: Word, 1989.

———. *Luke 9: 21—18: 34*. Word Biblical Commentary. Dallas, TX: Word, 1993.

Parunak, H. Van Dyke. "Structural Studies in Ezekiel," PhD diss., Harvard University, 1978.

Pietersma, Albert and Benjamin G. Wright, eds. *A New English Translation of the Septuagint and the Other Greek Translations Traditionally Included Under That Title*. New York: Oxford University Press, 2007.

Powell, Mark Allan. *What Is Narrative Criticism?* Minneapolis: Fortress, 1990.

Ressaguie, James. "Interpretation of Luke's Central Section (Luke. 9:51–19:44) Since 1856." *Studia Biblica et Theologica* 5 (1975) 3–36.

———. "Point of View in the Central Section of Luke." *Journal of the Evangelical Theological Society* 25 (1982) 41–47.

Rhoads, David, et al. *Mark as Story*. Minneapolis: Fortress, 2012.

Rius-Camps, Josep. "Lc 10,25-18,30 Una Perfecta Estructura Concentrica dins la Secció del Viatge (A Perfect Concentric Structure within the Travel Section) (9,51-19,46)." *Revista Catalana de Teologia* 8 (1983) 283–358.

Schneider, Walter, "Mellō." *New International Dictionary of New Testament Theology*, edited by Colin Brown, 1:325–27. Grand Rapids: Zondervan, 1978.

Seebass, H. "Righteousness, Justification." *The New International Dictionary of New Testament Theology*, edited by Colin Brown, 3: 352–56. Grand Rapids: Zondervan, 1978.

Talbert, Charles. *Reading Luke: A Literary and Theological Commentary on the Third Gospel*. Macon, GA: Smyth and Helwys, 2002.

Tannehill, Robert C. *Luke*. Nashville: Abingdon, 1996.

———. *The Narrative Unity of Luke–Acts: A Literary Interpretation*, 1. Philadelphia: Fortress, 1986.

Tiede, David L. *Luke*. Philadelphia: Fortress, 1988.

———. *Prophecy and History in Luke-Acts*. Philadelphia: Fortress, 1980.

Trible, Phyllis. *Rhetorical Criticism: Context, Method, and the Book of Jonah*. Minneapolis: Fortress, 1994.

Watson, Duane F., and Alan J Hauser. *Rhetorical Criticism of the Bible: A Comprehensive Bibliography with Notes on History and Method*. Biblical Interpretation Series, edited by Culpepper, R. Alan and Rolf Rendtorff. Leiden: Brill, 1994.

Welch, John W. *Chiasmus in Antiquity*. Provo, UT: Research, 1981.

Westermann, Claus. *Praise and Lament in the Psalms*, translated by Keith R. Crim and Richard N. Soulen. Atlanta: John Knox, 1981.

Wigram, George V. *The Englishman's Greek Concordance of the New Testament: Coded with the Numbering System from Strong's Exhaustive Concordance of the Bible.* Peabody, MA: Hendrickson, 1996.

Wiseman, Donald J. "Hiram." *The New Bible Dictionary.* Edited by D. R. W. Wood, et al., 475. Downers Grove, IL: Inter-Varsity, 1996.

Witherington, Ben, III. *Women in the Ministry of Jesus: A Study of Jesus' Attitudes toward Women as Reflected in His Earthly Ministry.* Cambridge: Cambridge University Press, 1987.

www.ingramcontent.com/pod-product-compliance
Lightning Source LLC
Chambersburg PA
CBHW062043220426
43662CB00010B/1628